GOD

IS FOR REAL

GOD

IS FOR REAL

AND SO ARE HEAVEN AND HELL

ANN MILLER

For information about this title or to order other books and/ or electronic media, contact the publisher:

Majestic Publishing, LLC
2232 Dell Range Blvd., Suite 245 #3235
Cheyenne, WY 82009

ISBNs:
979-8-9896712-2-9 (hardcover)
979-8-9896712-0-5 (softcover)
979-8-9896712-1-2 (eBook)

For Worldwide Distribution. Printed in the United States of America.

Cover and Interior design: 1106 Design

Dedication

In loving gratitude, I dedicate this book to:

Our Lord and Savior Jesus Christ. He is the true author of this book from start to finish. In loving obedience to His calling on my life, I have endeavored to faithfully communicate all that He has given me to share with His people. I hope and pray this book will accomplish His will, and help every Christian be prepared to stand before Him.

God Moments

For God may speak in one way, or in another,
Yet man does not perceive it.
In a dream, in a vision of the night,
When deep sleep falls upon men,
While slumbering on their beds,
Then He opens the ears of men,
And seals their instruction. (Job 33: 14-16)

And it shall come to pass in the last days, says God,
That I will pour out of My Spirit on all flesh;
Your sons and your daughters shall prophesy,
Your young men shall see visions,
Your old men shall dream dreams.
And on My menservants and on My maidservants
I will pour out My Spirit in those days;
And they shall prophesy. (Acts 2:17-18)

. . . but prophecy is for a sign, not to unbelievers
but to those who believe. (1 Corinthians 14:22 NASB 1995)

Preface

This book is my humble testimony of some amazing things God has done in my life during the last fifty-plus years. I call these "God Moments" because there are several different kinds of encounters and events that include visions, prophetic dreams, premonitions, revelations, miracles, and supernatural incidents.

Why am I writing this book? First and foremost, to be obedient to the calling God placed on my life in 2013 when He told me, "I have made you a watchman," and to share the things He shows me with His people. Most of these revelations are wonderful and encouraging, but some are specific warnings of judgment and difficult times ahead. It can be very distressing to deliver such messages, because most people reject them and the messenger who brought them. Many Christians as well as non-believers today do not want to hear anything that may upset their lives or doctrinal views. But God's watchmen are emphatically commanded to communicate whatever He gives them, whether His people want to receive it or not. And that is why I am writing this book.

In the Bible, Jesus tells those who have experienced God's miracles and supernatural grace to go and tell others about the wonderful things the Lord has done for them. Every born-again believer is expected to share their testimony of Jesus Christ and how He transformed their life—which is the greatest miracle of all. Sharing your personal testimony is probably the most powerful way to glorify God and lead others to Christ. It also builds everyone's faith!

> … *"Go home to your friends, and tell them what great things the Lord has done for you, and how He has had compassion on you." (Mark 5:19)*

Prophesied events are coming together very fast now, and the whole world senses that humanity has little time left. We are entering a very difficult period that will require great faith and courage to make it through. Now is the time to build up that faith to strengthen oneself and others. The Bible says that the fearful, unbelieving, and cowardly will not enter Heaven. (Revelation 21:8)

I believe that the miracles, prophecies, testimonies, and scriptures shared in this book provide strong "proof" that God, Heaven, and Hell are very real. Although most professing Christians believe this now, the trials and tribulations that are coming will severely test everyone's faith. Satan will also perform wonders and produce "evidence" that will cause believers to doubt and tempt them to abandon their faith. Hopefully, the evidence and information presented in this book will help Christians hold onto their faith and not fall away in the Great Deception and Strong Delusion that are coming.

Table of Contents

Introduction

As I mentioned in the Preface, during most of my adult life I have experienced visions, dreams, and spiritual experiences that I call "God Moments." Most have been open visions in which I am fully awake going about my day, when suddenly I enter into another spiritual dimension. Some have been premonitions in which I knew something specific was about to happen. Others have been prophetic dreams, which are similar to open visions but take place while sleeping. Several visions I share in this book occurred when I was a brand-new Christian, and had no idea that many of the things I had seen and experienced were actually described in scripture. But I soon discovered that fact, once I began reading through the Bible. This was especially true of the testimonies I share in "The Visitation."

Although I continued to receive visions and messages from the Lord for many years, I didn't understand why God was showing me these things. I was given supernatural information but wasn't told what to do with it. So, I was reluctant to share these experiences with people because I didn't really understand God's purpose for them, and my Lutheran church was very uncomfortable discussing supernatural works. I didn't want to make myself out to be anything special or weird, so I only shared a few things with some of my family.

Then in January 2013, the Lord finally told me why He had given me these visions and supernatural experiences, and what He wanted me to do with them. I was in the hospital battling a serious blood infection when I experienced another God Moment, as I opened my Bible one morning. The Lord spoke to me through scriptures I had randomly opened to in Ezekiel chapters 3 and 33. As my eyes fell upon the words written on those pages, the Holy Spirit spoke profoundly into my mind and spirit, saying, "I have made you a watchman." Then He gave me a mandate to tell His people to repent, and to share certain visions He has shown me that He calls "swords."

But I had no idea how to be a "watchman," what to watch for, where to look, or who to tell. So, I asked the Lord to teach me. And for the past ten years, He has been doing just that—showing me things, giving me understanding and Biblical validation, and leading me to other watchmen for confirmation and additional information. He has also given me wisdom to understand certain things happening in the world and how they play into what He has shown me and Biblical scripture.

God led me to write this book to share with His people the prophetic messages, miracles, and supernatural things He has performed in my life, the lives of my family, and certain other watchmen. I believe He has given us these experiences "for such a time as this," and to provide me the material to write this book—a book that glorifies Him and helps those seeking the truth to know that He is God and He still performs miracles and supernatural acts in the lives of His people. He is also warning us about what is coming, in order to build our faith and prepare us to be with Him for eternity in Heaven.

Does God Really Exist?

P*robably the most fundamental questions* that most people struggle to answer in life are: "Does God really exist?" and "Are Heaven and Hell real?"

Discovering the truth about God is arguably the most important purpose in life for every human being. And it has never been more important than it is today, as the world is faced with numerous civilization-ending threats on a daily basis. Whether it's the specter of nuclear war, economic collapse, cosmic calamities, or deadly pandemics, we are being bombarded with constant reminders of the perilous times we are now living in.

Is there proof that God exists?

I believe there is an abundance of proof that God exists, and that He is the God of the Bible. But how can one prove something that is spiritual to those who live in a physical reality? Through a preponderance of evidence—which is the accepted standard for proof in courtrooms every day. The reality of God can be proven by verifiable evidence of things that only He can do—miracles, supernatural acts, and fulfillment of prophecy. And that is what I will present in this book—an abundance of God's miracles and supernatural works in my life, and the lives of certain other people whose testimonies He has led me to share. These examples from just a handful of Christians' lives are more than enough evidence to convince a jury and most skeptics. But when similar stories from millions of Christians throughout the world over the last two thousand years are added to them, the evidence is overwhelming. And, when the multitude of witnesses recorded in the Bible are added to these, the evidence is irrefutable—God is most definitely real and Jesus Christ is God our Savior!

So, why is this important for those who already believe in Jesus Christ to understand? Because our faith is about to be tested big-time! This book is actually for Christians more than non-believers because Church members have never been more confused and divided in their beliefs than now. The apostle Paul prophesied that in the end-time God will send a "strong delusion" upon humanity, sealing the fate of all those who "did not accept the love of the truth." There will be a "great falling away" of professing "believers" and most people in the world will fall under the delusion, believe "the lie," and follow the Antichrist. It is important that every Christian ensures that they are believing *Biblical* truth and not "another gospel" or following "another Christ" different from what is described in the Bible. Those who are will likely fall under the strong delusion and be lost because they did not love *the truth*.

When the delusion comes, it will be so convincing that the whole world will believe it, except a small remnant of "the elect." I believe it will involve the disclosure of information and historical facts that have been withheld from humanity by nefarious players over the last two thousand years. The disclosures will likely be presented in a manner that implies Christianity and the Bible are not true because they didn't speak about these realities. It is possible that supernatural "aliens" will also be revealed with new convincing doctrines, as I theorize in Part III, "The Great Deception and Strong Delusion."

The coming of the lawless one is according to the working
of Satan, with all power, signs, and lying wonders, and with all

unrighteous deception among those who perish, because they did not receive the love of the truth, that they might be saved. And for this reason, God will send them strong delusion, that they should believe the lie, that they all may be condemned who did not believe the truth but had pleasure in unrighteousness. (2 Thessalonians 2: 9-12)

But regardless of how the delusion comes, remember that the Lord warned us ahead of time, so we will prepare and not be deceived. We need to build up our faith and understanding of God's words and prophecies now before that chaotic time arrives. I hope and pray the testimonies and information shared in this book will help Christians avoid the delusion, believe for miracles, and "do great exploits" in these last days!

Are Heaven and Hell for real?

Yes, Heaven and Hell are real, tangible places, not metaphors or ethereal realities. They are just like Jesus described them in the Bible. In Part III, "Heaven Is for Real and So Is Hell," I discuss these realities in greater detail and share several testimonies of Christians who God has taken to both places, then back to Earth—to witness to others. One of those persons was my late husband, Rhett. In 2012, the Lord gave him a tour of Heaven; then three years later in 2015, He allowed Rhett to experience a tour of Hell!

I share Rhett's descriptions of these places in detail, along with the stories of six other Christians whom the Lord led me to for confirmation of the things Rhett described. God gave all of them experiences very similar to Rhett's. Do their testimonies prove Heaven and Hell really exist? I believe they do, especially since they confirm what Jesus said. And, I think most people will agree.

Do Christians need proof that God, Heaven, and Hell are for real?

Yes and no. Born-again Christians have the Holy Spirit living within them. He witnesses the truth about God to them, causing them to believe and love God. This, together with God's written word, the Bible, is normally all the proof they need to know that God exists.

However, a lot of false doctrine has crept into the Church about the reality of Heaven and Hell. I have had PhD pastors tell me they didn't believe that demons or Hell really exist. If church leaders are uncertain about these things, then I believe Christians need to see convincing evidence that they not only exist, but are actually a more profound reality than the physical world we experience on Earth.

The Bible prophesies that demonic entities from Hell and Satan's fallen angels will come upon Earth in the end days. It is better to be spiritually and mentally prepared for such things now than to die from fright when they manifest. But even more important is to be able to take authority over them, as Jesus said He has empowered us to do. Study the scriptures and learn what you need to know now. (Luke 10:19; 21:26; Revelation 9:1-12; 12:7-9)

I believe we have entered into the period Jesus identified as "the beginning of sorrows" in Matthew chapter 24, Mark chapter 13, and Luke chapter 21.

> *And Jesus answered and said to them: "Take heed that no one deceives you. For many will come in My name, saying, 'I am the Christ,' and will deceive many. And you will hear of wars and rumors of wars. See that you are not troubled; for all these things must come to pass, but the end is not yet. For nation will rise against nation, and kingdom against kingdom. And there will be famines, pestilences and earthquakes in various places. All these are the beginning of sorrows. (Matthew 24:4-8)*

Let's be sure to study God's word and take heed that no one deceives us, as Jesus warned. We must follow the one true God of the Bible, and obey all that He has commanded us. Nobody wants to be one of those believers who loved "Jesus" and did many good works (including miracles) in His name, only to find out too late that the "Jesus" and gospel they loved was not the Jesus of the Bible. They loved a lie that told them they could get away with practicing iniquity and that preached lawlessness. (Matthew 7:23; Luke 13:25-27; Revelation 22:15).

I hope and pray the information and testimonies shared in this book will help build up the faith of God's people and will help inspire them to persevere through the challenging times ahead, share their testimonies with others, and be among the overcomers!

And they overcame him by the blood of the Lamb and by the word of their testimony, and they did not love their lives to the death. (Revelation 12:11)

Is God for real?
Come and see . . .

How to Navigate This Book

I*f there is one thing* that most people can agree on these days, it's that we just don't have enough time to sit down and do all the reading we would like to do. So, I have tried to organize this book in a manner that will enable the reader to easily move around and find the topic and information they wish to read.

The first four chapters are intended to help the reader get a "big picture" view of the purpose and layout of this book, and highlight specific topics that I feel are especially important for our faith and walk with Christ in these end-times.

The remainder of this book is then divided into Parts I-IV, as described below:

Part I: "God Is for Real"

The focus in Part I is on presenting evidence to support my assertion that "God is for Real," and that this fact can be effectively proven. To do this, I share numerous testimonies of supernatural and miraculous things that God has done in my life, and the lives of certain other people whose stories He has led me to share.

Why is it important to "prove" that God is for real? Because we are moving into a time when Christians will be attacked, persecuted, and impoverished for their faith; only those with the strongest belief in Jesus will overcome this perilous time. Many believers will fall away because of the "strong delusion," persecution, and "the great deception" that is coming.

I think the great deception will present what appears to be evidence that undermines the Bible, and especially Jesus. In today's world of AI and "deep fakes," anything is possible! When such evidence is combined with the persecution and discrimination that will be heaped on Christians, many people will be tempted to believe the lies and forsake Jesus. They will likely take "the mark" or deny Christ, and lose their salvation.

So, Christians will need all the strong evidence they can get to remind them that God is for real and that the Jesus Christ of the Bible is our Savior. They also need to know about the Lord's prophetic messages to prepare them mentally, physically, and spiritually for certain events that are coming. Then, when those things happen, they will remember His forewarnings, and it will strengthen their faith, enabling them to be an overcomer.

The information in Part I is presented in two categories:

+ Visions, Prophetic Dreams, and Revelations
+ Miracles, Supernatural Acts, and Wonders

Most of these testimonies have been witnessed or corroborated by numerous people, written about in news stories, recorded in public records, documented in medical records, validated by physical evidence, or verified through Biblical prophecy and scripture. These personal experiences cover a variety of topics, including several prophetic visions and messages about specific end-time events that are now unfolding.

Part II: Warnings of the Watchmen

This is probably the most important material in this book for most Christians to read right now. The things described by the watchmen are being fulfilled today. People need to get prepared psychologically and physically, but most of all spiritually, for what is coming!

My focus in Part II is on the "sword" visions that God has shown me and two other watchmen. The Lord led me to these other witnesses, in response to my prayers asking Him for confirmation of the visions and supernatural acts He has done in my life. I also needed to know if I was to share this information and the experiences of my late husband, Rhett, in a book. So, I asked Him to give me "two or three witnesses" for confirmation, as the Bible instructs us to do.

A few months later, in 2018, the Lord began answering my prayers. He first caused me to hear about a Romanian pastor named Dumitru Duduman. Then in 2019, He made me aware of a world evangelist named Henry Gruver. God had given each of us supernatural visions, dreams, and revelations about the same future events that will come upon America. The Lord also gave me strong confirmation that I was to share all of our testimonies. Following is a brief synopsis of some of the most urgent things the Lord has shown Dumitru, Henry, and me:

> When the United States goes to war with China over Taiwan, a group of people from the middle of the US will be fighting against the government, as if in a civil war. Then Russia, China, and other nations who have been conspiring against the United States will suddenly attack us with missiles and troops from all sides. Most Americans will be blindsided, oblivious that there was a threat.

Now, forty years after the Lord began showing Dumitru, Henry, and me such visions, our daily news headlines are speculating about the imminent war with China over Taiwan—and our need for a "national divorce" or civil war in the United States. These prophecies will soon be fulfilled.

So, please look at all the evidence, preparatory information, and what to watch for, presented in Part II. Then, take heed and prepare for the challenging situations ahead.

Part III: Heaven Is for Real and So Is Hell

In Part III, I share the details of my late husband's experiences in Heaven and in Hell. I also talk about the other six Christians whom the Lord led me to for confirmation of Rhett's testimonies. All of their stories are amazingly similar in their descriptions and what they experienced.

Among the most important things they shared were their passionate warnings that the "once-saved-always-saved" doctrine is not true. They said it is sending many "believers" to Hell!

> … "By the mouth of two or three witnesses every word shall be established." (2 Corinthians 13:1 NASB)

Their testimonies are also validated by the words of Jesus and His descriptions of Heaven and Hell, recorded in the gospels. Every human being will spend eternity in one of these two destinations. Read these compelling testimonies, and do what you must to ensure that you get into Heaven and don't end up in Hell. Time is of the essence.

Part IV: Connecting the Dots

In Part IV, I do a synopsis of the information and stories shared, to identify which visions and messages have been fulfilled or are now in process of fulfillment. Have any failed? Do they pass the Biblical tests?

What are the essential truths the Lord is telling His people in these prophetic messages?

Conclusion

In my Conclusion, I look at the plethora of testimonies and evidence presented in this book to determine if my assertion "God is for real" has been sufficiently proven. I also address some other important questions that many people struggle with, and offer my personal answers and understandings regarding them.

I then examine important prophecies, warnings of the watchmen, and witnesses of Heaven and Hell. I also look at whether there is evidence that the "end of the age" is imminent, and what a person needs to know and do if this is true.

Do you want to be saved?

I have saved the best for last—an invitation to come into a personal relationship with Jesus Christ. If you have never asked Him to forgive your sins and come into your heart and be your Lord and Savior, or if you have strayed down a wrong path, don't hesitate—come to Him *right now* and be saved. Our world can turn on a dime these days; you cannot presume upon tomorrow!

The Promise of Psalm 91

Why *is Psalm 91 so important?* To give us hope and comfort, build our faith, and help us be ready for the wedding. Most Christians believe that we are now entering the end-time events described by Jesus and the writers of the New Testament. Our world is changing rapidly, and we are beginning to see Biblical prophecies fulfilled almost daily now.

As described in Matthew chapter 24, Mark chapter 13, Luke chapter 21, and Revelation chapter 6, tyrants are going out to conquer other countries, and warmongers are trying to stir up wars and rumors of wars as they taunt and provoke each other. Nation is rising up against nation and kingdom against kingdom. Reports of calamities, new plagues, economic collapse, cosmic threats, and drastic weather catastrophes fill our daily news headlines. Lawlessness and injustice are upending constitutions and legal systems in first-world nations as well as third-world countries. It feels like the people have been rendered helpless, as many government leaders appear to be complicit with those working to destroy the nations!

Humanity is desperate for hope. And, that's what Psalm 91 gives Christians! It is one of the most beloved go-to scriptures in the Bible because of the Lord's strong, comforting promises for supernatural protection in times of trouble and calamity. Sounds like it was written for today, doesn't it? I think so.

This is why I have decided to share this encouraging scripture at the very beginning of this book—to help us see our lives through the lens of hope. We need to keep God's promises in front of our minds by reading this and Psalm 23 often. Believing these promises and trusting Jesus to do as He says really strengthens our faith to make it through tough times. He is Almighty God and nothing is impossible for Him!

But each of us has a part to play, if we want to receive these promises. Our lives must conform to the description of the person "who dwells in the secret place of the Most-High."

Your secret place can be anywhere—a closet, a room, a corner, under a tree, or whatever place you can find to be alone with the Lord. A place where you can rest in His presence, talk to Him, meditate upon His word, and experience Him as your refuge and the One who restores your soul.

I also want to say that Psalm 91 is not just a beautiful poem or metaphor. It is actually describing a prophetic event. In my vision, "In the Wings of an Eagle," I share how God allowed me to experience the things described in Psalm 91. As I describe in that testimony, when the attacks came upon America, God's angels instantly rescued me from the catastrophe and I was caught up in the wings of a very large, divine eagle—just as this Psalm describes!

God will save His righteous people from terrifying calamities, as described in Psalm 91. He will protect them supernaturally, like He did with Daniel, Shadrach, Meshach, and Abednego in the Old Testament book of Daniel. Whether it's in the wings of a divine eagle or some other way, make sure you're ready to go.

Psalm 91

He who dwells in the secret place of the Most-High
Shall abide under the shadow of the Almighty.
I will say of the LORD, "He is my refuge and my fortress;
My God, in Him I will trust."

Surely, He shall deliver you from the snare of the fowler
And from the perilous pestilence.
He shall cover you with His feathers,
And under His wings you shall take refuge;
His truth shall be your shield and buckler.
You shall not be afraid of the terror by night,
Nor of the arrow that flies by day,
Nor of the pestilence that walks in darkness,
Nor of the destruction that lays waste at noonday.

A thousand may fall at your side,
And ten thousand at your right hand;
But it shall not come near you.
Only with your eyes shall you look,
And see the reward of the wicked.

Because you have made the LORD, who is my refuge,
Even the Most High, your dwelling place,
No evil shall befall you,
Nor shall any plague come near your dwelling;
For He shall give His angels charge over you,
To keep you in all your ways.
In their hands they shall bear you up,
Lest you dash your foot against a stone.

You shall tread upon the lion and the cobra,
The young lion and the serpent you shall trample underfoot.

"Because he has set his love upon Me, therefore I will deliver him;
I will set him on high, because he has known My name.
He shall call upon Me, and I will answer him;
I will be with him in trouble;
I will deliver him and honor him.
With long life I will satisfy him,
And show him My salvation."

Get Ready for the Wedding

As *Christians, the Bible tells us* that we are meant to become "the bride of Christ," and our most important goal in life is to be worthy and ready for the Wedding Supper of the Lamb. But to do so, we must have wedding garments—and they must be spotless. So, how do we obtain these garments, and how do we keep them spotless?

When you are "born again" into the kingdom of God, you receive a wedding garment that is clean and white. You are expected to keep it such, and beautify your wedding garments as you grow into a mature and righteous adult. How exactly do you do that? The Bible says that a Christian obtains clean, bright linen for the wedding by their "righteous acts" (Revelation 19:8). That means believing and obeying God, walking as a disciple of Jesus, and doing good works (Matthew 22:37; John 13:35; Ephesians 2:10).

As you do these things, you are building a trousseau for a glorious wedding. But you must be ready at all times, so you can go immediately whenever the Groom comes for you. Therefore, you must always be wearing your wedding garments. So, the problem is, how do you keep them clean and spotless as you navigate through this dirty world?

Wedding garments are soiled by sin—sin that you choose to do, and your unintended sins done through ignorance or responding wrongly to the offenses of others. And, that pretty much describes daily life in this world. So, how does one cleanse their garments from sin? There is only one way—Jesus!

I call it "taking your daily shower." Confess your sins each day (or as you become aware of them) and Jesus will cleanse both your heart and your wedding garments. Then, "go and sin no more," as He commands. But if or when you do sin again, wash, rinse, and repeat. This is how we keep ourselves ready for the wedding.

> *If we say that we have no sin, we deceive ourselves, and the truth is not in us. If we confess our sins, He is faithful and just to forgive us our sins and to cleanse us from all unrighteousness. (1 John 1:8-9)*
>
> *Let us be glad and rejoice and give Him glory, for the marriage of the Lamb has come, and His wife has made herself ready." And to her it was granted to be arrayed in fine linen, clean and bright, for the fine linen is the righteous acts of the saints. (Revelation 19:7-8)*

There is a wonderful new movie that beautifully illustrates the deep spiritual symbolism in the Wedding of Jesus and the Bride. It is called *Before the Wrath*. I think you will be very blessed by this movie and the profound insights it gives us about this all-important event. The movie may still be available on Netflix, Amazon Prime, Hulu, or YouTube.

PART I

GOD IS FOR REAL

For since the creation of the world His invisible attributes, His eternal power and divine nature, have been clearly seen, being understood through what has been made, so that they are without excuse.

Romans 1:20 NASB

Visions, Dreams, and Revelations

In this section of Part I, I share numerous supernatural experiences including prophetic visions, dreams, and revelations that God has given me over many years. They are confirmed in Biblical truths, prophecies, and scriptures throughout the Bible. Some have been prophetic, and most of those have been fulfilled or are currently in process.

All of the supernatural experiences described in Part I came to me by the will of God, not my own thoughts or desires. I never asked for them nor sought supernatural experiences, like some people do. They all came unexpectedly, "out of the blue," and were permanently engraved in my mind. I remember every detail of all these dreams and visions, like a photographic memory, even though they span more than fifty years. In fact, this is the first time I have written any of them down. So, that's a pretty big miracle in itself, since I am now past the age of seventy!

When I received my first three God Moments, I was not yet a born-again Christian, although I did believe in God the Father, Jesus Christ, and the Holy Spirit. I don't know why the Lord began revealing Himself to me at that point in my life, but the Bible tells us that we are predestined to become born-again at a specific time. I think these first three experiences were gifts of God's grace at times when I really needed it, even though it was before my "appointed time." God is gracious to all!

Almost ten years later, I came to Jesus through Billy Graham ministries, just before Easter in 1983. Then, about six months later, I experienced "The Visitation," as I describe in this chapter. Although I had been a Christian for six months at that point, I had never read the Bible. So, I didn't realize that many of the things I saw and experienced in The Visitation were actually written in the Bible.

Immediately after The Visitation, the Lord led me into extensive research. As I began reading through the Bible for the first time, I realized that what God had shown me in visions and dreams, He was now verifying through His written word. He enabled me to experience certain prophecies and scriptures written in the Bible, as future events that would take place during my life in this world.

"I AM That I AM"

I *experienced my first "God Moment"* when I was nineteen. I had been thinking about some philosophers my friends and I had been discussing, as some of us were in college learning about "the great thinkers" for the first time. I was pondering Descartes's iconic statement, "I think, therefore, I am." I was trying to understand why this was considered such a great insight. It seemed obvious to me and not worthy of such acclaim. I wondered if it was so "deep" that I just didn't get it.

While walking around my living room perplexed in these thoughts, God suddenly broke into my world. I instantly stopped, aware of the overwhelming presence of God coming from above and behind me. As I turned in His direction, He profoundly spoke into my mind: "I AM that I AM—and I am a paradox in this world." I immediately understood that God is "I AM," and we are not to attribute Descartes's declaration to ourselves. I realized that Descartes's statement was actually blasphemous, and I should not honor him or follow him. I also realized that God's ways and truths are a paradox in our world. I knew that what we think is good, He may see as sin; and what He sees as good, we often find unappealing.

In this encounter I also *experienced God's perfect love, grace, and patience* toward us human beings, and felt *how deeply He cares about us.* I knew beyond any doubt that God exists, and that He is omniscient, omnipresent, and omnipotent and that He is aware of everything we think and do. But most surprising to me was how much He values a personal relationship with us!

Biblical validation of my encounter:
The things I experienced were later confirmed to me through Biblical scriptures:

> And God said unto Moses, I AM THAT I AM: and he said, Thus shalt thou say unto the children of Israel, I AM hath sent me unto you. (Exodus 3:14 KJV)

The "Paradox" of God is verified:

> "For My thoughts are not your thoughts nor are your ways My ways," says the LORD. "For as the heavens are higher than the earth, so are My ways higher than your ways, and My thoughts than your thoughts." (Isaiah 55:8-9)

Following are a few Biblical examples that illustrate the Paradox of God in this world:

Exaltation through humility: *Humble yourselves in the presence of the Lord, and He will exalt you. (James 4:10 BSB)*

Strength through weakness: *And He said to me, "My grace is sufficient for you, for My strength is made perfect in weakness." (2 Corinthians 12:9)*

Receive by giving: *I have shown you in every way, by laboring like this, that you must support the weak. And remember the words of the Lord Jesus, that He said, "It is more blessed to give than to receive." (Acts 20:35)*

"Give, and it will be given to you: good measure, pressed down, shaken together, and running over will be put into your bosom. For with the same measure that you use, it will be measured back to you." (*Luke 6:38*)

Freedom through servitude: *And having been set free from sin, you became slaves of righteousness. (Romans 6:18)*

Gain in losing: *But what things were gain to me, these I have counted loss for Christ. Yet indeed I also count all things loss for the excellence of the knowledge of Christ Jesus my Lord, for whom I have suffered the loss of all things, and count them as rubbish, that I may gain Christ. (Philippians 3:7-8)*

Rejoice in trials: *My brethren, count it all joy when ye fall into diverse temptations; knowing that the testing of your faith produces patience. (James 1:2 NKJV)*

A servant is the greatest of all: *Yet it shall not be so among you; but whoever desires to become great among you, let him be your servant. (Matthew 20:26; Mark 9:35, 10:44)*

Die to worldly things, and receive abundant life: *Do not love the world or the things in the world. If anyone loves the world, the love of the Father is not in him. For all that is in the world—the lust of the flesh, the lust of the eyes, and the pride of life—is not of the Father but is of the world. And the world is passing away, and the lust of it; but he who does the will of God abides forever. (1 John 2:15-17; Galatians 5:24; Matthew 6:19-21)*

Be Still and Know
That I Am God

This *God Moment happened* when I was twenty-five and had just gotten divorced. I had two small children and was living in an apartment on the ground floor next to a beautiful, forested creek. I was going through a difficult time in my life, certainly a low point. It was summertime and I had just put my kids to bed around 9 p.m., as the daylight was waning.

I closed Sean's bedroom door and began walking into the living room, when suddenly I felt myself entering God's presence and into another dimension. I was engulfed in a divine atmosphere filled with a profound peace that I had never experienced before. It seemed timeless, divine, deeper, and more real than the atmosphere on Earth. There was no stress or anxiety—just a surreal, beautiful peace that I wanted to last forever. I was in the natural world physically; I was standing in my home and observed my living room, dining room, the patio deck; but somehow the atmosphere of Heaven had invaded my world, encapsulating me in this divine reality. Then my spiritual eyes were opened, and I was able to see things in another dimension, at a cellular level.

As I was standing there looking around the room in awe, I was drawn to go out onto my deck. The trees, foliage, and creek seemed even more beautiful than before. They glistened, sparkled, and seemed to be dancing and rejoicing. I could see detail, shades, and nuances I had never seen before. I was relishing in this exhilarating experience and the deep beauty I was seeing for the first time. Then I went deeper, and my spiritual eyes were opened even more.

I saw *life*—the light of God's presence *within* His creation. His presence was in the leaves, foliage, and even the water. His light was in every living thing, and *His presence was like tiny golden ribbons of beautiful sparkling liquid light weaving in, out, and around all the cells—holding everything together in vibrating life and love.* What a treat and a blessing! I realized that regardless of how difficult life in this world may be, knowing God and being in His presence transcends all the stress and mundane drudgery of this world. He is *Reality*, our ultimate reward, and being in His presence makes the problems of this world seem insignificant—just a minor annoyance we must get through.

This God Moment was confirmed about ten years later, after I had become a Christian. I was reading the Bible one day and came across Psalm 46:10: *Be still and know that I am God.* Instantly, I had a flashback to my creek-side experience, and the Holy Spirit witnessed that my experience was a fulfillment of this scripture. It was also a fulfillment of these scriptures:

…for in Him we live and move and have our being…(Acts 17:28)

In Him was life, and the life was the light of men. (John 1:4)

One God and Father of all, who is over all and through all and in all. (Ephesians 4:6)

Therefore, we do not lose heart . . . for our light affliction, which is but for a moment, is working for us a far more exceeding and eternal weight of glory, while we do not look at the things which are seen, but at the things which are not seen. For the things which are seen are temporary, but the things which are not seen are eternal. (2 Corinthians 4:16-18)

Our Family's Salvation

Four years after our divorce, Rhett and I reconciled and were remarried. Then in 1983, God poured out His grace on our family and saved all of us, independently of one another within a few months. Rhett was the first to become a Christian but didn't tell me or anyone that he had been led to Jesus by a coworker.

Approximately six months after Rhett's conversion, one evening I was drawn to leave the dinner dishes and immediately turn on the TV. It was broadcasting a Billy Graham Easter crusade. The program was ending as they were giving a final "altar call," and displayed a phone number for the television audience to call and speak with a crusade counselor. Although I hadn't watched the crusade, I felt a strong urge to respond. So, I called the phone number on the screen and amazingly got right through!

I spoke with a lady who asked if I was a Christian, and I replied "yes." She asked what church or denomination I belonged to. I replied "Mormon." There was a gasp on the other end of the phone followed by a long pause, and I realized there was something wrong with saying I was a Mormon. She then began reading John chapter 1 to me, and I heard for the first time in my life that Jesus was *God*, not "my elder brother" or "the brother of Lucifer," as Mormonism teaches. What an epiphany!

I was thrilled! I had always wanted Jesus to be more than my "big brother," who was someone I was never able to love or worship. She then led me through the Sinner's Prayer and told me that I was now "saved." I was happy to discover that Jesus really is God, but thought she was presumptuous to declare that I was "saved." She then stressed that I needed to start attending a good Bible-believing church. Mormons claim to believe the Bible, and she didn't say to stop going to the Mormon Church, so I began attending Mormon church services for the first time in several years.

Then, six months later I fell into a spiritual and emotional crisis. I had been experiencing an increased hunger to know God; but whenever I went to Mormon services, I would feel angry, disgusted, and physically nauseated with what I was perceiving spiritually. I felt guilty for the negative thoughts and feelings I was having about the Mormon Church.

I started to think that it must not be possible to know God, because the more I went to church seeking Him, the more I couldn't find Him and the more I hated church! I began sinking into depression, feeling that life wasn't worth living if I couldn't have a meaningful relationship with God.

Then, one day everything suddenly changed. . . .

The Visitation

"The Visitation" was a very profound God Moment that encompassed thirteen open visions, most of which are described below, except for a few visions called "swords" that are shared in Part II. The Visitation includes "The White Light" through "The Baptism of the Holy Spirit."

These visions occurred consecutively within about a twenty-minute period, but the amount of spiritual truth and knowledge imparted to me would have taken much longer, if experienced in the physical realm. In God's presence in the spiritual realm, knowledge, understanding, and perception are instantaneous and most communication is through mental telepathy. It's amazing how fast and easy it is to learn and understand when you're in His presence!

As I describe in the testimonials below, one morning in October 1983, the Lord suddenly broke into my world and began revealing Himself to me through a series of visions. As I stood in my bedroom, it was suddenly transformed into a supernatural "event center!" My furniture disappeared and the perimeter of the room was lined with different spiritual-dimension "movie sets," or vignettes.

A divine Guide, whom I was not allowed to see, was standing behind me and would turn me toward each scene. I could discern Him enough spiritually, to know that He was large (over six feet tall), masculine, and divine. I believe this was either Jesus or an angel. As He directed my focus, we began viewing whatever scenario each set was meant to depict. After a few seconds of viewing the scene together, I would be supernaturally drawn into that scene, and would experience it in first-person. It was almost like "time travel." I went from one venue to another, depicting scenes from Jesus's time to future events on Earth and in Heaven, as described in the visions that follow . . . .

The White Light

I*t was a beautiful day in early October 1983,* my favorite time of year. As I was going through the mundane routine of cleaning my house, I glanced through the doorway from my bathroom into my bedroom, and something caught my eye—an unusual white light. It was like a fluorescent light hovering near the ceiling in the southeast corner of the room where there were no windows or light sources.

As I watched the light, the physical surroundings became even more surreal, and I began seeing everything transition between different dimensions. The light was inside my bedroom, then far away like across the face of the earth, traversing a variety of different landscapes. I was captivated by this supernatural perception, as the walls of my bedroom disappeared and reappeared. But even more fascinating was the light itself. It seemed to be alive, like a person. It was pure white and alluring—divine! The light seemed to be very polite, patiently waiting for me to acknowledge it.

Then, suddenly I was distracted by another light in the opposite corner of the room. It was yellowish like an incandescent light, and it was bouncing around trying to get me to look at it. It was playing loud circus music and tooting horns in an effort to compete with the white light for my attention. I laughed in amusement and derision at the cheap antics it was using to draw me away from the white light. It was so inferior to the white light that it was laughable it would even try to compete. Humiliated, the yellowish light shrunk away.

As my gaze returned to the white light, it suddenly moved closer and then stopped, waiting patiently for me to accept it. I could now see two beings within the light. The larger one was like a cloud in form; the other was the figure of a man. I perceived divinity, holiness, and utter perfection emanating from this enthralling light. While I stared in amazement, the light suddenly came closer and stood right in front of me. I realized it was God, as the word *Cosmos* came into my mind. At that moment, I knew He was immensely greater and different from what I thought or could comprehend, and I understood that His being fills the entire universe and beyond. I knew that He is Reality and the spirit of creation!

I then became aware that He was very pleased and excited about a mighty work that was taking place in China. Many Chinese people were believing in Him and sacrificially worshiping Him. They were doing great works of faith and He was blessed by their passionate love for Him.

As the Presence stood there before me, I perceived that there were three distinct persons in the light: a Cloud-like being and a divine Man, enveloped in an exquisite spiritual being. Three distinct "persons" wrapped together as one God!

Vision confirmed through scripture:

+ *This is the message which we have heard from Him and declare to you, that God is light and in Him is no darkness at all. (1 John 1:5)*

+ *"God is Spirit, and those who worship Him must worship in spirit and truth." (John 4:24)*

+ *. . . "Do I not fill heaven and earth?" says the LORD. (Jeremiah 23:24)*

+ *"Hear, O Israel: The LORD our God, the LORD is one! (Deuteronomy 6:4)*

+ *Believe Me that I am in the Father and the Father in Me . . . (John 14:11)*

+ *Go therefore and make disciples of all the nations, baptizing them in the name of the Father and of the Son and of the Holy Spirit . . . (Matthew 28:19)*

The understanding I was given about China was later verified: Although I had no idea of a Christian movement occurring in China at that time, a few years later I learned that what God had communicated to me was indeed happening in 1983. Below is an excerpt from an official document written in 2018, stating this fact:

"Deng Xiaoping's opening and reform policy changes triggered a religious revival in the *1980s*, with *Christianity* first spreading in house churches formed in rural areas. The second *major* event was the crackdown on democracy activists in Tiananmen Square in 1989." —The Council on Foreign Relations, October 11, 2018

The Fear of the Lord

I *was so excited that God* would condescend to appear to me that I immediately began to speak to Him as if He were on a human level. BIG MISTAKE! "God is not a man, that He should lie"—nor that we can approach Him like a man. Above all, we are to "fear the Lord" and revere Him with humility. We must honor and obey Him as Almighty God because He is neither man nor a created being. He is the self-existent One—spiritual, holy, terrifyingly wonderful, and all powerful. We are to *wait for Him*—and not be presumptuous, like I was.

> "The fear of the LORD is the beginning of wisdom, And the
> knowledge of the Holy One is understanding.
> (Proverbs 9:10)

My irreverence was met with extreme indignation by the Father. He began rising up like an explosion—a nuclear bomb going off in the universe! I began repenting fast and furiously in an effort to quell His billowing anger. In this brief moment, *I learned how devastating it is to offend the Lord, even in ignorance.* We are to fear Him and walk humbly before Him, as well as love and obey Him. His power, grandeur, and holiness are far beyond anything we can imagine.

Vision confirmed in scripture:

+ ... "The LORD will judge His people." It is a fearful thing to fall into the hands of the living God. (Hebrews 10: 30-31)

+ Let all the earth fear the LORD: let all the inhabitants of the world stand in awe of Him. (Psalms 33:8)

+ But I will show you whom you should fear: Fear Him who, after He has killed, has power to cast into hell; yes, I say to you, fear Him! (Luke 12:5)

The Dark Cloud

The Lord was quick to forgive as I repented. As I was standing there, devastated, and wondering if God would accept my apology, a very dark, thick cloud enveloped me. It was like a giant down-filled comforter saturated in perfect, unconditional love that penetrated every cell in my body, into my bones and marrow. I was experiencing the perfect love of my holy and compassionate Father God, cuddling me as He whispered into my spirit and soul, "I love and forgive you completely." Every cell in my body was vibrating in His profound love that seemed to go on and on.

You may be wondering how I knew it was a dark cloud. I perceived it with spiritual eyes, which are multidimensional. This is supernatural vision that is absorbed into the mind, and is much more encompassing than what our physical eyes can see.

Vision confirmed in scripture:

+ . . . *"Yes, I have loved you with an everlasting love; therefore, with lovingkindness I have drawn you." (Jeremiah 31:3)*

+ *Then Solomon spoke: "The LORD said He would dwell in the dark cloud." (1 Kings 8:12)*

+ *Clouds and darkness surround Him; righteousness and justice are the foundation of His throne. (Psalm 97:2)*

I believe the Lord often wraps Himself in clouds to manifest Himself to us. Otherwise, we would be evaporated by the intense light of His being.

We may perceive God's presence as a white cloud or a dark cloud. I personally experienced the Father's presence as a dark cloud and Jesus's presence as a white cloud. Why? Jesus said:

. . . My Father is greater than I. (John 14:28).

Perhaps the Father's presence is so powerful that He must wrap Himself in extra-thick dark clouds to visit us, even in a small manifestation of His being!

In the Wings of an Eagle

As I was basking in my Holy Father's gracious perfect love, I suddenly felt myself tumbling upward through dark, swirling clouds, as if being sucked out of a turbulent storm. I was disoriented and angry because my world had just been violently disrupted. Then, I found myself in a very still, dark place wondering, *What just happened?!* I finally got my bearings enough to grope around and pry something open with my hands, in an effort to see out.

I was amazed and perplexed to see that I was in the wings of a giant eagle, tucked inside its feathers in the middle of its right wing. I knew I had been rescued from something and knew that I wasn't the only person the eagle would rescue. I suddenly felt a deep wave of peace and security come over me, and knew that this eagle was Jesus. He lovingly spoke into my mind, saying, "Why were you anxious? Didn't you believe that I would protect you?" I felt disappointed in myself for forgetting His power and promises during this turbulent event. Then I looked down.

We were flying about ten thousand feet above the earth, out of harm's way. I looked at the earth below to try to figure out what was going on. It was semi-dark, like dusk, and hard to make out the landscape below. Everything appeared brown and hazy. Finally, I gained focus and I was able to see why it was so murky, and why I was in the wings of this eagle.

The earth beneath me had been devastated, scorched, and flattened. Everything had been evaporated! There was nothing green—only brown, void of any vegetation or structures except part of a blackened steel bar crookedly jutting out of the ground. This remnant from what must have been a tall urban building was all that remained in the wide valley that had previously encompassed a large city. Everything was still and lifeless. Then, one lone man emerged in the far corner of the valley, stumbling around in the devastation. He must have been deep underground when the event happened. It looked like the aftermath of a very powerful nuclear bomb, and my heart ached for the poor man who survived.

As another wave of God's profound peace came over me, I realized that I had been rescued from this horrific event—"in the wings of an eagle." And I wondered, *Who or what exactly is God—a giant eagle?!!*

I had been raised in Mormonism, which taught me that God was a man—flesh, blood, and bones man. But I had just *experienced* Him as a divine light, a dark cloud, and now a giant eagle. So, I did what any almost-sane person would do—I cried out, "Who are *You*—what is *Your name?*" (Continued in "The Glory Clouds.")

Vision partially fulfilled in scripture:

What I experienced in this vision is described in Psalm 91. Aspects of my experience are also described in several other scriptures in the Bible, which are shown below. I shared the entire Psalm 91 earlier, but I want to highlight a few passages below that I feel are especially significant in this vision:

Psalm 91 excerpts:

The promises of this Psalm are given *to "you [who] have made the LORD . . . your dwelling place"* and to the one who *"has set his love upon Me."*

I believe that if we conform our lives to be like the person described in Psalm 91, we are promised that when calamity comes, Jesus will rescue us.

+ *He shall cover you with His feathers, and under His wings you shall take refuge. (v. 4)*

+ *You shall not be afraid of the terror by night nor of the arrow that flies by day, nor of the pestilence that walks in darkness, nor of the destruction that lays waste at noonday. (v. 5-6)*

+ *. . . but it [calamity] shall not come near you. Only with your eyes shall you look and see the reward of the wicked. (v. 7-8)*

+ *Because you have made the LORD, who is my refuge, even the Most High, your dwelling place, no evil shall befall you nor shall any plague come near your dwelling. (v. 9-10)*

+ *For He shall give His angels charge over you, to keep you in all your ways. In their hands they shall bear you up, lest you dash your foot against a stone. (v. 11-12)*

"Because he has set his love upon Me, therefore I will deliver him;

*I will set him on high, because he has known My name.
He shall call upon Me, and I will answer him;
I will be with him in trouble;
I will deliver him and honor him.
With long life I will satisfy him,
And show him My salvation."*
(v. 14-16)

The Glory Clouds

Then God answered my question, *"Who are You?"*—but not how I expected. I began to accelerate upward at great speed through white, glistening clouds, swirling with streaks of pure gold. It seemed to go on and on and I was beginning to wonder if I would ever come out of these glorious clouds. Even though it was a wonderful experience infused with divine peace and joy, I didn't want to stay there forever. I wanted relationships and activities. I was beginning to panic, thinking I would never see "reality" or people again!

Then suddenly, the clouds parted and a heavenly man-like being was standing over me. He appeared to be made of the same glorious substance as the clouds. Holiness and perfect love emanated from Him. I knew that He was God and that He was a divine spirit (not the physical false god of Mormonism). I now understood that He could manifest in any form He needed to: a white light, a divine man, a dark cloud, a giant eagle, a lion, a fire, or however He desired for a particular situation. He is "I Am," the dynamic essence of all creation—God Almighty. And, I realized this divine man-like being was Jesus Christ Himself.

What I had just experienced was a foretaste of the Rapture. God answered my question: His name is "Jesus Christ!"

Partially fulfilled in scripture:

+ *Then the sign of the Son of Man will appear in heaven, and then all the tribes of the earth will mourn, and they will see the Son of Man coming on the clouds of heaven with power and great glory. And He will send His angels with a great sound of a trumpet, and they will gather together His elect from the four winds, from one end of heaven to the other. (Matthew 24:30-31)*

+ *Then we who are alive and remain shall be caught up together with them in the clouds to meet the Lord in the air. And thus, we shall always be with the Lord. (1 Thessalonians 4:17)*

I Will Rejoice over You with Singing

A *few seconds later I was back on Earth* standing in my house when Jesus appeared again, a few feet above me. Immediately my spirit left my body and joined Him, suspended about five feet above the floor. I was amazed that I was actually in two places at the same time. I was physically standing in my house looking up at my spirit, kneeling at the feet of Jesus a few feet above me.

I could hear my spiritual self, praising Him in a heavenly language that I didn't understand, but it sounded quite repetitive. I felt the emotions that my spirit-self was experiencing in His presence, as I was worshiping Jesus. The physical me (who was in awe of what was going on) and the spiritual me were connected and aware of each other while in two different realms. This is when I realized that we exist in three dimensions or realities: body, soul, and spirit.

Your *soul* is immortal and is essentially *you*—comprised of your mind, personality, your will, and a soul-body that has faculties similar to your physical body.

Your *spirit* comes to life when you are "born again." It is *the divine you* that is able to know God. It has the faculties of mind, personality, will, and a *spiritual body* that you receive in Heaven.

Your soul and spirit are united and go to Heaven as one, to stand before Jesus when you leave this world. When He takes you to the Father, the Father gives you a spiritual body and a new name.

Conversely, if you have not been "born again," your spirit is not alive, so your soul cannot enter Heaven. Also, if you harbor certain sins in your heart such as unforgiveness, hatred, and lust for the things of this world, you cannot enter Heaven. Satan claims your soul and takes you to his kingdom for eternity.

Once again, Jesus was bright white and appeared to be made from a substance similar to the divine clouds, but I could not see Him fully. I could see the features of His face as if they were outlined in this white cloud substance (it was similar to looking at the "negative" of a photograph).

He was laughing and rejoicing over me as if singing, like someone who was thrilled to have just run into his long-lost best friend! He had so much to tell me and was excited and eager to show me all His awesome things. I was enthralled with His presence, and deeply humbled that I was so valued by such a magnificent and important Person.

Partially fulfilled in scripture:

+ *The LORD your God in your midst, the Mighty One, will save; He will rejoice over you with gladness, He will quiet you with His love, He will rejoice over you with singing." (Zephaniah 3:17)*

+ *Jesus answered and said to him, "Most assuredly, I say to you, unless one is born again, he cannot see the kingdom of God." (John 3:3)*

+ *It is sown a natural body; it is raised a spiritual body. There is a natural body, and there is a spiritual body. (1 Corinthians 15:44)*

+ *"... And I will give him a white stone, and on the stone a new name written which no one knows except him who receives it." (Revelation 2:17)*

The soul body has the same form and feelings as the physical body but is made of a spiritual substance, as illustrated in the following scripture:

> *... The rich man also died and was buried. And being in torments in Hades, he lifted up his eyes and saw Abraham afar off, and Lazarus in his bosom. "Then he cried and said, 'Father Abraham, have mercy on me, and send Lazarus that he may dip the tip of his finger in water and cool my tongue; for I am tormented in this flame.' (Luke 16:22-24)*

Our Exciting Future
in Heaven

As *I was reflecting on the profound reality* I had just learned about our body, soul, and spirit, I suddenly found myself standing in the foyer of a heavenly building, where the interior looked like it was made out of ivory. Jesus then joined me, and He began to give me a taste of some of the things that life in Heaven holds for us. As He waved his hands toward the ceiling, a dome opened above us and straight into the universe. Then He opened up my mind, and pure intelligence poured in. I felt like my IQ had instantly taken an exponential leap, and there was nothing too difficult for me to learn or understand.

I then began to rise up into the black starlit sky above us, and was awestruck by the amazing beauty and vastness of the universe. Waves of amazement and exhilaration washed over me and I was filled with overwhelming excitement. The stars and worlds seemed to be created with their own unique beauty and personalities. I knew that one of our greatest blessings and most important activities in Heaven will be to traverse the universe doing God's will. I sensed that there are other worlds, and possibly universes that we don't know about on Earth. I can't wait to become a "space cadet" on mission for God!

This vision's reality is confirmed in scripture:

+ *. . . The heavens declare the glory of God, and the sky above proclaims His handiwork. (Psalm 19:1 ESV)*

+ *He counts the number of the stars; He calls them all by name. Great is our LORD, and mighty in power; His understanding is infinite. (Psalm 147:4-5)*

+ *When I consider Your heavens, the work of Your fingers, the moon and the stars which You have ordained, what is man that You are mindful of him, and the son of man that You visit him? (Psalm 8: 3-4)*

+ *But as it is written: "Eye has not seen, nor ear heard, nor have entered into the heart of man the things which God has prepared for those who love Him." But God has revealed them to us through His Spirit. For the Spirit searches all things, yes, the deep things of God. (1 Corinthians 2: 9-10)*

Blessed to Help Others

S*tanding back in my bedroom again,* my Guide directed me toward a vision of myself several years into the future. I appeared to be around sixty years old, an empty-nester and unmarried. I looked quite different and didn't recognize myself until I was supernaturally drawn into the scene and I began experiencing it in first-person.

I was looking out a small warehouse-looking window at a bleak gray sky. The setting appeared very grim and depressing. It was my new office, which was uncharacteristic of my personality and the way I normally did business. I sensed that we were in the midst of a very deep and serious financial recession and people were really hurting. There seemed to be a bleakness about it, as if it had been going on longer than normal and there didn't seem to be much optimism for recovery.

My office was furnished with a few folding tables and very modest décor. Everything was austere and basic because the focus of my business was not on impressing others or making a professional statement. It was on helping others—young families who weren't able to provide adequately for their children because of the painful recession. Many jobs were gone, and people needed financial help to provide basic necessities as the economy was languishing.

The only office equipment I had was a desktop printer and my small laptop computer, which seemed to be the workhorse of my life. However, this vision was in 1983, before desktop printers and laptop computers were invented. Yet, I saw these things and was continuously using them for everything I needed to do. My other go-to device was a compact cell phone, which was the only telephone I had—but again, such phones were not yet invented in 1983!

The purpose of my business that God had given me was to give money to the people He would bring to me. He would bless me, so I could help those in need. It would be my own money that I earned or was entitled to, but He would bless me with more than I needed, and I was not to hoard it. Freely I received; freely I was to give. I was only to give to those He brought to me through referral or learning of their need. There wouldn't be a lot of people, but some would need substantial help for an extended period of time. The money I gave was to be a gift with no strings attached.

Then He showed me that one unexpected day, He would suddenly pay me back all that I had given. It would be poured into my lap, filling up as if in an invisible container and overflowing—as if being dumped from the sky!

Vision fulfilled, 2012-2018:

This vision was largely fulfilled during "the Great Recession" but continues on an occasional basis today. The people the Lord brought to me included family members (close and distant), strangers, and acquaintances of people I knew. The Lord has not yet "paid me back," but I'm sure He will at the right time—maybe when He returns.

Aspects of this vision confirmed in scripture:

+ *"Give, and it will be given to you: good measure, pressed down, shaken together, and running over will be put into your bosom. For with the same measure that you use, it will be measured back to you." (Luke 6:38)*

✦ *"And behold, I am coming quickly, and My reward is with Me, to give to everyone according to his work." (Revelation 22:12)*

I have learned that when God fulfills such visions, the essentials are fulfilled quite literally, but some of the details may have been metaphors used to communicate feelings and truths in a deeper, more impressive way. So, they may not be fulfilled as expected. For example, with this vision, everything was fulfilled much as I was shown, except for my office.

When this vision came to pass thirty years later, I didn't have a stripped-down office, but a very nice one—in my home. I believe the austerity depicted in the vision was meant to communicate that I was not to waste money on unnecessary things. The economic times would be harsh, and I needed to be frugal, so I could give as much as possible to others. And, when that time came, I was able to work *frugally* out of the nice office that the Lord had blessed me with in my home!

"Follow Me"

Next, my Guide gently turned me toward the west, and I began viewing a scene from Biblical times. I watched as bearded men wearing tunics and long robes began gathering under a low-spreading tree on a dirt road. I perceived them to be Jesus's disciples. It was summertime and one-by-one they arrived, talking amongst themselves. Then a shorter, stocky man entered the scene facing the men with his back to me. He seemed to be in charge, as everyone was paying attention to him. There was something dynamic and authoritative about him, so I thought he must be Peter. He was talking to them and giving them instructions. Then he turned around and was facing me.

I was startled and felt exposed, like he had discovered we were spying on him. As he began walking slowly toward me, I felt anxious. My Guide put his hands on my shoulders to strengthen and reassure me. The man had very dark, shoulder-length hair and a beard, but I couldn't see the features of his face, even as he came closer. He was wearing a plain off-white tunic exposing his muscular forearms. He stopped about ten feet from me, but I still couldn't see the features of his face. Then typewritten words appeared across his chest: "Follow Me."

Astonished, I realized it was Jesus, and He was inviting me to become part of His group. But it was also a command to follow Him. I was thrilled to be invited and wanted to go more than anything, but then remembered my three children. I hesitated, pleading, "But, I can't leave my children!" He turned and walked away. He didn't try to persuade me or give me a comforting answer for my dilemma. He didn't even look back at me. He just began walking up the mountain path, as each of His disciples fell in behind.

I felt terrible, as I realized that I had rejected the Lord and chose someone over Him. He won't accept second place to anyone, not even a mother's young children. His invitation is a high honor, and those who don't treat it as it deserves are not worthy of Him. I wondered if I had blown my only chance to become one of His disciples.

Vision confirmed in scripture:

+ *"You shall have no other gods before Me." (Exodus 20:3)*

+ *He who loves father or mother more than Me is not worthy of Me. And he who loves son or daughter more than Me is not worthy of Me. And he who does not take his cross and follow after Me is not worthy of Me. (Matthew 10:37-38)*

The Things of Earth
or the Things of Heaven

My *Guide now turned me to the northeast*, and I began seeing a vision of some things that were my heart's desire. I saw a carved oak kitchen cabinet door, some woven baskets, and a granite rock. The trend in home décor had changed in the early 1980s from the dark Mediterranean look to rich natural oak and earthy textures. I desperately wanted to redo my kitchen, and these things were exactly what I wanted so much I could taste it. Except for the granite rock, that is. I was puzzled why that was in the mix. In 1983 granite countertops were not yet in vogue, so I had no desire for anything made of granite. But everything else—YES! That's exactly what would make my world and was my heart's desire. And, ten years later *granite* countertops were my heart's desire!

Then, beautiful pillars of transparent gemstones appeared next to the worldly items I desperately wanted. Radiant light was shining through the pillars as each one glistened with a different color in beautiful hues of red, green, blue, gold, and lavender. They were gorgeous in beauty, but even more thrilling was that each one was *alive and emanated different spiritual and emotional qualities.* Love, joy, peace, wisdom, knowledge, and other exquisite feelings radiated from these beautiful pillars, flooding my entire being in ecstasy.

I knew that these were the building materials of Heaven and are what our hearts *really* desire and crave. I now understood why things in this world never truly satisfy us—they're *dead*. But the things of Heaven delight our spirits and souls with their beauty and continuously envelope us in exquisite spiritual experiences—life to its fullest!

I no longer wanted the things I had been lusting for. They were like junk and garbage to me and I wanted them gone—out of my sight. How could I ever want something so *dead?!!* I felt disgusted with myself for being so shallow and blind. The things in this world are cheap, broken knockoffs of the things in Heaven and only a fool would choose them.

Vision confirmed in scripture:

+ ... *"Come, I will show you the bride, the Lamb's wife." And He carried me away in the Spirit to a great and high mountain, and showed me the great city, the holy Jerusalem, descending out of heaven from God, having the glory of God. Her light was like a most precious stone, like a jasper stone, clear as crystal.* (Revelation 21:9-11)

+ *The foundations of the wall of the city were adorned with all kinds of precious stones: the first foundation was jasper, the second sapphire, the third chalcedony, the fourth emerald, the fifth sardonyx, the sixth sardius, the seventh chrysolite, the eighth beryl, the ninth topaz, the tenth chrysoprase, the eleventh jacinth, and the twelfth amethyst.* (Revelation 21:19-20)

+ *"Do not lay up for yourselves treasures on earth, where moth and rust destroy and where thieves break in and steal; but lay up for yourselves treasures in heaven . . . For where your treasure is, there your heart will be also."* (Matthew 6:19-21)

+ *"They shall be Mine," says the LORD of hosts, "on the day that I make them My jewels. And I will spare them, as a man spares his own son who serves him." (Malachi 3:17)*

+ *. . . My soul shall be joyful in my God; for He has clothed me with the garments of salvation. He has covered me with the robe of righteousness, as a bridegroom decks himself with ornaments, and as a bride adorns herself with her jewels. (Isaiah 61:10)*

Come Away with Me

Now my Guide turned me toward the northwest, and I began observing some people that included many of retirement age. I saw a woman from the back whom I thought looked like my younger sister. Then I suddenly entered into her body and realized it was me! I was part of a group of Christians preparing for the return of Jesus, while going about their daily lives.

Then the scene changed, and I was standing in my home looking out a window overlooking the Salt Lake Valley. I had an unobstructed view of both the sky and valley below, which was important to me. I was intently watching things happening in the world and for signs from Heaven. There seemed to be a lot going on, but I felt frustrated because I couldn't get adequate information from the news media. The news reporting was watered down and vapid, like they were trying to keep the people dumbed down, passive, and in the dark—while cheery and entertained. It seemed so fake!

As I walked over to a glass sliding door, I saw a vision in the sky of a group of people getting ready to go on an especially important mission trip. (*This was weird because I was seeing a vision within a vision.*) They seemed like a special group who had been chosen for this trip, and were very disciplined and focused on getting everything ready to go. I really wanted to be part of this group, but they had been preparing for a while and their flight was leaving soon. I felt that they would be going to another continent, possibly South America.

It wasn't easy to get into their group—you had to qualify and be invited. I felt discouraged and regretful that I had allowed myself to be distracted by so many "important" things in the world, and could miss this opportunity.

Then suddenly, I got the call! Jesus was inviting me to join the group, but there was something I had to do first. I had to sell everything I owned and give the money to the poor—then I could get my ticket for the flight. Amazingly, I had no problem wanting to comply. My only issue was doing it fast enough. I had a lot of stuff and little time before they would be leaving. I was afraid I couldn't do it in time and would miss the flight.

So, I asked Jesus if I could just give everything to my children and their families. He said, "No, they won't need it. You are to sell everything and give the money to the poor." I felt overwhelmed, frustrated, and dismayed because I had so much stuff. The things I thought were a blessing suddenly became a great burden, like a ball and chain around my neck tying me to this world. I felt like I had been deceived and played for a fool by accumulating so much *junk!*

Then I looked at the woman standing at the window, but didn't realize it was me. I was in my seventies, heavier with shorter blonde hair, and was standing in a specific home overlooking a valley.

This Vision is now being fulfilled:

Thirty years after this vision, Rhett and I bought a home in the southeast foothills of Salt Lake Valley. It is the exact home and location where I saw myself in this 1983 vision—and I look just like the woman I saw standing at the window!

During the last few years, as I have been learning how to be a watchman, I have become increasingly frustrated with the lack of professional journalism and truthful information available through television and the mainstream media. So, I have become like an investigative journalist doing my own research, as the Lord has led me to His own quality experts and independent news sources.

This 1983 vision portrayed me as a watchman, which is exactly what God called me to do. It is literally being fulfilled now as watching, researching, and connecting the dots through the guidance of the Holy Spirit is my main activity!

> *"Watch therefore, and pray always that you may be counted worthy to escape all these things that will come to pass, and to stand before the Son of Man." (Luke 21:36)*

Baptism of the Holy Spirit

I *was back in my home now*, standing in awe of the extraordinary things I had just experienced. Leaning on the doorframe, I gazed into my bedroom as I was regaining my bearings in the natural world. I was amazed and wondering why God had given me this experience.

Then suddenly, the Holy Spirit came upon me like a rushing wind (just like the Bible says). As the Spirit entered my body, the wind changed into a rushing river surging through me from head to toe and back again. My blood turned into effervescent bubbles of joy, energizing me with excitement and strength, surging throughout my body!

Then the river of joy welled up in my heart (around my solar plexus) and began gushing out of me like a fountain of unconditional love! It was impossible not to love anyone or anything that came into my presence. The unconditional, perfect love of the Father was filling me as if it were my nature. It was the most wonderful feeling ever, and I was hoping it wouldn't go away. It made it so easy to "love others as yourself!"

Then it got even better, as heavenly peace descended upon me like soft spiritual blankets, permeating deeper and deeper into my mind, body, soul, and spirit. I perceived beautiful layers of blue and purple resonating with different nuances of perfect peace. Basking in this wonderful love, joy, and peace, I thought, *"This is what true life feels like—and it is the atmosphere of heaven!"*

I enjoyed this divine experience for a few minutes, then it started lifting as the Holy Spirit began moving on His way. So, I begged God not to take it away from me completely. He graciously granted my request and allowed His divine presence to linger, gradually waning over the next three days.

The effervescent joy of the Lord Jesus, profound love of the Father, and indescribable peace of the Holy Spirit had changed me forever! The baptism of the Holy Spirit infused me with spiritual power, boldness, unshakable faith, and a deep passion for God. I had tasted Heaven—and now I was addicted. I have been pursuing Jesus ever since, craving more of Heaven. Nothing in this world can satisfy or get you excited once you have experienced God and Heaven. This is what our souls *really want!*

Vision confirmed in scripture:

+ John the Baptist said: *I indeed baptize you with water unto repentance, but He who is coming after me is mightier than I, whose sandals I am not worthy to carry. He will baptize you with the Holy Spirit and fire.* (Matthew 3:11)

+ *". . . for John truly baptized with water, but you shall be baptized with the Holy Spirit not many days from now."* (Acts 1:5)

+ *"But you shall receive power when the Holy Spirit has come upon you . . ."* (Acts 1:8)

+ *". . . how much more will your heavenly Father give the Holy Spirit to those who ask Him!"* (Luke 11:13)

+ *. . . to know the love of Christ which passes knowledge; that you may be filled with all the fullness of God.* (Ephesians 3:19)

+ *". . . for the joy of the LORD is your strength." (Nehemiah 8:10)*

+ *You will show me the path of life; In Your presence is fullness of joy; At Your right hand are pleasures forevermore. (Psalm 16:11)*

This is the conclusion of "The Visitation" experience.

Salvation of My Extended Family

A *few days after The Visitation,* I had a prophetic dream that seemed to be a continuation of my "Judgment of the Wicked" dream that I share in Part II.

My extended-family dream:

> I was very alarmed that Jesus was coming soon to judge the world, so I frantically tried to reach out to warn my parents and siblings. I realized that if they were Mormons, they would suffer the judgment I had witnessed in my "Judgment of the Wicked" dream.
>
> I ran to the phone but could only reach my mother and one sister. Although my mother seemed to believe me, I had a feeling she might stand in the way of my siblings hearing or believing my message. And since most of us were not very close, I didn't think they would listen to me without my mother's endorsement.
>
> Unfortunately, that turned out to be true. So, I continually prayed over the following years that the Lord would grant them the grace to be saved.

Mostly fulfilled:

This dream has been largely fulfilled now. For many years, my mother would agree with me about the Biblical gospel, but she seemed to hinder my brothers and sisters from hearing or believing my testimony.

However, God heard my prayers and worked around this obstacle. As it turned out, I was able to lead my father, two brothers, and three sisters to the Lord. I was also in the process of witnessing to another sister and brother, but sadly each suddenly died before I could lead them into a born-again relationship with Jesus.

When my husband, Rhett, went to Heaven in 2012 (as I write about in Part III), he was met by my father, brother Verl, and a sister who was miscarried before birth. But my mother and oldest sister were not there. My other siblings were still living at that time.

I now have one sibling remaining, for whom I am praying the Lord will grant the grace for salvation. So hopefully, most of my family will be together in Heaven!

The Black and White
Mormon Temple

A *few days after The Visitation*, I was standing at my kitchen sink washing dishes while gazing out the window in front of me. Suddenly, the scene changed and instead of looking at my neighbor's house, my eyes were viewing a Mormon temple looking beautiful with its stately, pinnacled architecture dressed in bright white.

As I was watching this scene in front of me, admiring the temple, a thick black cloud appeared above it and began oozing down, draping the beautiful white structure in inky blackness. Then the temple began flashing black to white over and over again. I immediately understood that God was telling me that the Mormon Church appears to be holy but is actually evil.

This bold visual message was shocking to me. Even though the Lord had been telling me for a few days at this point that Mormon teachings were off-base and even false doctrine, this stark picture was screaming in my face that the Mormon Church was "evil!"

Vision confirmed in scripture and my research:

> *"Woe to you, scribes and Pharisees, hypocrites! For you are like whitewashed tombs which indeed appear beautiful outwardly, but inside are full of dead men's bones and all uncleanness. Even so you also outwardly appear righteous to men, but inside you are full of hypocrisy and lawlessness. (Matthew 23: 27-28)*

For twelve months following my Visitation experience, the Lord led me to do about two thousand hours of deep research into the books and history of the Mormon Church. I also studied the Bible and researched most of the major religions and cults in today's world. My research into the Mormon Church proved it to be a Luciferian religion much like the Freemasons.

Mormonism is also a fulfillment of the prophecies of Jesus and the apostle Paul, foretelling that deceivers and false gospels would emerge in *the latter days*. They both warn that these imposters would teach "doctrines of demons" and preach "another Christ" and "another gospel" that is different from what God's written word, the Bible, describes. (Matthew 24:4-5; 2 Corinthians 11:4; 2 Timothy 4:1)

It is also interesting that another name for the Mormon Church is "Latter-day Saints." Satan likes to dress up in camouflage, and then write his cryptic signature in plain sight—as if mocking foolish human beings!

Changed Lives

After my Visitation experience, I was a new person. I had been baptized in the Holy Spirit and His presence was strong within me. I had a certainty about God that nothing could shake. My faith skyrocketed. I knew the truth—Jesus—and He became the passion of my life!

But I am certainly not the only one. Over the years, I have been blessed to see others come to Jesus, and I have watched God miraculously change them and move in their lives, as He has in mine. It's been like observing the "scientific method" operating in human beings instead of test tubes: Apply the necessary inputs, sit back, and watch—voila! As the Holy Spirit comes into their heart, most people demonstrate the same result: They feel a miraculous love for God and have a passion to learn about Jesus, and their behavior becomes more Christ-like.

Many of those I saw come to the Lord have continued this "formula" and led others into a born-again relationship with Jesus, and a changed life. Some have pursued careers in the Church, theology, ministry, and doing great work for the Lord! Although we all have suffered through "desert experiences" and hard times that have tested our faith, none have fallen away. Having a personal relationship with Jesus sustains us, as we continue to trust in Him, our "First Love!" He is our Refuge, our Strength, and our Song—even as we "walk through the valley of the shadow of death!"

Confirmed in scripture:

+ *But you shall receive power when the Holy Spirit has come upon you; and you shall be witnesses to Me . . . to the end of the earth." (Acts 1:8)*

+ *And do not be conformed to this world, but be transformed by the renewing of your mind . . . (Romans 12:2)*

+ *He has put a new song in my mouth—Praise to our God; Many will see it and fear, And will trust in the LORD . . . (Psalm 40:3)*

The Eyes of Jesus

About three years after we became Christians, Rhett and I attended a three-day Marriage Encounter weekend at a hotel in Park City. After a morning in which we had fasted, prayed, and meditated on the Lord, we were assembled together and told to look silently into our spouse's eyes.

After doing so for about five seconds, Rhett's eyes began to transform. They changed color from dark brown to golden brown and they changed shape. They weren't Rhett's eyes—they were Jesus's eyes! As my eyes locked with His, I was mesmerized, as perfect love poured into my entire being.

Jesus was looking deep into my soul with such powerful love, compassion, and adoration—that I felt like I was going to melt. It was humbling and overpowering. He knew everything about me, and yet He loved and valued me deeply, and wanted to be my companion and Lord!

What I felt was probably similar to what Peter experienced when he said: "Depart from me, for I am a sinful man, O Lord." And what the Centurion expressed when he replied, "Lord, I am not worthy that You should come under my roof" (Matthew 8:8). I too felt the conviction of realizing I was face-to-face with the Son of God, who valued me so much that He took my punishment and died in my place to save me. I had to look away, as my soul cried out, "I'm not worthy of you, Lord. I don't deserve Your sacrifice."

But thankfully, Jesus didn't listen to me.

It is heart-wrenching to contemplate the degree of His suffering and heartbreak, as He paid for the sins of billions of people—knowing most of them would reject His gift. How tragic that they will die and suffer needlessly in Hell.

Confirmed in scripture:

+ *When Simon Peter saw it, he fell down at Jesus' knees, saying, "Depart from me, for I am a sinful man, O Lord!" (Luke 5:8)*

+ *. . . to know the love of Christ which passes knowledge; that you may be filled with all the fullness of God. (Ephesians 3:19)*

+ *For "whoever calls on the name of the LORD shall be saved." (Romans 10:13)*

Rhett's Greater Purpose

About five years into our Christian lives, I began feeling very dismayed and concerned about Rhett's lack of spiritual growth. I felt we were growing apart because he didn't seem to have any desire to read the Bible or grow in his faith. He traveled a lot with his job and most of his associates were not Christians, but very worldly people. I could see him slipping back into ungodly ways. So, one day I cried out to the Lord, telling Him about my fears for Rhett, and that we were growing apart because of his worldly attitude and immaturity as a Christian.

The Lord answered my prayer in an unexpected way. He gave me a vision of Rhett and myself, as if we were spirits rising up toward Heaven. Rhett was ahead of me, higher on the path toward Heaven. I understood the Lord was telling me that His purpose for Rhett would actually be greater than my calling—and that he would fulfill it.

Over the next twenty years, I began to doubt the validity of this vision. As Rhett continued down his worldly path, I began to think this vision would not be fulfilled for some reason. But then one day after many twists and turns in our marriage and lives, God began fulfilling His purpose for Rhett's life.

The Lord had to take Rhett down and humble him, to get him to repent. In 2005, after thirty-one years of marriage we got divorced. By

2010 Rhett had lost his marriage, his health, and his career within a five-year period. When he was sixty-two years old, he suffered his third heart attack, which left him disabled and financially devastated. But unfortunately, that's what it took to remove his arrogance and get him to humble himself, confess his sins, and return to Jesus.

Then God began restoring him to the man he was created to be, and Rhett fulfilled his calling before he left this world six years later. The Lord gave him some experiences He gives very few people. He took him to Heaven and later to Hell, and gave him an incredible testimony to share with others. A testimony that is especially powerful for the time we are living in today.

The Lord took Rhett home to Heaven about eighteen months after He gave him the tour of Hell experience. He wasn't in good enough health to write about his experiences when they occurred. But his testimonies need to be shared, as they contain critical information for Christians to understand, as well as for unbelievers. His testimonies will shock you, bless you, and hopefully keep you from being deceived.

I believe the Lord wants me to tell Rhett's story and share his important testimonies. So, that is what I try to do in Part III: "Heaven Is for Real and So Is Hell." I pray that our testimonies, together with the testimonies of other watchmen in this book, will help Christians know the truth, be prepared for the trials ahead, and get ready for the wedding!

And you have forgotten the exhortation which speaks to you as to sons: "My son, do not despise the chastening of the LORD, nor be discouraged when you are rebuked by Him; for whom the LORD loves He chastens, And scourges every son whom He receives." (Hebrews 12:5-6)

"It's a Girl!"

In *January 1987, I gave birth to Kelli,* my fourth and last child. I had just turned thirty-eight, and having another baby at that age was hard on me. I felt exhausted, as I was working full time while raising my other three children. Kelli was a surprise baby whom Rhett nicknamed "Princess Mai Tai," because she was conceived while we were on vacation in Hawaii. Ironically, she was born exactly seven years after my previous child, Greg, whose birthday is one day later. That in itself seemed like a God Moment!

During my pregnancy I had an ultrasound done to tell us whether we would have a boy or a girl. The ultrasound results said we were having a boy. But truth be told, I was dreading having another boy. The thought of another seven years of little league football seemed more than I could take. The games, practices, and other things required to be a good football parent for my first two boys took so much of the little time and energy I had that I felt exhausted even thinking about it. But I really liked the idea of having a little girl. So, I asked the Lord to please make the baby a girl instead.

The next several months went by with no problem. We had to buy all new baby furniture and provisions, since I had long ago given away what I had. We prepared everything with a boy theme and colors. Most of the clothes from my baby shower were for a boy. So, when I went to the hospital for delivery, I packed the cutest little black and white tuxedo suit with a red bowtie to bring him home in.

The delivery was more difficult than my previous children. If not for my highly skilled and experienced doctor, Kelli may not have lived due to some complications that happened during delivery. But thank God we got through it and my doctor heroically delivered her, although he had to break her collarbone to do so!

As she was being delivered, the doctor asked us if we were expecting a boy or a girl. Rhett and I both said, "It's a boy." Then a few seconds later the doctor proclaimed, "Congratulations, you have a beautiful baby girl!" What??!! Doctor Barton had quite a sense of humor, but at that moment I didn't appreciate his joke, and retorted with something like, "Yeah, right." But he wasn't joking—it was a girl!

So, what happened? Did God change the baby from a boy to a girl? I don't know, but it's possible. It's also possible they didn't interpret the ultrasound correctly. But regardless, the Lord then let me know that it was His will to give me a girl.

While I was lying in the recovery room, wondering why the ultrasound saw her as a boy, the Lord gave me a vision. I saw myself and Kelli eighteen years into the future. She was a beautiful young woman just out of high school with long, dark hair. But I looked quite different. I was fifty-seven, had straight blonde hair, and didn't look as old as my age. Then the Lord told me that at that time in my life I would get divorced, and my daughter would be a friend and companion to me.

Vision fulfilled:

Eighteen years later, in September 2005, this vision came true exactly as the Lord had shown me. Rhett and I finally separated and got divorced a few months after Kelli graduated from high school. And she was a real comfort and companion to me for the next few years.

+ *Delight yourself in the LORD and He will give you the desires of your heart. (Psalm 37:4).*

+ *"For with God nothing will be impossible." (Luke 1:37)*

Demonic Vultures

During the first two weeks of August 2005, the Lord enabled Rhett and me to observe a phenomenon in the spiritual realm. Every night we would go outside and sit on the patio swing together around 10:00 p.m. to relax, talk, and view the stars on the warm summer nights. Then the show would begin . . . .

We saw huge demonic-looking birds flying in the night sky above us. They looked like whitish cloud-like figures flying in random patterns over the city but especially over us. They were flying at about the level of clouds, and each one was at least a mile across in size.

We both saw the same things at the same time and would comment on the strange shapes, patterns, and erratic behavior of different birds. They always came from the north and would fly across the Salt Lake Valley in random circular patterns as they worked their way southward. We only saw them on cloudless nights, which was the case for most of the first two weeks of August. They looked like evil vultures circling erratically, as if fiendishly looking for a meal!

We listened to the news for reports from other people who may also have seen this phenomenon, but there was nothing. Apparently, Rhett and I were the only people who saw them. Another interesting thing was how we reacted to them. Ironically, Rhett hated seeing them and was afraid of them, but I enjoyed the show. I appreciated that God had given us spiritual eyes to see what was actually going on in the unseen realm of our world—and I had no fear of them because I felt God's presence surrounding me.

Vision fulfilled one month later:

In the Bible, vultures carry a negative image as unclean, hated birds, and such birds are also likened to demons. When several vultures are circling, it is to scavenge something that is in the process of dying.

At the time, Rhett and I both sensed this supernatural phenomenon was a harbinger of evil, but neither of us realized exactly what it meant. Were they planning something for Salt Lake Valley? Were they targeting us? Were they always there but this was the first time we were able to see them? The answer turned out to be "yes" to all three questions.

On a personal level, they were a harbinger of the death of our marriage. God opened our spiritual eyes and enabled both of us to see these demons that were targeting us. One month later they succeeded, and our marriage, which had been declining for a while, finally came apart and we got divorced.

Demonic Vultures:
Their Purpose

In *February and June 2020,* the Lord led me to discover two watchmen (Pastor Donna Rigney and Pastor Dana Coverstone) who had some amazing encounters with the Lord. In their encounters, Jesus gave each of them additional information about demonic vultures and their purpose. This is my summary of what these two watchmen shared:

> Demonic vultures are some of the most evil and powerful demons to come out of Hell, where they delight in torture. But their favorite thing to do is create hatred on Earth, because that is a very effective way to keep Hell supplied with fresh victims. Hatred is the environment of Hell and it is the most powerful strategy they have to feed Hell's voracious appetite. They know that no one can enter Heaven if they harbor hatred, wickedness, or unforgiveness in their heart—which means they get them!

How they gain access:
These evil, demonic birds gain access to come upon the earth through portals that are opened up through hatred and grow larger as hatred

and strife increase. The bigger the portals become, the more vultures of all sizes are released. In addition to stirring up hatred, they also create depression, anxiety, and thoughts of self-hatred and suicide in people—and they especially like to target children.

Demonic vultures are invisible to our natural eyesight, which is what makes them so effective. They come in all sizes, from small shoulder-size to the huge creatures Rhett and I saw. And they are everywhere, looking for an opportunity to access a person. What gives them access to a person? Sin. A person's sinful actions, beliefs, and attitudes. These demons especially love evil speech and word curses because it gives them easy access to both the person speaking such things as well as to the object of the evil words or curses.

So, if you think you can speak evil, judgmental, or condemning words about others and get away with it—watch out! Doing so can open you up to these evil entities. However, if evil words or a curse are spoken about someone but it has no validity (it's not the truth or deserved), they cannot come upon that person.

Like a flitting sparrow, like a flying swallow,
So a curse without cause shall not alight. (Proverbs 26:2)

The sins of the flesh are also huge open doors for these evil demon birds: fornication, adultery, lust, lying, unforgiveness, slander, greed, theft, maliciousness, practicing the occult, and evil. And of course, every kind of hatred: strife, meanness, abusiveness, envy, jealousy, disrespect, bigotry, disdain, haughtiness, arrogance, and pride.

Those who *act* like Hell are rich targets.

Their purpose is to find an opening to gain access and drag as many people into Hell as possible. They especially like to capture believers who are not walking with the Lord, such as hypocrites or backsliders. But unforgiveness, offense, and speaking evil about others may provide their greatest supply of victims. So, take heed!

I believe one of the reasons Jesus tells us to forgive others, pray for our enemies, and do good to those who mistreat us is to prevent these demons from being able to access us. And, if we stop to think about it, those who offend and mistreat us are actually their victims and need to be freed. So, pray for them. But if you return evil with evil, these evil demons can access you.

Love and obedience to God's word is how we defend ourselves from these demon vultures!

Jesus on the Cross

In *September 2005*, my thirty-one-year marriage was coming to an end. Our relationship had been going downhill for a few years, and the Lord had now given me permission to end it.

Not only did my marriage end, but my career in real estate and mortgages was beginning to end, as the national housing boom was turning into the "Great Recession." I was feeling vulnerable and insecure about my future on many levels. So, I just dug in with Jesus, clinging to Him and trusting Him on a day-to-day basis, as if on a roller coaster ride!

I reordered my daily routine, spending the first hour or two each morning in God's word, praying and meditating on Him and His words. This routine became my default and refuge whenever I began to feel anxious. I was relying on the Lord to carry me through each day, in a world that was quickly falling apart! He was literally my rock, comforter, and guide.

One such morning, I had just finished my devotional time, reading the Bible for about an hour. I got up from my sofa and began making my way into the dining room. But suddenly I was no longer in my home. I was walking up a small hill, sparsely dotted with tufts of wild grass. It was a dark and depressing atmosphere. Thick gray and black clouds hung low over the land. It felt like it should rain but there was no wind. Everything felt eerily still, heavy and ominous. As I lifted my eyes to gaze ahead, I saw something very unusual. Yet, somehow it wasn't unusual; it seemed normal and fitting. A rustic carved door was standing near the top of the hill—just this heavy door in its frame, standing by itself as if it were supposed to be there. I could easily go around the door on my way up the hill, but I felt that I was supposed to go through the door. As I approached it, I was impressed with how heavy and rustic it was, yet somewhat regal with its deep carved design. It seemed to be magnified by the morose, somber atmosphere enveloping the land.

Cautiously, I pushed the heavy door open and gazed through it. There was Jesus by Himself, hanging on a cross! The cross was made of rough-hewn wood and set lower to the ground than usually depicted. I was pained at how alone, dark, and dreary His situation seemed. He was in physical and emotional distress but it almost seemed incidental, like something He had to endure while accomplishing a much greater goal. His face was steadfastly looking ahead, and his eyes were fixed on something in front of Him.

I peered around the door to see what Jesus was so intently looking at in the distance. Straight ahead was the opening of a cave that descended down into the earth. An extraordinarily strong evil force was emanating out of the cave. It is difficult to describe it, just like it's almost impossible to describe what the peace of God feels like. Why? Because they are both spiritual environments that are not normally present on Earth, so we haven't developed the vocabulary to articulate them. But with that said, I'll try my best to describe the approaching presence.

It was intense evil so strong that Jesus would only allow me to glance in its direction for two to three seconds at a time, and He only allowed me two glimpses. The evil was palpable, resonating an oppressive heaviness, like a crushing vise. Powerful fear enveloped everything it came near, and I perceived malevolent personalities of intense hatred, mayhem, and evil within it.

As I looked back at Jesus hanging on the cross, I realized that the worst part of His crucifixion was this—having to go into this horrendous environment called Hell. I knew that the deeper one goes into this pit, the more gruesome the evil becomes. But although Jesus dreaded having to enter this unspeakably evil atmosphere, He had no fear. He was absolutely resolute and focused on getting the job done and defeating the powers of Hell. He would enter the depths of the pit and overcome all the devils and demons to save His people.

Deep gratitude and humility swept over me, as I saw how awesome Jesus is and the intense love and compassion that He has for us. He is our all-powerful Savior, the lover of our soul, the hero who fearlessly fights to save His friends. And He is victorious because He is Almighty God and the Lion of Judah. There is nothing as powerful as Jesus. No devil, demon, Satan, nor any created thing can take us out of His powerful hand!

> *My sheep hear My voice, and I know them, and they follow Me. And I give them eternal life, and they shall never perish; neither shall anyone snatch them out of My hand. (John 10:27-28)*

Only we can remove ourselves from His hand—if we forsake Him, reject His words, or blaspheme the Holy Spirit. (John 12:48)

My personal problems seemed to pale in comparison to what I had just witnessed. I knew that Jesus had confronted and defeated the horrendous powers of Hell for us, and He would help me overcome the ugly storm I was facing.

Although I went through some difficult times for the next seven years, Jesus was guiding my path. He carried me through a dark valley and the shadow of death, to some wonderful blessings on the other side!

This vision is affirmed in scripture:

+ Then Jesus said to them again, "Most assuredly, I say to you, I am the door of the sheep. All who ever came before Me are thieves and robbers, but the sheep did not hear them. I am the door. If anyone enters by Me, he will be saved . . ." (John 10: 7-9)

+ I gave My back to those who struck Me, and My cheeks to those who plucked out the beard; I did not hide My face from shame and spitting. For the LORD God will help Me; therefore, I will not be disgraced; therefore, I have set My face like a flint, and I know that I will not be ashamed. (Isaiah 50:6-7)

+ Now from the sixth hour until the ninth hour [while Jesus was on the cross] there was darkness over all the land. (Matthew 27:45)

+ . . . For the joy set before Him He endured the cross, scorning its shame, and sat down at the right hand of the throne of God. (Hebrews 12:2 NIV)

+ I am He who lives, and was dead, and behold, I am alive forevermore. Amen. And I have the keys of Hades and of Death. (Revelation 1:18)

+ Having disarmed principalities and powers, He made a public spectacle of them, triumphing over them in it. (Colossians 2:15)

+ Yea, though I walk through the valley of the shadow of death, I will fear no evil; for You are with me; Your rod and Your staff, they comfort me. (Psalm 23:4)

The Golden Spear

In *May 2008, after being divorced three years,* Rhett came to my home to discuss a life insurance policy he wanted to get. His health was deteriorating but he wanted me to see if I could get something to cover final expenses, as he didn't want to be a burden to his children.

When he arrived, he didn't look very well and immediately sat down on my staircase, as if exhausted. As I stood there looking at him, suddenly I was shown a vision. I saw a golden spear about ten feet long speeding toward my back. As it hit and went through me straight into Rhett, I was filled with tremendous compassion for him. But it wasn't my compassion; it was Jesus's compassion—and His righteous anger about what Satan had done to him. I realized how the Lord had gifted Rhett to be a great man, but the devil had deceived him and destroyed God's plans for his life.

Jesus was sad and angry at how Satan had destroyed Rhett. I perceived what God had gifted him to be and it was quite impressive. Unfortunately, his failure to stay close to Jesus resulted in such a tragic loss. But He loved Rhett and was going to stop Satan's plot to destroy him. Jesus was going to use me in His plan, but first He had to change my heart to have compassion for Rhett.

This began an evolving friendship over the next two years. Rhett began calling me, and we had some good conversations about a variety of topics. Occasionally we would go to dinner, a movie, or other events together. All wasn't smooth, however. There were periods of disagreement and tension that reminded me how happy I was not being married to him. Being intermittent friends was fine with me.

Then in April 2010, Rhett had a serious heart attack and emergency surgery that left him unable to return to his profession. He was severely weakened and functionally disabled, requiring oxygen 24/7. He was left incapacitated and financially damaged at the age of sixty-two.

But the Lord once again gave me His compassion for Rhett, and a desire to take care of him. I couldn't bear the thought of leaving him alone to die like that. Rhett had his faults, but he had always been there to help me and everyone else who needed assistance throughout his life. He was always willing to make big personal sacrifices to help and provide for others, and he deserved the same kind of respect, support, and friendship in his hour of need.

I took care of him in my home when he was released from the hospital, and worked hard to help him get the financial and healthcare benefits he was supposed to be entitled to. This whole experience humbled him, and he became a much nicer, thankful person, despite his physical and psychological tragedy. But after a few months, living together without being married began to bother my conscience as a Christian. If we were going to live like this, I felt we should be married, so as to not give the impression of impropriety. Rhett was very much in agreement and grateful that I would want to marry him in his condition. But I felt it was what the Lord wanted us to do.

On November 20, 2010, we remarried in a wedding ceremony in our home, with all of our adult children and their families present. It was somewhat awkward, as many had mixed emotions about us remarrying, and understandably so. They had gone through a lot of unpleasant emotions with our divorce, and didn't want to face that kind of experience again. But I felt certain the Lord was behind it, and would bless our remarriage, which He did!

Once remarried, we established new routines and traditions. We began having morning Bible studies and praying together every day. Then, one day about six months later, Rhett came to me and asked me to help him pray the Sinner's Prayer—he wanted to repent and have the kind of personal relationship with the Lord that I had. So, I prayed with him.

Things soon began changing in our lives, like a major breakthrough! Problems we had been struggling with were suddenly turned in our favor, and God was beginning to bless us. The Lord was hearing our prayers for our children, granting repentance and blessing in their lives. He then led me to just the right person to help us get Rhett's VA benefits, since he had served several years in the military, but the corrupt Department of Veteran Affairs at that time was trying to deny that he was even in the military!

But after a two-year battle with the VA, the Lord gave us a sudden breakthrough and blessed us with the compensation Rhett deserved, since his health problems were caused by exposure to "Agent Orange" when he was in Viet Nam. This greatly improved our financial lives. The Lord also used our victory to begin cleaning up the corrupt VA system, resulting in justice and compensation for thousands of other veterans!

The Holy Spirit began working with Rhett, leading him into deep confession of his sins and repentance. It was like he was taking a daily shower in holy water. He would frequently come to me and confess specific sins and ask my forgiveness, saying he felt the Lord wanted him to do so. He enjoyed learning more about God in our daily Bible studies and began drawing closer to the Lord in frequent prayer. He would go out on our patio and pray and talk to God for hours at a time, like in conversation.

Watching how God was moving with him reminded me of the question Jesus posed about who loves Him the most—the one who was forgiven little or the one who was forgiven much? Rhett loved Jesus much.

Therefore, I say to you, her sins which are many,
are forgiven, for she loved much . . . (Luke 7:47)

Then one beautiful spring morning in May 2012, the Lord answered a question Rhett had been earnestly praying about. He wanted to know if we could be married in Heaven. I had told him that the Bible says there is no marriage in Heaven, but my answer really upset him. He couldn't imagine how Heaven would be that great if we couldn't be married. He was determined to get a better answer, so he kept pursuing the Lord for an answer that he could accept.

The Lord heard his prayers and gave him his answer—and He sent two angels to do so! They took Rhett to Heaven, where he was given one of the most fantastic experiences I have ever heard. He was given a complete tour of Heaven. His question about marriage and many more truths about Heaven were shown him in a magnificent way!

Then three years later, in February 2015, God deepened His call in Rhett's life. He showed him the other side as well—by taking him on a tour of Hell! His testimonies about these experiences are detailed in Part III.

The visions, precepts, and experiences shared in this testimony are also affirmed in the following scriptures:

+ *The LORD is gracious and full of compassion, slow to anger and great in mercy. (Psalm 145:8)*

+ *But go and learn what this means: 'I desire mercy and not sacrifice.' For I did not come to call the righteous, but sinners, to repentance." (Matthew 9:13)*

+ *And above all things have fervent love for one another, for "love will cover a multitude of sins." (1 Peter 4:8)*

"Remain, Remain . . ."

Just before Christmas in December 2013, I was preparing for our family Christmas party and asked the Lord to give me the message He wanted me to share with my four adult children and their families. I was expecting the Holy Spirit to lead me to an edifying message of love and comfort, as He usually does. But not this time! Instead, He spoke the word "remain" into my mind very strongly four times. I heard the *audible* voice of the Lord in my head, and it was definite and resonating.

I was taken aback and puzzled by the word "remain." *What did it mean?* So, I prayed and asked the Lord to tell me the meaning. But there was no reply. Then, I felt the Holy Spirit telling me to look up the word in my concordance. I was reading my small Bible, which has an extremely limited concordance, and didn't expect that word would be in its index. But to my surprise, there were four citations for the word "remain!"

Two of the scriptures were in John chapter 15, one was in the book of 1 John chapter 2, and another in Revelation chapter 3. As I read all of these scriptures, I realized they were centered around a specific premise—that we must diligently seek and obey the Lord to remain in Him. I sensed that some of my family had strayed onto dangerous paths, and He was warning us to repent and obey Him, in order to remain in Him.

Perplexed, I wondered why He was saying this, since most Protestants are told: "Once-saved-always-saved—you cannot lose your salvation." Are those who backslide or go down wrong paths in danger of not remaining in Christ? Was Jesus saying that we can lose our salvation?

Message confirmed in scripture:

+ *If you keep my commands, you will remain in my love, just as I have kept my Father's commands and remain in his love. (John 15:10 NASB)*

+ *"I am the vine; you are the branches. If you remain in me and I in you, you will bear much fruit; apart from me you can do nothing. If you do not remain in me, you are like a branch that is thrown away and withers; such branches are picked up, thrown into the fire and burned." (John 15:5-6 NIV)*

+ *As for you, see that what you have heard from the beginning remains in you. If it does, you also will remain in the Son and in the Father. (1 John 2:24 NIV)*

+ *. . . "I know your works, that you have a name that you are alive, but you are dead. Be watchful, and strengthen the things which remain, that are ready to die, for I have not found your works perfect before God." (Revelation 3: 1-2)*

The Bride and
the Kingdom

In *early January 2014*, Rhett told me about the tour of Heaven experience God had given him in May 2012. The reason it finally came out is because I pinned him down and made him tell me how he knew the advanced Biblical truths and information he periodically expressed during our morning Bible studies. I knew that he rarely studied the Bible himself, and that he had never taken any classes in these things. Yet, he knew things that most theologians don't understand, and there was no wavering or fuzziness about the statements he made. He spoke as if from firsthand experience.

He was reluctant to tell me because he thought I wouldn't believe him and might think he was crazy. He didn't want to be put in a "funny farm," so he kept it to himself. I won't go into all the details of the things he was shown in Heaven and in Hell here, because I cover them in Part III: "Heaven Is for Real and So Is Hell."

But there was something Rhett saw at the gate of Heaven that I do want to discuss here. His description of what he was shown confirmed what I felt the Holy Spirit had been telling me whenever I studied the New Testament. And that message was that the "once-saved-always-saved" (OSAS) doctrine is not true!

When Rhett arrived at the gate of Heaven, he saw a large group of believers waiting their turn to go before Jesus, Who was standing before the gate. This group included high-profile Christian leaders, evangelists, pastors, theologians, and Sunday school teachers, as well as many non-clerical, everyday believers. Exactly the kind of people you would expect to be standing at the gate of Heaven.

They were all excited, eagerly anticipating the rewards they would receive for all the good works they had done in the Church. But as each person came before Jesus when it was their turn, Rhett was shocked at what he saw. Many of these model Christians were rejected and Jesus told them, "I don't know you." Then, Satan's evil angels would swoop down, grab them, and fly off with them—as they were crying, pleading, and trying to justify themselves by citing all the good works they had done for Jesus!

Stunned, I asked Rhett why they were rejected. "Because their heart wasn't right," he replied matter-of-factly. When pressed for more details, he said that there was sin in their heart or they loved something else more than Jesus. Many people were rejected because of unforgiveness in their heart, and numerous pastors and clergy were rejected because they didn't really love Jesus and His people. They were doing a lot of good works in His name but their motivation was for money or to promote themselves in some way. Such persons were held to a stricter standard than those who were not clergy. Rhett said, "If there is anything in your heart that would offend the Father, Jesus will not let you into Heaven."

So, the standard is high—not lenient, as the "once-saved-always-saved" doctrine leads people to believe. We are called to glorify God with our lives in this world, and be conformed to Jesus's image through sanctification. God does not allow hypocrites or rebellious, willful children who love and act like the world to enter Heaven.

But God is merciful. He gives grace, forgiveness, and cleansing to those who will humble themselves, confess their sins, and repent. And that's "the good news." So, if you have been harboring unforgiveness, hatred, or bitterness in your heart, or have been a worldly, self-serving, or hypocritical believer, you can confess your sins and return to Jesus as your First Love, now.

What Rhett saw and learned at the gate and in Heaven changed him dramatically. Prior to this experience, he was the most adamant OSAS believer I knew, and his lifestyle reflected it. But after his trip to Heaven, he became the most anti-OSAS believer I knew—and *very* repentant!

I found Rhett's testimony to be reassuring but unsettling at the same time, because many Christians today love and practice the OSAS doctrine, which most believers in the United States have been taught. So, I prayed and asked the Lord to help me understand the truth about how we are to live out the Christian life, if OSAS is not the way we are to practice Christianity.

The Lord answered me almost immediately. He began showing me a vision of the world, as if it were being designed by an architect laying out plans on a table. The architect held up the OSAS doctrine, as if it were a template for Earth. But it was obviously too small in size. It had a weird jagged hole in the middle and a narrow shape and size that could never fit over the earth.

Then, the Lord spoke into my mind and said that the correct model is "the Bride and the Kingdom." I instantly understood that "the Bride" is the righteous Church, and that "the Kingdom" is referring to God's kingdom of believers on Earth, as depicted in the parables. They illustrate how God deals with His people, and the precepts they must understand and obey to enter His kingdom in Heaven.

The parables show us examples of the attitudes and behavior of those who have been born again, thus becoming citizens of God's kingdom while on Earth. Through true-to-life stories, they illustrate how God deals with His people in this world, and they give us glimpses into the reality of Heaven and of Hell. They also show us examples of kingdom citizens on Earth who will or won't be able to enter His kingdom in Heaven, due to their conduct in this world.

The parables lay it all out for us, with entertaining stories rich in metaphor, allegory, and engaging word pictures that we can relate to. In fact, the parables constitute about one-third of the teachings of Jesus in the New Testament, which indicates their importance. But Jesus also said that they are a type of code language that only those who have "ears to hear" and "eyes to see" can understand. This may be why many people gloss over and ignore them. I think another reason they are avoided is because they often contradict the OSAS doctrines—so, many of today's believers refuse to listen to anything like that. Just as the apostle Paul prophesied to Timothy:

> Preach the word; be prepared in season and out of season; correct, rebuke and encourage—with great patience and careful instruction. For the time will come when people will not put up with sound doctrine. Instead, to suit their own desires, they will gather around them a great number of teachers to say what their itching ears want to hear. They will turn their ears away from the truth and turn aside to myths. (2 Timothy 4:2-4 NIV)

What if we were led to study the parables, and examined all their examples and consequences of right and wrong behavior, as our "Christianity 101" training? How many mistakes, wasted years, broken relationships, disgrace, hypocrisy, and failures of every kind might have been prevented? How many more people would have been attracted to Christianity and become saved?

How would those results compare to the fruits that have been produced by the permissive OSAS doctrine: a plethora of disgraced pastors who fell into sin, salacious scandals that have brought shame to the name of Jesus, and Christians who are largely regarded as deluded hypocrites in the eyes of the world?

Jesus and the apostles never taught the OSAS doctrine. In fact, they taught the opposite—that one's behavior is enormously important to their salvation, as the parables illustrate.

So, if the OSAS teaching is wrong, how did it come into the Church? My understanding is that it originated with Martin Luther during the Protestant Reformation. He was thrilled when God showed him that we are saved by grace through faith and not by the onerous works the Vatican was requiring of people. God used him mightily to confront the sins and corruption of the Vatican and bring the Bible and truth to the masses. Luther was bold and accomplished many good and vital victories for the truth. He was the kind of strong-willed man God needed for a very tough job and to launch the reformation.

But then he went too far and began developing his own doctrines and editing scripture to make it agree with his theology. Luther wanted to believe that salvation was by grace "alone" through faith "alone" and that God requires no works from humanity for salvation. He then committed some MAJOR transgressions by adding to and taking away from God's written word, the Bible, in very significant ways. This is absolutely forbidden and one of the most egregious sins a person can commit, according to Revelation 22:18-19 and Hebrew practices that have been meticulously followed for thousands of years.

In a class taught by a Lutheran theologian in 2019, I learned for the first time that Martin Luther had committed some egregious violations when creating the first German translation of his Protestant Bible. He not only added the word "sola" (alone) into certain scriptures (adulterating important doctrine), he also removed numerous books from the canon of scripture that had comprised the Bible for over one thousand years. Those seven books and their teachings are now referred to as "the apocrypha." They have been marginalized and mostly disregarded by Protestants for the last five hundred years.

But he didn't stop there. Luther also wanted to remove several books from the New Testament, because they contained scripture that conflicted with his new doctrines. However, he received so much pushback from other theologians that he relented and relegated his unloved books to the back of the Bible instead. My theologian teacher indicated that Luther didn't like any of the books from Hebrews through Revelation, and made some very disparaging remarks about them and their scriptures.

Did God tell him to do any of that? No. Luther presumed he knew best, and arbitrarily added to and took away from God's written word to make it agree with his own doctrines. Hearing this reminded me of someone else who had audaciously adulterated the word of God.

When the Lord was leading me out of Mormonism in 1984, He began by showing me the egregious sins of its founder, Joseph Smith. The first thing He showed me was how Smith had done violence to the word of God by adding his own words to scripture and fabricating heretical doctrines. Although Joseph Smith didn't remove any books from the canon, he effectively removed the entire Bible from his followers, Mormons. Smith said that God told him the Bible had been mistranslated and couldn't be trusted. He and subsequent Mormon "prophets" taught that only the church leaders can correctly interpret the Bible.

Although today's Mormons claim to believe in the Bible, they don't trust it and cannot understand it. They actually believe the doctrines of men, while claiming to be Christians—and are fatally deceived by doing so.

All professing Christians need to know and understand the Bible for themselves, so they don't believe and trust in the doctrines of men. Beware of anyone who behaves like a wolf (or a goat), while claiming to be a sheep. Those who teach and worship another Christ, another gospel, or a different spirit from what is depicted in the Bible, and those who tamper with the written word of God, are a huge red flag! "Take heed that no one deceives you."

I am not going into the details of all that Luther did to establish his doctrines, nor of Calvin and others who added their own doctrines to Luther's teachings, resulting in today's "once-saved-always-saved" doctrine. I encourage the reader to do their own research on this topic. His treatment of God's written word was arrogant, reckless, and shocking, in my humble opinion. And it spawned the erroneous OSAS doctrine!

Scriptures that confirm this vision:

+ *Let us be glad and rejoice and give Him glory, for the marriage of the Lamb has come, and His wife has made herself ready." And to her it was granted to be arrayed in fine linen, clean and bright, for the fine linen is the righteous acts of the saints. (Revelation 19:7-8)*

+ *And the disciples came and said to Him, "Why do You speak to them in parables?" He answered and said to them, "Because it has been given to you to know the mysteries of the kingdom of heaven, but to them it has not been given. (Matthew 13: 10-11)*

+ *Jesus answered and said to him, "If anyone loves Me, he will keep My word; and My Father will love him, and We will come to him and make Our home with him. He who does not love Me does not keep My words . . ." (John 14:23-24)*

+ *Blessed are those who do His commandments, that they may have the right to the tree of life, and may enter through the gates into the city. But outside are dogs and sorcerers and sexually immoral and murderers and idolaters, and whoever loves and practices a lie. (Revelation 22: 14-15)*

"Connect the Dots"

A *few minutes after* "The Bride and the Kingdom" vision, I went into my living room and sat down to reflect on what I had just learned. I suddenly perceived in the Spirit that Jesus was standing in front of me. As I gazed up in His direction He spoke into my mind, "You have to connect the dots. It's time to start connecting the dots." Dots appeared scattered in a random pattern in front of Him. He began pointing to them one at a time, and I understood that once they are connected, I would see the truth about a given issue. Then, He wrote "Connect the dots ministry" across the scattered dots!

These two visions occurred in 2014, but a year earlier in January 2013, the Lord gave me a profound God Moment experience that I titled "I Have Made You a Watchman." I have placed this testimony in Part II, "Warnings of the Watchmen." So, when I received the "Connect the Dots" vision in 2014, I understood why He was telling me this. A watchman must know how to connect the dots, as he observes the landscape and receives information from his sources. It makes sense that Jesus would tell me that I was to start connecting the dots—it's essential if you're going to be a good watchman.

But I didn't really know how to be a watchman or how to connect the dots. So, I asked the Lord to teach me. And that's what He has been doing for the past several years. He has shown me many visions and prophetic dreams about our world, and inspired me to think like an investigative reporter. He has also connected me with several other watchmen around the world, to whom He is showing many different things. And, with the help and inspiration of the Holy Spirit, we are getting very good at connecting the dots!

Fulfillment of this vision:

This vision is in the process of being fulfilled right now. The Lord has been helping me connect the things He has shown me, with Biblical prophesies and events that are happening in the world today.

He has also connected me with many other watchmen He has called, as if we are His own reconnaissance team. Most are devout Christians with all kinds of expertise: pastors, scientists, investigative journalists, theology scholars, political experts, military experts, financial experts, professors, intelligence agents, movie directors, and certain believers with prophetic gifts. His desire is to warn His people about the time and season we are living in, so we can prepare ourselves mentally, physically, emotionally, and most of all spiritually for what lies ahead.

As iron sharpens iron, so one person sharpens another.
(Proverbs 27:17 NIV)

The Seeker-Sensitive Church

In the 1980s, a new phenomenon began emerging in Christianity called the "Seeker-Sensitive Church." Then, by the early 1990s, this popular model for doing church evolved into the "Emergent Church." Nobody ever said where it emerged from but it did spring up fast!

This hot new thing in Christianity certainly grew like a weed—as believers began leaving traditional churches and flocking to these world-friendly congregations. Studies show that most of their growth has come from attracting believers away from other churches, rather than evangelizing new Christians.

In 2015, after three years of visiting several of these congregations, I was led by the Lord to discover how this new model for church originated. The agnostic business guru Peter Drucker (world-famous for turning around the economy of Japan and reviving large corporations) was the author behind the "Seeker-Sensitive" church model and movement. Representing a group of like-minded wealthy men, he identified and approached certain promising young pastors across the US with an offer they couldn't refuse: his expert coaching and tailor-made business models to create highly successful Christian churches!

So, why did these ultra-wealthy non-believers say they wanted to promote Christianity? Because they felt the Church taught the kind of positive values that would create morality and turn around the declining character of American society, which they desperately wanted to do. You might say they were the original "Make America Great Again" promoters. Or, so they claimed.

It seemed plausible, and these gifted young Christian leaders, who included Rick Warren and Bill Hybels among others, were undoubtedly flattered to have been chosen. It was a very enticing offer wrapped in many week-long training retreats at Drucker and associates' fabulous homes. And, they were guaranteed success—a large, thriving church and the ability to make a very good living promoting Christianity.

But their model for success came with some significant compromises: To appeal to their target market they needed to minimize the physical cross (because it allegedly offends many young adults) and add coffee shops and rock bands for worship services. If they followed this formula, their target market (average age of thirty-two) would flock to their church in droves, they promised. And they did!

They gave the people what they wanted, as determined by their marketing surveys—a cool, modernized religion that felt like a casual social club, and guaranteed salvation by grace without conditions. What's more to love?!!

Everything was designed to be appealing to the tastes and lifestyles of the contemporary group they wanted to attract. They avoided anything that might be considered controversial or unappealing in the eyes of the world—like blatantly displaying the cross or talking about the supernatural gifts and power of the Holy Spirit.

Peter Drucker's church model was to be comfortable, entertaining, and inspiring—an inviting place where people from all backgrounds and beliefs could walk in and enjoy the service. It was a new way of doing evangelism. Church could be an enjoyable experience that didn't offend their target market. And, it would keep them coming back, bringing their friends with them. Now, all those unsaved people who were turned off by traditional Christianity could learn about Jesus.

But who is this contemporary Jesus they love and worship? Is He the self-sacrificing, righteous Jesus of the Bible or "another Christ"? If the leaders and congregation experience the prosperity they are often promised, do they use the extra money to help the poor in their congregation and elsewhere? Or do they use it to enlarge their own estate? We are told to judge the tree by its fruits. Are they producing the fruits of the Biblical Jesus—or the fruits of a worldly impersonator?

Do they believe in the supernatural Holy Spirit of the Bible, or "a different Spirit"? When people believe that the Holy Spirit is no longer needed for supernatural gifts, miracles, or works in the modern Church, they believe in a different spirit from the Holy Spirit who empowered Jesus and His apostles. If they only want the Holy Spirit to do an occasional baptism or salvation but otherwise reject His supernatural gifts and power, they have insulted, denigrated, and rejected Him, in my humble opinion.

Before long, many of the traditional churches also adopted Drucker's church model, in order to compete for a dwindling number of believers. And they likewise don't teach or promote the works of the Holy Spirit; some actually teach against it!

But now, the world is coming apart at the seams and Christians will need the gifts and power of the Holy Spirit more than ever. Will they repent and stop suppressing Him? Will He return with supernatural power to the churches who do? Let's hope and pray that He does!

+ *For the wrath of God is revealed from heaven against all ungodliness and unrighteousness of men, who suppress the truth in unrighteousness.* (Romans 1:18)

✦ *Of how much worse punishment, do you suppose, will he be thought worthy who has trampled the Son of God underfoot, counted the blood of the covenant by which he was sanctified a common thing, and insulted the Spirit of grace? (Hebrews 10:29)*

Miracles, Wonders, and Supernatural Events

The following testimonies are of miracles and wonders that display God's supernatural power and amazing love in many different ways. The Lord desires to demonstrate his goodness and power in the lives of His people, that they and others will believe and be blessed. God is supernatural, so when He acts it is in supernatural ways—from astonishing miracles that impact nations to supernatural wonders that whisper His love in very personal ways. But we must believe in order to receive such things, as the New Testament writer James states:

> But when you ask, you must believe and not doubt, because the one who doubts is like a wave of the sea, blown and tossed by the wind. That person should not expect to receive anything from the Lord. Such a person is double-minded and unstable in all they do. (James 1:6-8 NIV)

Sadly, many Christians have been misled into believing that God no longer does miracles and supernatural works in our modern world. So, they have doubt that prevents them from receiving such blessings. Hopefully, this book will help to dispel those doubts and build faith to receive and walk in the power and gifts of the Holy Spirit in these last days!

"Very truly I tell you, whoever believes in me will do the works I have been doing, and they will do even greater things than these, because I am going to the Father." (John 14:12 NIV)

In the first half of the Miracles section in Part I, I share several testimonies of supernatural acts the Lord has done in my life, and in the lives of my late husband and our four children over the past fifty-plus years. Then, I share several amazing miracles God performed in the life of a godly man named Henry Gruver. He was an unusual evangelist the Lord led me to in 2019, when I asked for confirmation of certain visions God had shown me. I discuss those specific visions in Part II, "Warnings of the Watchmen."

But the Lord also impressed me to include in this book some of the astounding miracles that He performed in Henry's life. They are powerful evidence that God absolutely exists—and that He still performs supernatural works in the lives of His people. I think you will be greatly blessed and your faith will be increased when you read about these amazing works of God that have been done in today's world!

Premonition of Imminent Disaster

In 1969, Rhett and I were married and he was working in my father's business, together with my oldest brother Merrill and Lenny, a family friend. One hot summer day in late July, I suddenly became gripped with a strong foreboding and a premonition that my father would be seriously injured the following day at his business.

The foreboding consumed me the entire day. That evening it was so strong that I told Rhett something violent was going to happen to my father the next day at work, and to stay close to Dad because he would need his help. I didn't know what was going to happen, but I knew it would be violent and my father would be seriously injured. Ironically, I didn't feel any threat to Rhett nor anyone else, just my dad. But I knew all of the guys would be present in the event.

The next morning, I continued to be consumed with this foreboding and couldn't think about anything else. I knew that my mother would need my help when the event happened, so I drove to her home. As I was getting out of my car, I heard the phone ringing in her house. Instantly, I knew what the phone call was about—the event had just happened!

I ran up the steps into the house as Mother was answering the phone, and I began telling my younger sister that Dad had just been injured and that's what the phone call was about. I was right. The caller gave Mom the horrific news, and she was beside herself. My dad's business had just blown up in an explosion and my father was injured and taken to the hospital! Amazingly, Rhett and Merrill were not injured. Lenny had been hit by a four-hundred-pound machine and buried under heavy equipment and debris—yet inexplicably, not seriously injured. But tragically, Dad had been blown through a large bay window and sucked back into the burning building, where he was buried under the collapsing wreckage.

It was a miracle that any of them survived. But most amazing of all was how God protected Rhett and Merrill in this horrific event—two strong guys whom He used to save the others. Rhett had been talking with my dad in his office when the building exploded from gas fumes hitting the water heater. The office was the only part of the building that had a basement underneath, where the furnace room was located. When the building exploded, the office floor collapsed, and Rhett was blown straight up two stories, hitting his head on a steel beam in the roof. He then fell three stories into the furnace room beneath the office.

He was surrounded by fire, and the basement staircase was gone, blown to bits as were all the walls in the building. Somehow, Rhett was able to scramble his way up to ground level and then through the fire and shambles until he saw my father's hand poking out from under a huge pile of debris. He frantically began digging through the rubble to rescue my father. At the same time, he saw Merrill at the other end of the building, pick up a four-hundred-pound machine, and hurl it off Lenny like a tinker toy. He picked up Lenny's unconscious body and carried him out of the burning building, dodging and weaving through the flames. Then with superhuman strength and speed, Rhett and Merrill frantically threw off a huge pile of bricks, glass, and wreckage in the midst of the raging fire to rescue Dad.

When I arrived at the shop about forty-five minutes after the phone call, the fire department and news media were there, and it was a devastating scene. My father and Lenny had been taken to the hospital. The fire was put out and all that remained was a charred brick structure, around a black, sooty interior. The building was completely gutted, windows blown out, equipment melted. Cars were demolished, and the acrid smell of water-soaked charred wood hung in the air. It was devastating and heartbreaking.

Rhett came over to my car when I arrived and began telling me what had happened. Miraculously, he was unhurt. He had only suffered a small scratch from a piece of glass when digging my father out. Then, he pulled out his wallet and showed me his driver's license. It was melted. But amazingly, he wasn't knocked unconscious when he smashed his head on the roof beam, he didn't suffer any broken bones from falling three stories, and he didn't have any burns, cuts, or even bruises, nor was his clothing burned. Just a scratch—and his hair was singed.

Merrill likewise was unscathed. Both Rhett and Merrill were strong men and in good shape. But what they were able to survive and do that day was superhuman. The fact that God had given me foreknowledge about this event was another miracle, and confirmed that the Lord Himself had graciously forewarned and was present in the event, protecting and performing a series of miracles—showing Himself to be God!

My premonition was fulfilled within twenty-four hours, on July 29, 1969.

I Feel Your Pain

On a cold January day in 1985, about two years after we became Christians, Rhett was on assignment working at an industrial facility about 250 miles from home. Around 5 p.m. as he was leaving work, he slipped on an icy sidewalk and fell hard on his right shoulder, tearing his rotator cuff. Excruciating pain ripped through his shoulder and he was unable to lift his arm!

At the exact time of his accident, I also experienced his injury. I was at home in our kitchen preparing dinner when I bent down to pick up something on the floor, and suddenly I felt a sharp, deep pain in the rotator cuff area of my right arm. The pain was excruciating, and I could not lift my arm. Shocked at what had just happened for no reason, I remember looking up at the clock on the wall above me—it was 5:09 p.m. The pain continued for about thirty minutes before it began subsiding and I regained normal use of my arm. My daughter Michelle was with me in the kitchen when it happened and still remembers this unusual incident.

How and why did I experience Rhett's pain? I don't know but this event was supernatural! Was it a demonic attack? Did they attack both of us simultaneously? Was it retaliation for the twenty-page letter we sent to the Mormon Church two months earlier, telling them in detail why we were withdrawing our membership? Or were Rhett and I so closely connected by the Holy Spirit that I felt his pain? I don't know, but for some reason this supernatural incident occurred.

As a result of this event, the Holy Spirit impressed upon me to always pray for angelic protection over my family, which I have done every day since!

Spiritual Gifts

About three years after my Visitation experience, a Holy Spirit-filled man with amazing gifts for healing and words of knowledge began attending the Lutheran church we had joined. His name was Ken Yahvah. "Yahvah" is another holy name of God. Most Christians are familiar with His holy name "YHWH," which is pronounced "Yahwey." However, Hebrew scripture also shows His name as "YHVH," pronounced "Yahvah." I have often wondered if Ken may have been a special messenger of God in human form. He was the most supernaturally gifted Christian I have ever known, and there was something mysterious about him.

My reason for bringing up Ken Yahvah is the influence he had on our new Christian lives. One afternoon, he came to our home, ministered to our family, and healed my neck, shoulders, and knee of arthritis that was setting in, due to a car accident I was in fourteen years earlier. Then he led Rhett, our daughter Michelle, and me to receive our spiritual prayer tongues.

This is a Biblical gift that the apostle Paul talks about in some of his epistles. Paul said that all Christians should pray in their spiritual tongues often. Why? I believe that it is the perfect prayer of the Holy Spirit and, therefore, the Father hears it. *And if we know that He hears us, whatever we ask, we know that we have the petitions that we have asked of Him.*

(1 John 5:15). So, it is highly effective prayer that accomplishes the will of God. Praying in your spiritual tongue is also extremely effective in doing spiritual warfare—a fact I have personally witnessed. (Ephesians 6:18)

But unfortunately, most churches today no longer teach or believe in the powerful gifts of the Holy Spirit that God gave to His people at Pentecost. The unbelief and politically correct gospel that have infiltrated Christianity in the last forty years have greatly weakened the Church and squelched the Holy Spirit.

Christians are soon going to wish they had God's supernatural power, as our world descends into very dark and dangerous times. We will need every Holy Spirit gift the Lord has for us, to persevere and maintain our faith. As we enter into a time of intense spiritual battle between the forces of good and evil, the Holy Spirit's supernatural gifts of Miracles, Faith, Prophecy, Words of Knowledge and Wisdom, Healings, and Gifts of Tongues can make the difference between victory and defeat. That's why God gave them to us!

Jesus Himself bestowed a spiritual tongue upon me, as I described earlier in The Visitation, and that same tongue was later confirmed through Ken Yahvah. Then, the Lord told me to use it in spiritual warfare, as I describe in "The Deliverance," where it broke through the power of demons. Those who say the Lord did away with supernatural works of the Holy Spirit because they are no longer needed in the Church are speaking absurdities that are doctrines of demons, in my opinion and experience.

And take the helmet of salvation, and the sword of the Spirit, which is the Word of God; praying always with all prayer and supplication in the Spirit, being watchful to this end with all perseverance and supplication for all the saints. (Ephesians 6: 17-18)

Jesus wants us to receive our prayer tongue, as well as the other supernatural gifts, and use them to pray to the Father, heal the sick, cast out demons, and do all the supernatural acts that He did and we are supposed to do. (Mark 16: 17-18; John 14:12)

> *Now to each one the manifestation of the Spirit is given for the common good. To one there is given through the Spirit a message of wisdom, to another a message of knowledge by means of the same Spirit, to another faith by the same Spirit, to another gifts of healing by that one Spirit, to another miraculous powers, to another prophecy, to another distinguishing between spirits, to another speaking in different kinds of tongues, and to still another the interpretation of tongues. (1 Corinthians 12:7-10 NIV)*

Which "manifestation of the Spirit" did God give you? Have you ever used it?

We as Christians need to wake up and ask the Lord for every supernatural gift we can get. We are entering into the most challenging time in world history, and we will need everything God has for us to fight both the spiritual and physical encounters that are coming—*before* the Rapture!

It is extremely offensive to reject or scoff at a gift someone offers you—especially if it is from God Almighty! Will He scoff at the cries of those who scoffed at Him? (2 Peter 3:3; Galatians 6:7; Proverbs 1: 24-28, 3:34)

Confirming scriptures:

+ *So what shall I do? I will pray with my spirit, but I will also pray with my understanding . . . (1 Corinthians 14:15 NIV)*

+ *Likewise, the Spirit also helps in our weaknesses. For we do not know what we should pray for as we ought, but the Spirit Himself makes intercession for us with groanings which cannot be uttered. (Romans 8:26)*

+ *Now this is the confidence that we have in Him, that if we ask anything according to His will, He hears us. And if we know that He hears us, whatever we ask, we know that we have the petitions that we have asked of Him. (1 John 5: 14-15).*

+ *"Therefore, I tell you that people will be forgiven for every sin and insult to God. But insulting the Holy Spirit won't be forgiven." (Matthew 12:31, CEB)*

"Get Out of the Boat!"

When our oldest daughter, Michelle, graduated from high school, we rewarded her with a vacation to Hawaii. She and five of her girlfriends all went together for a week by themselves. They were good girls, so all of the parents trusted them, especially since there was a group of best friends going together. But I still covered them in prayer morning, noon, and night.

They had a fabulous time seeing the sights, playing in the ocean, and enjoying the culture of such a beautiful tropical paradise. One such day, as Michelle and her friend Kim were floating on rafts in the ocean, some guys approached them and offered to give them a free tour of the islands in their boats. That sounded great! The girls wanted to do an island tour but couldn't afford to pay for it, so this was the perfect answer. They returned their rafts to the dock and proceeded toward the guys waiting for them.

Excited, the girls started getting into their boats. But as soon as Michelle stepped foot into the boat, she heard the *audible* voice of the Lord: "GET OUT OF THE BOAT!!" It was a loud, male voice reverberating in her head and struck terror in her. She immediately jumped out of the boat and motioned to her friend to come with her, frantically making excuses that they had to go tell their friends where they were going. All she knew was that she was to get away fast, and not get into the boat!

Scriptural confirmation:

+ *"The fear of the LORD is the beginning of wisdom, and the knowledge of the Holy One is understanding." (Proverbs 9:10)*

+ *Knowing, therefore, the terror of the Lord, we persuade men . . . . (2 Corinthians 5:11)*

+ *Yea, though I walk through the valley of the shadow of death, I will fear no evil; for You are with me; Your rod and Your staff, they comfort me. (Psalm 23:4)*

This scripture was my peace of mind and assurance while they were gone:

Be anxious for nothing, but in everything by prayer and sup-plication, with thanksgiving, let your requests be made known to God; and the peace of God, which surpasses all understand-ing, will guard your hearts and minds through Christ Jesus. (Philippians 4: 6-7)

Amazing Grace

My oldest son, Sean, loves to have a good time. He has always had a great sense of humor and can keep you laughing with his amusing stories and comical way of looking at life. He has a talent for turning an awful event into a really funny story full of irony and hilarious observations!

An example is this story about something that happened to him one day when he was in high school. This is a story that I didn't learn about until many years later when he was an adult, and it came out in casual conversation, an "oh, by the way" type of comment.

Sean's friend Mark had just gotten a hot new sports car for his birthday and wanted to show it off. It didn't take much persuading to convince Sean to cut class and go with him on a joy ride. But as they were driving down the road returning to school, the traffic light suddenly changed, so Mark stepped on the gas pedal to get through the light. The car's turbocharged engine quickly accelerated as they entered the intersection. Unfortunately, their joy ride came to an abrupt end, as they met another car turning left in the intersection!

Sean was ejected through the windshield (this was before you *had* to wear a seatbelt). He remembers his head hitting the windshield, flying through the air, and his neck and shoulder hitting a cement curb as he landed about fifty feet away, next to a gas station. He jumped up dazed, and rushed over to the crumpled sports car to check on his friend, who was slumped over the steering wheel, bleeding from his nose with a cut around his ear. Mark regained consciousness and asked Sean how he had gotten out of the car. Pointing to a man-sized hole in the front windshield, Sean told him that was how he had gotten out. But Mark couldn't grasp what he'd heard and kept asking Sean over and over again how he had gotten out of the car.

People who had witnessed the accident rushed over to the scene, insisting Sean lie down—because he had to be in shock. But he ignored them and focused on Mark, as the intersection began filling with people. Then the police began arriving—and Sean was terrified! He didn't want to get in trouble for sluffing school again. So, he blended in with the crowd and went over to the gas station, where he called another friend to come and pick him up. Sean finished the rest of his classes that day, then came home after school like it was just another day. He had no cuts, bruises, or obvious injury—except a goose egg on top of his head.

Miraculously, his friend and the driver of the other car had only minimal injuries. I do remember hearing that Mark had totaled his brand new sports car, and thinking how upset his father must have been. But I had no clue Sean was with him.

How many people thrown through a windshield come away unscathed? How many people thrown fifty feet, hitting their head and neck on a concrete curb, jump up like they'd just tripped? This was a miracle—the grace of God and His guardian angels that surrounded Sean that day!

> *For He shall give His angels charge over you, to keep you in all your ways. In their hands they shall bear you up lest you dash your foot against a stone. (Psalm 91: 11-12)*

It's quite an amazing story, and the funny part is that he never told me about this incredible event until twenty years later. Am I the only mother who doesn't find out about the shenanigans and near-death experiences of her children until many years after?!

Back from the Dead

In 1997, around my son Greg's seventeenth birthday, he went out one cold January night with his friends to celebrate. They were partying and drinking beer like teenage boys often do. At the time, Greg happened to be on a certain medication for muscle spasms he was having in his neck, from a football injury a few years earlier.

As a result of the medication and alcohol, he had a drug interaction, leaving him unconscious. His friends panicked, probably being drunk, and drove him to the nearest hospital, where they dropped him off near the emergency entrance. They were likely scared about what had happened and afraid of getting in trouble with the law, so they just left his unconscious body there on the ground. Not long after, an ER doctor arriving for the night shift almost ran over him! But thankfully he didn't, and they got Greg inside before he froze to death.

They worked frantically to save him, not knowing who he was or what was wrong with him. There was no one to tell them what had happened, and Greg had no ID on him, so they couldn't call anyone. After working on him for over an hour, they lost him. Greg flatlined and was dead—for about twelve minutes. Then, he suddenly came back to life! From what they told me later, Greg was quite the event in the emergency room that night—a lot of stress and drama!

For about a year before this happened, I had an uncomfortable feeling that something like this was going to happen to Greg. So, I always covered him in prayer whenever he went out. But on this particular night, it was my daughter Kelli whom the Lord was speaking to about Greg. She was ten years old at the time, and *knew* that she needed to stay up that night to answer the phone because something was going to happen to Greg. So, unbeknownst to me, she did.

Around 2:30 a.m. the phone rang, and Kelli answered it. Cottonwood Hospital was calling for me, so she came into my bedroom to wake me up. It was that awful phone call that we all hope never to get, especially at 2:30 a.m.! The hospital emergency room staff were saying my son was there and I needed to get to the hospital ASAP. Rhett was working out of town that night, so Kelli went to the hospital with me.

When we arrived, everything seemed quiet and orderly; there was no drama. I was led into a small room where a nurse was sitting quietly beside Greg's bed. He was awake and sitting up and seemed fine. The nurse proceeded to tell me how glad they were to finally reach me. Everyone had been terribly upset, not knowing who to notify—until he unexpectedly came back to life. Then, he gave them the information to call me.

I got the impression they didn't have many people suddenly come back to life after being dead for twelve minutes—and be fine. It really shook them up!

So, what happened to Greg during those fateful twelve minutes?

He told me that he "went down into silence." He was conscious but everything was very dark, pitch black, and still. It wasn't Heaven and it wasn't the traditional description of Hell, but was it "outer darkness"? It was nothingness. Living in a black nothingness with no one else around—profound aloneness. It was its own kind of Hell.

The dead do not praise the LORD, nor any who go down into silence. (Psalm 115:17)

Why did Greg come back to life? Did he cry out for Jesus to save him? No, he didn't—the thought never crossed his mind. He seemed to be helpless to do so, like he had no concept of God. But he did feel an ominous fear approaching him. Then, suddenly he was out—free! Back in the world, awake and alive again—rescued from spiritual prison and a terrifying reality!

I believe it wasn't Greg's time to die, and the Lord had important plans for his life. But he wasn't right with God for some reason, giving Satan the ability to seize him. The spiritual realm is governed by spiritual law, much like we on Earth are governed by physical law. Greg was raised in the Church and he was a believer, but he had fallen into the world and wasn't walking with Jesus. If you die and are out of fellowship with Christ, Satan apparently has power over your soul!

I believe the Lord wanted to save Greg, but there had to be a legal right to release him from Satan's claim. Greg needed a spiritual "trump card!" I think that trump card was found in faith, love, and intercessory prayer together with God's will. My faith and intercessory prayer that night before I went to bed, plus Kelli's love for her brother and obedience to the voice of the Holy Spirit, together with the will of God for Greg's life, created a strong three-cord spiritual rope that Jesus used to yank him out of the devil's grip. Or maybe God could have done so anyway, because it wasn't Greg's time to go.

Something usurped the laws of life and death that night. But is my theory Biblical? I think it is, based on the following scriptures:

+ The apostle Peter was miraculously released from prison through intercessory prayers. God sent an angel to break his chains and take him out of the jail cell. Intercessory prayers together with the love and faith of a group of Christians gave God's angel the authority to intervene and free Peter from jail. (Acts 12)

+ The prophet Elijah prayed in faith for the dead body of the widow's son, and God heard his prayer. The boy came back from the dead, through Elijah's love, faith, and intercessory prayer. (1 Kings 17: 17-24)

When we ask in faith for things that are within God's will, nothing is impossible. The apostle John tells us:

Now this is the confidence that we have in Him, that if we ask anything according to His will, He hears us. And if we know that He hears us, whatever we ask, we know that we have the petitions that we have asked of Him. (1 John 5: 14-15)

There is exponential power when Christians get together to pray in agreement about something. Jesus Himself joins us. And when He is the third cord, nothing is impossible! Christians are going to need great faith and spiritual power in the days ahead, so we need to learn and practice God's precepts now!

+ *"Again, truly I tell you that if two of you on earth agree about anything they ask for, it will be done for them by my Father in heaven. For where two or three gather in my name, there am I with them." (Matthew 18:19-20 NIV)*

+ *Though one may be overpowered by another, two can withstand him. And a threefold cord is not quickly broken. (Ecclesiastes 4:12)*

Kelli's Winter Camp

During junior high school, my daughter Kelli was involved in the Youth Group at our church, and would attend both the summer and winter camps each year. I was always a big fan of these camps because of the life-changing spiritual growth and good times the kids always experienced. However, a week before she was to attend her eighth-grade winter camp, I began to feel a strong foreboding about the camp—that there would be serious injury. I didn't know what the event would be, but I felt that Kelli would be impacted by it. So, I began praying, and even considered not letting her go to the camp.

The kids left for Camp Utaba on Friday, and were supposed to return Sunday afternoon. On Saturday, I began having unsettling feelings about the camp and knew that I needed to pray for Kelli, so I did. It was a strong ominous feeling that I couldn't shake, like what I had experienced many years before when my father's business was demolished in an explosion.

On Sunday morning, I attended church at Good Shepherd, but couldn't shake the strong foreboding hanging over me. At 12:30, as I was leaving the church parking lot, I suddenly experienced a "God Moment" and knew I had to pull over immediately and pray hard for Kelli! So, I did. Then I drove home. About twenty minutes after arriving home, the phone rang. As Rhett was answering it, I knew immediately that something had happened to Kelli!

One of the pastors was calling to tell us they were taking Kelli to the hospital in an ambulance. She had fallen about forty-five minutes earlier while ice skating, and hit hard on the back of her head. She was unconscious and her blood pressure was extremely low, near death. They said everyone was praying for her and they would call us from the hospital when they had more information. About an hour later they called, and the news was good. She had regained consciousness and her blood pressure was normalizing.

Once we had her safe at home, Kelli related her experience to me. She described how she was lying on her back after the accident and everything was very still and dark, but she sensed that others were gathered around her praying and trying to revive her. Then, a beautiful white light appeared above her, and she reached her hand up toward it. She wanted to go with the light—it was filled with the most wonderful love and peace she had ever experienced!

Later, her camp counselor called to tell me what had happened. She described the same events that Kelli and the pastor had related, but made a big point about how Kelli was unconscious but kept reaching her arm up while they were trying to revive her. The counselor had gone with Kelli in the ambulance and was praying for her while the paramedics were working on her. She talked about what a battle it was to keep her from dying, as her blood pressure was at the point of no return! Later, the doctors told me that it was a miracle she recovered and didn't have brain damage, given the critical level she was at.

The supernatural power of God through love, faith, and intercessory prayer—again!

I believe this was a demonic hit-job that the Holy Spirit had warned me was going to happen, because intense spiritual warfare would be required by me and everyone at the camp.

Surely the LORD God does nothing unless He reveals
His secret to His servants the prophets. (Amos 3:7)

The white light was the Lord Jesus who came to Kelli's bedside with supernatural comfort and power to protect and sustain her, defeating the powers of evil as we all prayed. Jesus's presence was the only thing Kelli wanted—and what she was reaching for while unconscious!

For we do not wrestle against flesh and blood, but against
principalities, against powers, against the rulers of the darkness
of this age, against spiritual hosts of wickedness in the heavenly
places. Therefore, take up the whole armor of God, that you
may be able to withstand in the evil day, and having done all,
to stand. (Ephesians 6: 12-13)

A Medical Impossibility

When *I was thirteen years old,* I was diagnosed with psoriasis, a chronic skin disease that is unsightly and embarrassing. Itchy patches of flaky skin called "lesions" would develop mostly around my joints—knees, elbows, and even my knuckles. Sometimes it would spread to my arms and legs. It was awful to live with, especially as a teenager and young adult. So, I had to wear long sleeves and pants most of the time. And for the next thirty years, I periodically had to take a dangerous drug called methotrexate to clear up my skin, so I could enjoy different activities.

I struggled with this bothersome disease for almost forty years, before it dawned on me to ask the Lord to heal my skin. Why hadn't I asked before? Because it was medically impossible to be cured of psoriasis and I had lived with it for so long, I had just accepted it and never considered that I could be cured.

But then one day, several years after I had become a Christian, I was praying and a thought suddenly came into my mind to ask the Lord to heal my skin of psoriasis. So, I did. I went on with my life and didn't think about it again for a few weeks. Then, I began to notice that my psoriasis had improved, even though I hadn't done anything different. This continued and a short time later, my skin was 100 percent clear.

That was over twenty years ago, and I have remained clear ever since—healed of the incurable genetic disease, psoriasis!

Thank you, Lord Jesus!

Bless the LORD, O my soul, and forget not all His benefits:
Who forgives all your iniquities, who heals all your diseases,
Who redeems your life from destruction,
Who crowns you with lovingkindness and tender mercies,
Who satisfies your mouth with good things,
So that your youth is renewed like the eagle's.
(Psalm 103: 2-5)

Deliverance

I *will not give details about the identity* of the individual central to this event, but the Lord used Rhett, Michelle, and me to deliver this person from demons. The event took place on September 16, 2012, which also happened to be the beginning of Rosh Hashanah.

It was a dramatic demonstration of the power of the Holy Spirit together with the name of Jesus, scriptures, and our faith as we did battle with various demons, commanding them in Jesus's name to leave the person. As soon as we confronted the demons, the "strongman" took control of the person and bound them. The person became aware of the demons' presence within them and could hear the demons talking amongst themselves.

They began manifesting through their victim in various ways: redness around the eyes, nose, and mouth; inability to speak (the demons constricted the person's voice box, as if choking them); eyes rolling back in their head; moving in and out of consciousness; rolling their head around to prevent the person from looking into our eyes; and the demons speaking out their names in their individual demonic voices, when commanded to do so.

The first demon stated his name in an Arabic-sounding accent as "Ka." But the second demon spoke with an Indian-sounding accent, speaking his name "Rakhi." I later did a little research and found that "Ka" is an Egyptian god that attempts to capture the soul. And Rakhi is the Indian god of brother/sister love. It targets brothers and sisters, and attempts to bind them together through a ritualistic kind of brotherly love.

We did battle for about two hours and got out the weaker demons, but the "strongman" remained stealthily hidden, refusing to manifest or identify himself, while keeping the person bound. In desperation and exhaustion, I prayed and begged Jesus to help us—we couldn't leave the person in this condition! The Holy Spirit impressed me to pray in my prayer tongue, so I did. Rhett and Michelle also interceded in their prayer tongues.

Immediately, the Holy Spirit began moving and Jesus showed up in great power as a bright white light, standing behind me. When that happened, the demons freaked out and began screaming and "running around" inside the person—they were terrified! (All of these details were related to me afterward by the person who was delivered.) Then, the Lord put it in my mind to ask the person a certain question, and give them an ultimatum. They had to choose whom they loved more—their family members or the demons. This may sound absurd, but demons make you love what they love and hate what they hate, so their victims often want to keep the demons more than anything else—even their parents, spouse, or children.

The person struggled with all their strength to respond to my question, trying to mouth "yes" when I asked if they chose their loved ones over the demons. The strongman was restraining their body and choking their voice box to prevent their ability to respond. But as soon as I saw their answer, I seized it and exclaimed, "WE HAVE AGREEMENT!" Then I commanded the demons in the name of Jesus to release the person and leave them. A few seconds later, the person began violently dry heaving several times, releasing the demons with each heave. After they finished, we saw the most amazing miracle of all: The person went from looking like a hardened worldly person to looking like an angel!

We then led the person through a prayer of confession and repentance, and they asked Jesus to come into their heart and become Lord of their life. Later, the person told me that the strongman was the first demon to gain entrance into them, and that it was a demon of sex. They got this demon from watching a pornographic movie when they were a child. Their father was watching the movie late at night and didn't know the child had awakened and come into the room, and was able to see the movie. (The father was a "believer" in Jesus. The victim was also a believer, a member of our church for about twenty years who participated in ministry.) Apparently, the person learned the identity and origin of the strongman while we were in the process of casting out the demons.

So, let this be a warning to whoever reads this: If you watch porn, demons will enter you. If they can enter a child who inadvertently watched it, they will enter a person of any age who watches it!

If this happens, confess your sins ASAP, repent, and ask Jesus to forgive, cleanse, and renew you. But do so before the demons get a stronghold controlling your heart so you don't want to repent. Then, you'll need to have them cast out. But good luck finding Christians who can do so!

Needless to say, nobody who has demons can enter Heaven.

Confirmed in scripture:

+ *And He said to them, "Go into all the world and preach the gospel to every creature. He who believes and is baptized will be saved; but he who does not believe will be condemned. And these signs will follow those who believe: In My name they will cast out demons . . . ." (Mark 16: 15-17)*

+ *Behold I give you the authority to trample on serpents and scorpions, and over all the power of the enemy, and nothing shall by any means hurt you. (Luke 10:19)*

Mysteries

As I share in my testimony titled, "Out of the Blue" in Part II, on May 5 and 8, 2014, I was given two prophetic dreams that were partially fulfilled two months later on July 17 and 18. At the time they were fulfilled, the Lord impressed on me that there is something significant about those dates, having to do with numerology and nefarious power. I felt that nefarious events would happen on those dates in the future.

Exactly two years later, on the morning of July 17, 2016, my husband Rhett, who had been terminally ill with heart problems for seven years, suddenly developed carbon dioxide poisoning and his behavior changed dramatically. Medical professionals call it "carbon dioxide psychosis." He was incoherent, stumbling around, and he had a completely different personality. I had to call the paramedics, who took him to the VA hospital. Soon after arriving, he fell into a coma and died ten hours later on July 18.

Was his sudden death an evil attack somehow empowered on those dates? I don't know, but it felt like that to me. I wasn't psychologically ready for him to leave when he did. Until that day, his health was weakened but about the same as it had been for the past year.

The Bible says that sometimes God will show us "mysteries" regarding spiritual realities. I think that's what He did. The Lord showed me a mystery regarding the dates July 17 and 18, that these dates or the numbers themselves may have nefarious power. There are also two other dates that He has shown me that seem to have nefarious power—March 11 and September 11. Most of us remember the ominous September 11, 2001 attacks on America's power symbols—the Twin Towers in New York City and the Pentagon. But few are aware that other detrimental schemes have been launched on March 11 and September 11 in the years since that event.

Perhaps we should pay attention to situations shaping up around all of these dates, and focus on praying against the plans of evil!

Scriptures about God's mysteries:

+ *He reveals deep and secret things;*
  He knows what is in the darkness,
  And light dwells with Him. (Daniel 2:22)

+ *'Call to Me, and I will answer you, and show you great and mighty things, which you do not know.' (Jeremiah 33:3)*

+ *And Jesus answered them, "To you it has been granted to know the mysteries of the kingdom of heaven, but to them it has not been granted." (Matthew 13:11 NASB)*

God's Fingerprints

Although Rhett had been terminal for several years, I wasn't expecting him to die when he did. I really thought he still had a few years left. I guess it was wishful thinking, but I felt that if I focused on positive things, it wouldn't happen before I was ready.

There was nothing really different about Rhett's condition, nothing to indicate his time was about to end. Except that about a month earlier, he told me he was going to leave soon. He said I would be okay because I was strong enough. I didn't ask for details about what he was alluding to, because the Holy Spirit impressed me that Rhett knew things about the future that He didn't want him to tell me. So, I didn't ask.

Then he said, "When I get into Heaven, I'm going to ask Jesus if there is some way to let you know that I made it—I got through the gate! I know I can't come back—no one can come back to Earth from Heaven. But I'm going to ask Him for some way to let you know I am there."

Jesus honored Rhett's request. God's fingerprints were all over his funeral in supernatural ways. For example:

Lindsay's Poem
Our granddaughter Lindsay asked to be a speaker at her Papa's funeral, so in preparation for her talk she went online to find an inspirational poem

or quote to underscore the things she wanted to say about Rhett's life. A short time later she called, excited to tell me that she had found the perfect poem for her speech. It was titled "Broken Chain," by Ron Tranmer.

The Book of Poetry

Rhett had a military funeral held at Camp Williams Memorial Center. Working with military liaisons, we arranged for a full honor guard and military ceremony, including the "taps" salute, which was performed at the burial site by three retired Marines. After the funeral and ceremony was finished, one of the Marines who played taps gave a book of poetry he had written to one of our family members as a condolence gift to give to me, Rhett's widow. The title of the book was *The Chain Will Link Again*. Inside the book was the very poem that Lindsay had found online, "Broken Chain."

The Lord had inspired Lindsay to find and select that poem, and then He arranged for its author, Ron Tranmer, who was also a former Marine, to participate in honoring Rhett at his funeral—and give me a published copy of his book with Rhett's poem inside. Too many "coincidences" not to be a God Moment. Jesus was announcing: "Rhett is in Heaven!"

The Marine and Cindy's Haircut

Another amazing coincidence occurred with Rhett's niece, Cindy, who is a hair stylist. A few days before Rhett's funeral, a young man came to her salon for a haircut. In the course of conversation, he said that he had to get a haircut for a military funeral in which he would be part of the honor guard. Knowing Rhett's funeral was in two days, she asked, "For whom?" It was Rhett's funeral!

This young Marine was one of those who performed the flag ceremony at the gravesite. In a community of over one million people, what are the odds of that person coming to Cindy (who had never met him before) and telling her that he was there to prepare for Rhett's funeral? Jesus was declaring: "Rhett is in Heaven!"

The Hummingbird

Rhett was drafted into the military in 1970 during the Viet Nam war. He decided to go with the Marines as part of the air wing, and he trained as a helicopter specialist. He served three tours in Viet Nam as a helicopter crew chief in which he was involved in a lot of action, as they transported troops in and wounded out of the battle zones. Even though he was shot down three times and all of his closest friends were killed, he miraculously left the war virtually unscathed—only a small scar on his left calf from a bullet that had grazed him.

After the war, he spent another six years in the Corps in administrative positions. He was promoted quickly and was therefore planning to stay in as a career. But the stress became too hard on his health and our marriage, so he left in December 1979.

His funeral highlighted his time in the war and his aviation experiences as a defining part of his life, like a theme. Many of the visuals and speeches focused on his time in the military. During the gravesite ceremony in which the honor guard was performing the flag ritual, a little hummingbird suddenly flew into the scene. It hovered about a foot directly above the middle of the flag that was stretched out between two Marines, as if over a casket.

The hummingbird continued to hover directly over the flag as if supervising what they were doing, while the Marines performed the ceremony. When they finished, the hummingbird turned toward our family members sitting in the front row and began moving up the line as it looked directly into the face of each person. When it came to me (last in the line), it stopped and hovered for several seconds, looking directly into my face. Then it did a couple of loops as if a cursive signature before flying off into the sky. The hummingbird's performance lasted about 3-4 minutes. I could hear several people in the audience behind me, gasping and talking about the incredible performance of the little hummingbird!

Although I was taken aback, I immediately recognized this as the Holy Spirit acting on behalf of Rhett, to show his "attendance" and approval of his funeral. Rhett used to supervise military funerals as part of his administrative duties after Viet Nam. The hummingbird's cursive "signature" at the end represented his signature (he did calligraphy as a hobby), saying, "Thank you!"

God used a little hummingbird as the "icing on the cake" to tell me that Rhett had made it—he was in Heaven with Jesus. I then turned to the crowd, who had witnessed this amazing demonstration, and told them that a few years earlier, Rhett had nicknamed me "Hummingbird," and that I felt God had just used the hummingbird to let me know Rhett was in Heaven!

After the ceremony, most people went back into the military chapel and were visiting. Several came up to me and expressed what a wonderful and impacting funeral it had been, and how glad they were to have come. They all commented on the miracle of the hummingbird, some saying that when they saw it, they thought it was like a little helicopter and felt they had witnessed something supernatural!

Steve's Astonishing Declaration

Then my brother Steve excitedly came up to me, looked me in the eyes, and said in all seriousness, "You watch now—that little hummingbird is going to follow you home and come to visit you every day!" I laughed and thanked him for his comment but didn't take it seriously. Steve was a kind, loving, good-hearted guy who was always trying to make people feel better, but he wasn't religious at all. So, I just took it as Steve being his lovable self.

The Hummingbird

The Lord had used Steve to make a prophetic proclamation. The very next day that beautiful little hummingbird did exactly as Steve had predicted. It came to my living room window in Draper (several miles from where the funeral was held), and it hovered, looking into my house until I came to the window to acknowledge it. Then, it continued to come to my house every day thereafter for the next six weeks!

The hummingbird would often come two to three times a day, and if I went out onto my deck, it would make a "beeline" around the building to see me. It would stop at my deck and hover in front of me, looking into my face, waiting for me to respond to it. Sometimes it would come and wait for me, flying from one window to the next in my living room and then to the other side of my house and hover at my kitchen window, as if looking for me.

My son Greg was staying with me during that time and witnessed the phenomenon of the hummingbird several times himself. He is a very logical-thinking CPA and tends to be highly skeptical and reluctant to believe anything supernatural. But even he had to admit that the miracle of the hummingbird defied any other explanation. Jesus was proclaiming again and again that Rhett is in Heaven!

Steve's prophetic proclamation was fulfilled from July 28 to September 8, 2016.

The Obstructive Tree

In *June 2018, I returned* from a three-week vacation to find that a wild Russian Olive tree behind my property had a big growth spurt, and was completely blocking the view of the city from my backyard deck. I was upset because the primary reason I had bought my home on the side of the mountain was for the views.

My west view had also become blocked by trees that had grown up directly behind my home. However, since a developer was now going to build a big complex of apartments at the base of the mountain on the other side, I was thankful for those trees, which would be prettier than looking at a bunch of buildings. Besides, my west view wasn't that great anyway; it was my north view that was the best. But now that was gone, and I knew our community's HOA wouldn't pay to have the wild tree removed. They were being very tight with the money, even for necessary repairs. So, I was feeling quite unhappy about this issue.

About two weeks later, Greg and I were enjoying a quiet Friday evening in my home. It was about 10 p.m. and dark outside when the wind suddenly began blowing violently. There was a huge noise and the whole house started to shake. It sounded like a freight train was rushing straight at us out of the dark!

Living on South Mountain, we were accustomed to some sudden and intense winds—but this was different. The wind was howling like never before and the house shook, as it ripped directly in back of my home. We looked at each other in shock, frozen with fear as we realized a tornado was coming straight at us and we were helpless to do anything!

Then, as quickly as it came, it was gone. We had dodged a bullet—it had barely missed us. Reeling from this terrifying experience, we stared at each other wide-eyed and exclaimed, *"What the hell was THAT?!!"* I opened the sliding door and went out on the deck but couldn't see much in the dark. There was a little bit of wind and it was wet, but the storm was gone. It had lasted less than three minutes!

The next two days were beautiful, and on Sunday I attended church and returned home around noon. I went out on the deck to relax and get some fresh air and sunshine. But something was different: I had a beautiful view of the valley—the tree was gone. I couldn't believe it. Had my HOA actually removed the tree yesterday?

I ran downstairs and out my basement entrance, into the backyard. I had to check this out with my own two eyes. And what I found was even more astonishing. That large 30-foot tree was lying on the ground. It was completely uprooted and had fallen in the *opposite* direction it should have fallen. It had fallen toward the southwest, across a dirt hiking path that surrounded our community. It had fallen *toward* the direction the wind was blowing from two nights before.

Had it fallen toward the northeast as it should have, it would have hit my neighbor's kitchen and dining room windows, and done a lot of damage to their home. But miraculously, it fell in the only direction that would not hurt or damage anyone—toward the wind. The HOA hadn't taken out the tree—God had. He sent a special little tornado to uproot that one tree, spin it around, and drop it across the dirt path.

There were about seven other trees in close proximity to this tree, but they were all spared. They were all good and beneficial trees. He only targeted this one obnoxious tree. Rhett knew how important the view was to me. Did he "pull some strings" with Jesus to take out the tree? I felt like it was another "hummingbird" kind of miracle. Tornados almost never occur in Utah, especially near the mountains. But nothing else can explain what had happened!

+ *Delight yourself in the LORD and He shall give you the desires of your heart. (Psalm 37:4)*

The Two Eagles

July 17, 2019 was a beautiful summer day. It was the three-year anniversary of Rhett's passing. I decided to do my devotional time out on the deck that morning, where I could enjoy some fresh air and sunshine while reading the Bible and reminiscing. After reading for about fifteen minutes, I casually looked up and gazed over the valley below, deep in thought. Suddenly, something caught my eye—a dark object flying directly into my airspace just above the trees thirty feet in front of me. It was an eagle! This was the first time I had seen an eagle in over twenty years, and never so close or flying so low.

As soon as it was directly in front of me, it began ascending, flying in tight circles up into the sky. When it was about five hundred feet above me, another object caught my eye. It was another eagle flying from the opposite direction. When it reached the first eagle, they began flying together, spiraling upward into the sky. I watched them for a few minutes until they disappeared out of sight.

I was awestruck at what a unique and serendipitous experience this had been. I felt like the eagles were soulmates who God reunited at my house before taking them into Heaven. What a special show it had been—and a tremendous blessing on a bittersweet day!

+ *But those who wait on the LORD shall renew their strength; they shall mount up with wings like eagles . . . (Isaiah 40:31)*

+ *My beloved spoke, and said to me: "Rise up, my love, my fair one—and come away." (Song of Solomon 2:10)*

Thundering in the New Year

I *spent New Year's Day 2020* quietly at home, alone. Earlier that morning I emailed a rather lengthy essay to my four adult children, which the Lord had inspired me to write on Christmas Eve and Christmas Day. The title of the essay was "Who Do You Say That I Am?"—which was the iconic question Jesus asked Peter in Matthew 16:15.

The main point of my essay was that this statement is of paramount importance. The entire Bible comes down to this one question, and your answer will determine whether you spend eternity in Heaven or in Hell. I knew the Lord wanted me to give the essay to my children, and felt New Year's Day would be the ideal time.

Around 3 p.m. Greg texted, thanking me for sending my essay. Then just before 6 p.m. Sean texted and thanked me, saying he had just read it. As soon as I finished reading Sean's text, it thundered! Loud thunder began rolling right over my house, directly over the kitchen where I was standing. It felt and sounded like it was right on top of my roof and kept rolling, as if in crescendos for about twenty to thirty seconds!

Shocked, I couldn't believe what I was hearing—it was the middle of winter. We never get thunderstorms on New Year's Day—it was freezing outside! I went to the window and looked out. It was very calm with no wind, just gentle snowflakes streaming down in the twilight. It looked peaceful and serene. I opened the door to listen for sounds of thunder off in the distance, but there was nothing.

I realized this was some kind of God Moment, but why? What did it mean? It was definitely a supernatural event but what was God saying? Was He speaking to me in the thunder? Was He commenting on the essay I had sent to my kids? Was it an affirmation or a rebuke? I began praying, asking Him to please tell me the reason for the thunder and what He was saying to me. Nothing happened. I prayed again, but no response. I continued praying for the next week, asking the Lord to please let me know what this was all about. Then, I just left it with Him, and forgot about it.

About two weeks later, I was on YouTube looking for a particular video when a thumbnail a few rows down caught my eye. It was a man I recognized, Sadhu Sundar Selvaraj. He is a Christian evangelist from India whom I had become aware of about two years prior.

The caption on the thumbnail read "Sadhu Sundar Selvaraj 2020 Prophetic Message," so I decided to watch it. He was sharing a message that he said the Lord had given him to deliver to the Church for 2020. His video was recorded on New Year's Day and lasted about an hour, as he spoke the things the Lord had shown him for various countries in the world.

At the end of his message, Selvaraj gave a very unusual real-time prophecy about something God was showing him in an open vision, as he was speaking. He said that he saw two mighty angels whom the Lord was sending to the homes of different people throughout the world. He described a lion-like angel that God was placing at the front of their houses, and a mighty warrior angel stationed at the rear of their houses. Then he said the lion-like angel was roaring, and it sounded like thunder rolling over the homes of these people.

The Lord had finally answered my question. The thunder over my house on New Year's Day was a lion-angel stationed at my front door. I guess God liked my essay!

Is Sadhu Sundar Selvaraj's prophetic vision Biblical? Scripture seems to corroborate it:

+ *I saw still another mighty angel coming down from heaven . . . and cried with a loud voice, as when a lion roars. When he cried out, seven thunders uttered their voices. (Revelation 10: 1, 3)*

+ *No evil shall befall you, nor shall any plague come near your dwelling. For He shall give His angels charge over you, to keep you in all your ways. (Psalm 91: 10-11)*

The Miracles
of Henry Gruver

I *now want to talk about a humble* prayer-walking evangelist named Henry Gruver, whom God led me to discover in 2019, for confirmation of some visions I have been shown that I describe in Part II. Jesus used Henry Gruver to demonstrate to the world that God exists, through his evangelism and some of the most amazing miracles I have ever heard. I am sharing a few of those in this section of Part I.

The Lord also gave Henry a specific prophetic vision in 1986, which was very similar to visions He showed me in 1983, and for several years after. I share Henry's vision, which I have titled "Russian Submarines," in Part II. Henry's vision is beginning to play out right now, and it is astounding!

Following is a synopsis of some of the miracles God performed through Henry Gruver. You can also watch Henry's personal testimonies about most of these incidents and more on www.stevequayle.com. Click on the picture titled "A tribute to Henry Gruver," which will take you to another page. There you will need to click on the caption beneath the picture to go from one video to the next.

As you read or listen to these amazing miracles, keep in mind what Jesus said:

"For with God nothing will be impossible." (Luke 1:37)

"Part I" video:

In this cozy and inviting conversation before a rustic fireplace with Steve Quayle, Henry describes some of the most profound miracles God had performed in his life:

First, Henry talks about a tragic event that happened several years earlier when he was raising his family. His three-year-old son's finger got slammed in a car door and was mostly severed, just hanging by a thread of skin. Henry immediately grabbed his tiny hand and commanded his son's finger to be "put back on" through the power of the blood and name of Jesus. And it was! Immediately, his tiny finger flipped back up into place. Then, his little son lifted his hand up and exclaimed, "Daddy, it's okay. Jesus put it back on!" He began wiggling it back and forth—it was fully functional. Of course, Henry then took him to the doctor to ensure everything was good, and the doctor confirmed that his finger was functioning and all was well!

Next is the story of another son who fell while climbing on a pegboard in his junior high gymnasium. He fell about twenty feet, landing on his head, and was paralyzed from the neck down. When Henry arrived at the scene of the accident, his son was lying on the floor unable to move, and he asked Henry to pray for him. So, Henry prayed several times—and each time his son was progressively healed from his neck on down. Before long, he was able to stand up and walk. The principal, school nurse, policeman, and everyone surrounding him were astonished. Henry's son was no longer paralyzed or injured—he was just fine. God had miraculously healed him, for all to see!

Next, Henry talks about another son who was born dead, in a home delivery. The umbilical cord was tightly wound four times around the baby's neck. Henry carefully removed the cord and prayed over the baby, commanding him to live, "in Jesus' name!" Suddenly, he opened his mouth and gasped for air, then began to breathe. He began turning from black to deep purple, to a beautiful pink, as life came into his little body. The child was completely healed—and perfectly healthy from that day on!

Then Henry talks about a fourth son (Henry had thirteen children) who at ten years old was hit very hard in his left eye by a rock, knocking it out of the socket and shearing off the front part of his eye. But once again, the Lord used this tragedy to perform a tremendous miracle, in front of five ophthalmologists who were called in to examine him. Henry prayed and commanded his son's eye to be healed. And, God supernaturally recreated a brand-new eye for Henry's boy, right in front of these doctors, who watched in amazement. Henry said that all five doctors later wrote personal letters of attestation about this miracle!

"Part II" video:

Near the end of this video, Henry talks about an amazing prophetic word-of-knowledge that the Holy Spirit spoke through him to two large families, who came into a house meeting where he was preaching in Vancouver, BC, Canada.

These families were best friends who had built their dream homes next to each other along a river in Texas. They had just sold their homes and were on their way to Alaska. A few months prior, God gave each husband and wife (four people) the same prophetic dream on the same night, in which He instructed them to sell their homes and move to Alaska. They were all devout Christians and recognized this as a direct command from God Almighty. They immediately put their homes on the market, and both sold very quickly for cash.

As these families were on their way to Alaska, they heard that Henry Gruver would be speaking at a certain place in Vancouver and wanted to hear him. So, they hustled to get there but arrived about thirty minutes late.

As they walked into the assembly and were sitting down, the Holy Spirit moved upon Henry and he proclaimed to these families, whom he didn't know: "Thus saith the Lord: 'I have uprooted you because I have given you a purpose and a plan for this day. And do not fear, for you are in my will, saith the Lord, and I will bless you. And before this day is over, you will see it!'"

Later that night, they were back in their hotel rooms watching the nightly news when a report came on about a devastating flood in Texas. Then, right before their eyes they watched both of their former homes floating down the river!

Needless to say, they thanked and praised God that they were protected from that tragedy and had the money from their homes safely in the bank. These couples had believed their visions from God and boldly obeyed Him in faith, even though they had to leave their dream homes and go to Alaska, not knowing what they were to do there. The Lord had protected and blessed them, and they saw the reason for God's urgent command the very night Henry spoke this proclamation—just as the Lord had said they would!

"Part III" video:

In this video, Henry shares an incident that happened when he was seven years old, in a Sunday school class. The teacher showed the children a flannel board illustration of the planets and universe and told the kids about

God's promise to recreate a new Heaven and Earth in the future. And, she told the children that they could stand by Jesus and watch him do it!

Henry was so moved by this story that when he got home from church, he went to his own "secret place," which was under his father's camping trailer. There he crouched under the trailer and prayed, asking Jesus if he could be one of those standing with Him when He rolls up the universe and creates a new one.

Many years later when he was an adult, Jesus appeared to Henry one day while he was teaching about prayer-walking to a Baptist church in Texas. Suddenly, Jesus came up behind him as he was lecturing at the podium and said, "Henry, I thought I would just let you pass through and see the heavens before I roll them up as a scroll and create a new Heaven and Earth." Instantly, Henry flashed back and heard himself as a seven-year-old boy under his father's camper praying his request.

At that moment, Henry had a total meltdown while standing at the podium, and began crying over and over, "Thank you, Jesus. I love you, Jesus," as he was overcome by the Lord's presence and His gracious honoring of his childhood request. Then the congregation started crying, as they too were overcome by the divine presence of Jesus. Henry remarked at how gracious God was to bless these Baptists with such an experience of His real presence, since most Baptists teach that God doesn't do supernatural acts or appear to people in today's world.

A few years after that experience, the Lord fulfilled His promise that Henry would "pass through the heavens before I roll them up as a scroll."

In this next testimony, Henry and his family were traveling in a Volkswagen bus from their home in Portland, Oregon, to Arizona for the wedding of one of their daughters. As Henry was catching some much-needed sleep, his wife was driving through the mountains of northern California when she lost control of the van. As it began jerking around, Henry awoke just in time to see that they were about to crash. The vehicle flipped over and was skidding down the highway upside down. A steel bar from the luggage rack on top ripped through the roof and straight into Henry's forehead—killing him!

Henry goes on to talk about the excruciating pain he experienced until he felt his soul separate from his body. Then he felt wonderful—no pain and more alive than he had ever been. He had all his faculties like a body has—memories, feelings, etc.—and understood what had happened. Then his soul went into a "tunnel" and began rapidly ascending away from Earth, through the heavens (Earth's atmosphere) and into outer space. He describes the beauty of the earth and what it looks like from outer space, and then talks about his up-close view of the moon. Then he tries to describe something that was astonishing. There is a plethora of unknown planets just beyond the moon. We don't see them because Earth's atmosphere obscures them from our view. Henry says they are glorious in beauty and each has its own personality and sings a unique song!

Henry then burst into a realm that he identifies as the Milky Way, and what a fantastic experience that was. He describes an explosion of planets of all sizes; again, each had its own unique color, personality, and sound! He talks about how there are many more colors than on Earth, and postulates that there may be "eighty-eight spectrums of color" rather than the mere eight-color spectrum on Earth. (This is also what my late husband, Rhett, described in his testimony about Heaven.) Then he breathlessly tries to describe how all of these heavenly bodies are singing in the most beautiful massive choir imaginable! As he is describing this awesome, ecstatic experience, Steve Quayle recalls scriptures that seem to speak about such things:

+ ... *"Eye has not seen, nor ear heard, nor have entered into the heart of man the things which God has prepared for those who love Him."* (1 Corinthians 2:9)

+ *The heavens declare the glory of God; And the firmament shows His handiwork. (Psalms 19:1)*

Then suddenly, Henry was back in his body! He could hear voices of people who were working on him but he couldn't see, speak, or move. He heard the forest ranger tell a dispatcher over the radio, "The woman and the eight children are fine, but we don't know about the man." When Henry heard this, he prayed in his mind, "Lord, whatever is missing on me, You can put it back together. I am going to my daughter's wedding—I am not going to any hospital!"

Suddenly, he felt something hot, like two cutting torches on each temple of his face, that began moving down throughout his entire body and out through his toes. As this happened, he regained his vision and he could talk. The profuse bleeding from the wound in his head stopped, and he began moving. He got up, brushing off everyone's efforts to keep him still, and began turning his head back and forth, insisting that he was fine. He was not going to the hospital—he was going to his daughter's wedding. And that's what he did!

Those who witnessed the accident told Henry that he was dead for at least thirty minutes. They also remarked about how astonished they were, as they watched their vehicle skidding on its top down the highway—and seeing all the children sitting undisturbed in their seats—upside down!

I believe guardian angels were holding them in place.

But this story doesn't end there. For several years following this extraordinary experience, Henry was called on to share his testimony with many other people in speeches before large audiences across the country. In doing so, several astrophysicists and astronomers came to hear him. Some became close friends and associates of Henry, as he was able to provide them information to confirm or refine their theories. And they were also able to help Henry understand a strange phenomenon that happened after his galactic adventure.

For a few weeks after this experience, Henry saw time—the second hand on clocks—as moving backward, rather than forward as they normally do. He was beginning to think he was going crazy. But NASA's leading astrophysicist, who became a close friend to Henry, assured him that he wasn't crazy. He told him that this phenomenon also happens to astronauts. Time is different in the dimension of outer space, so when a person comes back to Earth their brains have to readjust to the dimension of Earth time. Until they do, they perceive time as moving in reverse, like Henry did!

What an extraordinary series of events and experiences the Lord took Henry through, in answering his request to see the universe! All of this reminds me of the scripture:

> . . . *God causes all things to work together for good*
> *to those who love God, to those who are called*
> *according to His purpose. (Romans 8:28 NASB)*

"Part IV" video:

The Dragonfly Miracle: This miracle took place around 2015, in Taiwan, where the Lord had taken Henry to prayer-walk. On the morning they were about to embark on Henry's mission trip, his guide was suddenly notified that a very deadly type of malaria was spreading quickly in the southern part of the island where Henry was supposed to minister. There was no antidote or cure for this plague, which killed people bitten by these mosquitoes within four days. But the Lord had told Henry to go there, so he and a faith-filled local pastor decided to trust the Lord and go to this area anyway. And a group of about fifty faith-filled Christians went with them.

On the bus trip to their destination in southern Taiwan, they stopped along the way for a break and the local pastor traveling with him showed Henry a beautiful fertile valley below the mountain road they were on. He said that the Taiwanese government wanted to build a dam that would destroy this farmland where most of his congregation lived. He asked Henry to pray for them. So he did.

In the middle of his prayer, God interrupted Henry and showed him a vision—he saw a single dragonfly flying in front of his face. This was the answer to the malaria plague: Dragonflies eat mosquitoes! Immediately, Henry exclaimed, "Yes, Lord! Send clouds of dragonflies—millions of dragonflies across southern Taiwan!!"

Immediately, dark clouds of dragonflies appeared over the heads of the people standing around Henry, who had been on the bus. They all gasped in astonishment at this instant miracle—many of them had never seen a dragonfly in their lives. Henry then commanded the dragonflies in the name of Jesus, to be dispersed over the entire country and end the plague over Taiwan. Instantly, clouds of dragonflies began to take off in every direction!

Their whole group got back into the bus and resumed their journey, rejoicing along the way. Periodically, the local pastor would have the bus driver stop so he could tell people along the road that the plague was over—and about the miracle of the dragonflies. As he did, the people began clapping and rejoicing wherever they went!

But that wasn't all—there were more amazing miracles that God performed after they reached their destination, having to do with gold raining down on his audience! I highly recommend you listen to Henry describe these miracles in Steve Quayle's videos.

Four days later, Henry left Taiwan to go to Japan. On the day he left, the Taiwanese media suddenly announced that the plague was over, but they didn't know why.

Then in October 2016 Henry returned to southern Taiwan, and when the people heard he was there, they came to see him in droves at a large church that he was visiting. News about Henry's miracle had spread throughout the southern Taiwan communities. The people there had witnessed a supernatural work that had ended a devastating plague—and they wanted to see for themselves the person who had brought their miracle!

"Part V" video:

The Curse of Habu Island: This miracle took place in October 2000 on Habu Island, which is just off the Japanese island of Okinawa. Henry was on Okinawa to prayer-walk and break some curses operating over that island. As he was looking down from a mountaintop overlooking the area, the Lord showed him Habu Island and told him to go there the next day, and prayer-walk all the way to the top of the mountain on that island.

When Henry told his interpreter that God had told him to go to Habu Island the next day, the man adamantly refused to believe that God had told him to do that—and refused to go there. Why? Because it was saturated with Habu snakes, one of the ten deadliest snakes on Earth. Nobody goes there!

But Henry did—and so did his son Peter and his interpreter! What gave them the courage to go where few men dared to tread? Henry understood his authority and the dominion given by God to man over every other creature on Earth. There was no way he was going to let a snake intimidate him. Besides that, the Lord commanded Henry to go there—and he feared God far more than any snake! Then, Henry relates the following experience to Steve Quayle:

Determined to obey God, their small group finally made their way through the jungle and up the mountain on Habu island. After stopping to rest near the top, they looked around and down into a large ravine, where they noticed the opening of a massive cave. So, they hiked down and found that there were several caves with all kinds of ancient shaman altars and idols inside. Excited by their find, they began exploring what was actually a labyrinth of caves. A few years after Henry was there, archaeologists came to Habu Island and began exploring these caves. They have now determined some of the artifacts inside to be over five thousand years old!

Suddenly, as Henry and crew were coming out of the third cave, they were startled by a wild-looking native man who confronted them, saying, "What you doing in my cave?!" Henry replied, "I'm praying to my God!" To which the native man replied, "Oh, this is good! Do you want to find more altars? I'll show you." So, he proceeded to take them along a perilous and difficult trek deep into the caves that descended under the ocean, all the way to the altar of the most powerful shaman god. As they proceeded from one site to another, Henry put his foot on each altar, and canceled every curse in the name of Jesus—rebuking the satanic rituals and casting out demons.

When Henry did these things, the wild-looking cave-man began shaking, exclaiming, "You have such strong spirit, you make me shake all over!" Henry replied, "I have the Holy Spirit!"

"I never hear of Holy Spirit," the wild man responded, somewhat mystified.

Once they had finished canceling the evil strongholds in the caves, Henry and crew, including the wild-man, continued scrambling their way through the fierce terrain, until they reached the very top of the mountain. Then Henry placed his foot on top of the highest peak and took authority in the name of Jesus, over every snake and evil spirit on the island—commanding the snakes to die and proclaiming that the island now belonged to the Lord Jesus Christ. Then he spoke a blessing over the island, declaring that the island would be filled with people, farms, vegetables, fruits, and animals!

Hearing Henry's proclamations, the cave-keeper again exclaimed, "You have very strong spirit—I never meet anyone with such strong spirit!" Henry replied, "I have the Holy Spirit!"

The cave-keeper's voice broke as he humbly asked Henry, "Do you think maybe I can have Holy Spirit? I want strong spirit. I stay here from a little boy. They make me stay here; my family make me stay here. I grow up in this cave. They bring me food. I don't like it here—I'm alone so much. Could I have Holy Spirit . . . how do I get Holy Spirit?"

Henry replied, "It first begins when you ask Jesus Christ, the Son of God, to come into your heart."

"Oh, so if I ask Jesus to come into my heart, I get Holy Spirit?"

"Yes, you do," Henry assured him.

"I want Jesus in my heart! Jesus come into my heart, come into my heart—I want Holy Spirit!" he cried.

"Now, I feel like I am so much lighter. I feel like if I flap my hands I could fly like a bird. Does that mean I have Holy Spirit?" he cried, tears streaming down his face.

"Yes, it does—it means all your wrongdoing is gone . . . all your sin is gone . . . . You're totally clean," Henry told him.

Rejoicing, he exclaimed, "Oh, I like that! I have Holy Spirit! I have Holy Spirit!"

This wild-looking cave-keeper had been oppressed and forsaken by his family, but not by God. Jesus brought Henry Gruver across the face of the earth, through a treacherous jungle of deadly snakes, to save this precious soul—and cleanse this island that had been cursed as a stronghold of evil for millennia!

How compassionate, gracious, and powerful is our Lord God, Jesus Christ!

Six years later, Henry went back to do ministry on Okinawa and found that Habu Island was being developed! They had built a large, modern bridge from Okinawa to the island. There were electric power lines, people, farms, and fields filled with different kinds of fruits, vegetables, and animals—just as he had declared!

Then in 2016, Henry returned to Okinawa again, and Habu Island had continued to be developed. There were more farms and crops being raised. The side of a mountain had been cleared and was now filled with solar collectors. And the formidable occultic caves had been transformed into a tourist attraction and archaeological site. Habu Island had been transformed from an evil blight to a wonderful blessing for the people—because one man, Henry Gruver, chose to obey God regardless of the threats!

The Word of God says:

+ ... *Behold, to obey is better than sacrifice, And to heed than the fat of rams. (1 Samuel 15:22).*

+ If you keep My commandments, you will remain in My love, just as I have kept My Father's commandments and remain in His love. (John 15:10 NIV)

Very often, obedience also requires sacrifice, as Henry's life beautifully demonstrates. Henry Gruver obeyed God, sacrificed much, and as a result, the Lord used him to bring blessings to many and glory to God! The Lord also used Henry to fulfill prophecies and promises written in the Bible. For example:

Mark 16:15-18:

And He said to them, "Go into all the world and preach the gospel to every creature. He who believes and is baptized will be saved; but he who does not believe will be condemned. And these signs will follow those who believe: In My name they will cast out demons; they will speak with new tongues; they will take up serpents; and if they drink anything deadly, it will by no means hurt them; they will lay hands on the sick, and they will recover."

John 14:12:

"Most assuredly, I say to you, he who believes in Me, the works that I do he will do also; and greater works than these he will do, because I go to My Father."

Henry Gruver went into all the world and preached the gospel and led many people into salvation and right doctrine. He cast out many demons (e.g., Habu Island) and annihilated millions of poisonous serpents. God also used him to perform the same kind of miracles that Jesus did: healing paralytics, restoring limbs, commanding the dead back to life, instantly stopping gushing blood, and miraculously healing open wounds.

And in fulfilment of scripture, God used Henry Gruver to perform miracles that even Jesus didn't perform on Earth, as far as we know. For example:

+ Instantly ending plagues of deadly mosquitos; destroying millions of poisonous snakes; eradicating demonic strongholds and curses that had devastated lands for thousands of years.

+ Raining down pure gold flakes upon congregations where Henry preached. Henry said that one pastor in Kentucky swept up all the gold and paid off the church's mortgage!

+ At other times, God rained down all kinds of precious jewels on Henry's audiences. There are video interviews on YouTube and other platforms in which Henry describes these incidents and even pours out a container of a small remnant of those jewels.

But Henry was simply obeying God and following in the footsteps of his Master—Jesus Christ! Jesus's life was the greatest sacrifice the world has ever seen. And, look at all the good His obedience to do the Father's will has accomplished!

There are many more testimonies about miracles God performed through Henry Gruver that can be found on the internet.

Henry Gruver went to be with the Lord on October 10, 2019.
What a celebration that must have been in Heaven!

PART II

WARNINGS OF
THE WATCHMEN

"So, you, son of man: I have made you a watchman for the house of Israel; therefore, you shall hear a word from My mouth and warn them for Me." (Ezekiel 33:7)

Do not quench the Spirit. Do not despise prophecies. Test all things; hold fast what is good. (1 Thessalonians 5: 19-21)

Who Are God's Watchmen?

The Bible describes different kinds of "watchmen." During Biblical times, the Israelites would appoint military watchmen who were trained to act as scouts and guards for their communities. They would station them on high walls or watchtowers, to watch for signs of enemies or potential threats and quickly warn the people.

There are also prophetic watchmen whom God Himself calls, as described in Ezekiel 3:17:

> "Son of man, I have made you a watchman for
> the house of Israel; therefore, hear a word from
> My mouth, and give them warning from Me"

As with Ezekiel, the Lord communicates with His prophetic watchmen today through visions, dreams, and revelation. The watchman is sternly commanded to deliver God's warnings to His people, whether they want to hear them or not!

+ he said, "Listen to my words: When there is a prophet among you, I, the LORD, reveal myself to them in visions, I speak to them in dreams." (Numbers 12:6 NIV)

+ *'And it shall come to pass in the last days, says God, that I will pour out of My Spirit on all flesh; your sons and your daughters shall prophesy, your young men shall see visions, your old men shall dream dreams. And on My menservants and on My maidservants, I will pour out My Spirit in those days; And they shall prophesy.' (Acts 2:17-18)*

+ *But if the watchman sees the sword coming and does not blow the trumpet, and the people are not warned, and the sword comes and takes any person from among them, he is taken away in his iniquity; but his blood I will require at the watchman's hand. (Ezekiel 33:6)*

In addition to His prophetic watchmen, pastors are watchmen over their flock to keep them on the path of righteousness. But Jesus actually commands all believers to be watchmen over their own lives, especially in the last days. We are commanded to watch our lifestyles and watch for the signs of Christ's return.

In the parable of "The Ten Virgins," all were believers expecting to leave with the Groom. But only five were able to go when the bridegroom came in the middle of the night. Believers who had not adequately prepared were left behind, and not given another chance. Those disciples whom Jesus "knows" will have prepared themselves, as stated in Revelation 19:7:

> "Let us be glad and rejoice and give Him glory,
> for the marriage of the Lamb has come,
> and His wife has made herself ready."

Parable of the Ten Virgins:

"At that time the kingdom of heaven will be like ten virgins who took their lamps and went out to meet the bridegroom. Five of them were foolish, and five were wise. The foolish ones took their lamps but did

not take along any extra oil. But the wise ones took oil in flasks along with their lamps. When the bridegroom was delayed, they all became drowsy and fell asleep.

At midnight the cry rang out: 'Here is the bridegroom! Come out to meet him!'

Then all the virgins woke up and trimmed their lamps. The foolish ones said to the wise, 'Give us some of your oil; our lamps are going out.'

'No,' said the wise ones, 'or there may not be enough for both us and you. Instead, go to those who sell oil and buy some for yourselves.'

But while they were on their way to buy it the bridegroom arrived. Those who were ready went in with him to the wedding banquet, and the door was shut.

Later the other virgins arrived and said, 'Lord, lord, open the door for us!' But he replied, 'Truly I tell you; I do not know you.'

Therefore, keep watch, because you do not know the day or the hour." (Matthew 25:1-13 BSB)

Jesus warns His people to always be watching and ready to stand before Him, because we do not know the day or hour that has been appointed for each of us.

. . . Therefore, if you will not watch, I will come upon you as a thief, and you will not know what hour I will come upon you . . . He who overcomes shall be clothed in white garments, and I will not blot out his name from the Book of Life; but I will confess his name before My Father and before His angels. (Revelation 3:3,5)

In this Part, I share the things God has shown me and two other watchmen, Dumitru Duduman and Henry Gruver, regarding specific end-time events. These are other Christians whom the Lord led me to for confirmation of certain visions He has shown me.

. . . *"Every matter must be established by the testimony of two or three witnesses." (2 Corinthians 13:1 BSB)*

The Lord always shows His watchmen before judgment or calamity occurs, so they can warn His people to repent and make preparations for what is coming.

Surely the LORD God does nothing, unless He reveals His secret to His servants the prophets. (Amos 3:7)

I feel that I also need to address the question many people have about the validity of prophets and watchmen in the Church today. "Since we have the Bible, isn't that all we need? Didn't God do away with all those supernatural things in the Church Age?" they ask.

The short answer is that God has not done away with these callings in the Church Age. In fact, they are more important today than ever before! Everyone needs to read the information I discuss in "Warnings of the Watchmen," to understand how and why God has preserved these important callings in the Church. Jesus promises He will never leave nor forsake those who believe and follow Him; and working through His called watchmen is one of the ways God keeps this promise. As the apostle Paul writes:

And He Himself gave some to be apostles, some prophets, some evangelists, and some pastors and teachers, for the equipping of the saints for the work of ministry, for the edifying of the body of Christ, (Ephesians 4:11-12)
. . . prophesying is not for unbelievers but for those who believe. (1 Corinthians 14:22)

The apostle Paul tells us that God gave the Church prophets to edify the body of Christ. Think about it . . . when would the Church need prophetic messages from God and edification more than in the perilous end-times? Do you really think a loving Father would withhold this blessing from those who must endure the time of testing?

In recent years, the Lord has been showing numerous watchmen similar end-time events that are now beginning to unfold. It is as if God has pulled out all the stops, taken out His megaphone, and is shouting to a world immersed in noise, distraction, and unbelief: "Wake up and repent! Prophecy is rapidly being fulfilled and your time is very, very short!!"

As a called watchman, I am commanded to tell God's people what He has shown me. It's not a job most people would ask for, but I must fear God and not man. I hope and pray this information will help those who read it to recognize the time we are now entering. I pray that it will help you to repent and prepare. Then, as you see these things come to pass, your faith will be strengthened rather than devastated—as most people in this world will be.

"Now when these things begin to happen, look up and lift up your heads, because your redemption draws near." (Luke 21:28)

"I Have Made You a Watchman"

In January 2013, the Lord finally told me the reason for the visions, miracles, and supernatural works He has done in my life. He revealed that He has called me to be a "watchman" and these experiences were part of my calling. He has provided me with testimonies (both mine and others) to write this book and demonstrate that He exists—God is for real—and He is still performing miracles and supernatural acts in the lives of His people!

I'm not sure why He waited until that point in time to tell me about my calling, because I was in bad shape. I was lying in the hospital with multiple life-threatening conditions: a serious blood infection (MSSA), sepsis, osteomyelitis, pneumonia, and pleurisy. All of this was the result of a tainted needle from a vitamin B-12 shot! But I think the Lord revealed my calling at this time as comfort; to let me know that I wasn't going to die because there was something I was called to do.

By my third day in the hospital, I was feeling strong enough to sit up and do a little reading. So, I reached for my Bible, intending to read the gospels. The book fell into my lap, opened to Ezekiel chapter 3. As I picked it up, my eyes fell on Ezekiel 3:17-19:

"Son of man, I have made you a watchman for the house of Israel; therefore, hear a word from My mouth, and give them warning from Me: When I say to the wicked, 'You shall surely die,' and you give him no warning, nor speak to warn the wicked from his wicked way, to save his life, that same wicked man shall die in his iniquity; but his blood I will require at your hand. Yet, if you warn the wicked, and he does not turn from his wickedness, nor from his wicked way, he shall die in his iniquity; but you have delivered your soul."

Instantly, I experienced a strong God Moment! I knew the Lord was telling me this was my calling, and the primary purpose behind the miracles and spiritual experiences He had done in my life. As my eyes locked onto these verses, the words "I have made you a watchman" seemed to jump off the page, deeply impacting my spirit and soul!

As I lay there reflecting on the profound experience that had just happened, I randomly turned to Ezekiel chapter 33. Again, my eyes fell on almost the very same words that were written thirty chapters earlier. The Lord was confirming my watchman calling by immediately repeating it to me. But this time, He added something else:

"'But if the watchman sees the sword coming and does not blow the trumpet, and the people are not warned, and the sword comes and takes any person from among them, he is taken away in his iniquity; but his blood I will require at the watchman's hand.'

"So, you, son of man: I have made you a watchman for the house of Israel; therefore, you shall hear a word from My mouth and warn them for Me." (Ezekiel 33: 6-7)

I was to warn God's people about any "swords" He has revealed to me. As I continued to read, I understood that swords were visions of calamities and judgment that He shows His watchmen. All that "gloom and doom" stuff that nobody wants to hear! The kind of messages that got prophets killed in the Old Testament. The Lord has shown me several of those kinds of visions—and now He was commanding me to tell His people about the things I have seen!

So, that is what Part II is about—the swords that God has shown me and the other watchmen He led me to for confirmation. These swords are visions and prophecies of our current time and events that are now coming to pass. The Lord has shown these and other events to numerous watchmen throughout the world. We are to warn His people and help them be prepared mentally, physically, and spiritually for the end-time events ahead.

Watchmen are also commanded to warn God's people to repent, so they don't die in their sins. Remember, Lucifer was thrown out of Heaven because sin was found in his heart—the sin of pride! Jesus will not allow anyone into Heaven if there is sin or wickedness in their heart. But "the good news" is that our hearts can be cleansed when we obey God's word:

If we say that we have no sin, we deceive ourselves, and the truth is not in us. If we confess our sins, He is faithful and just to forgive us our sins and to cleanse us from all unrighteousness. (1 John 1: 8-9)

God's watchmen must warn of His judgment upon those who die in their iniquities. But we are also to declare His grace and forgiveness to those who confess and forsake their sins:

When a righteous man turns away from his righteousness, commits iniquity, and dies in it, it is because of the iniquity which he has done that he dies. Again, when a wicked man turns away from the wickedness which he committed, and does what is lawful and right, he preserves himself alive. Because he considers and turns away from

all the transgressions which he committed, he shall surely live; he shall
not die. (Ezekiel 18: 26-28)

I spent a total of thirteen days in the hospital and another three months recovering from my illnesses. But as soon as I got out of the hospital, I began planning a family reunion. I knew the Lord expected me to share my testimonies with others, beginning with my extended family. So, at our reunion, I began by sharing my testimony about how I became a born-again Christian, many years prior. Most of my family were not Christians, but at least three persons came to the Lord soon after our reunion!

I thought my job was done. But the following year, the Lord began giving me more visions and prophetic experiences; and by 2018, I knew that He expected me to do more. I was to share the things He had shown me and the miracles He had done in my life, with a much larger audience—His Church.

I began by writing down all of the visions, prophetic dreams, and miracles God has done in my life over fifty-plus years. It went surprisingly fast, almost as fast as I could type, in many cases. The Lord has given me a photographic memory for the visions, dreams, and supernatural acts He has performed in my life. So, each testimony was like watching a movie. I not only saw everything in detail, but remembered my thoughts and the social and political environment present at the time. This in itself was a miracle, since I was about seventy years old when I began writing these things down!

But it wasn't just my experiences that God wanted me to share. I was to share my late husband Rhett's spiritual experiences as well. And also, the testimonies of the other watchmen and witnesses I speak about in this book—those whom He had shown visions corroborating my own and those whom He had taken to Heaven and Hell, as He did with Rhett.

Most of the following testimonies are in chronological order, beginning with the first vision the Lord showed me during my Visitation experience in 1983. This vision, "In the Wings of an Eagle," corresponds with God's promises in Psalm 91. It is prophetic—these things will actually happen, and I believe I will experience them in my lifetime. But this beloved Psalm together with Psalm 23 also provide strong hope, comfort, and assurance of God's promises and protection for His people in the turbulent times ahead.

In the Wings of an Eagle: Part 2

In *Part I, "Visions, Dreams, and Revelations,"* I shared my testimony titled "In the Wings of an Eagle," which was an experiential vision of the things described in Psalm 91. You may want to refer back to that testimony for all the details of this vision.

Psalm 91 is a wonderful, heartwarming scripture with God's love and comfort woven between the lines. It is one of the most beloved and quoted Psalms in the Bible, providing hope and strength to His people for millennia. But for me, it also describes a prophetic vision God gave me about events that would take place later in my life, and how the Lord will protect and rescue His faithful people in these situations. Although calamities will come, He will save those described in this Psalm in supernatural ways, much like He did with Daniel, Shadrach, Meshach, and Abednego in the Old Testament book of Daniel!

I was thirty-four at the time of these visions but I knew that the events would happen about forty years later, when I was in my mid- to late seventies. I saw myself living in my current home, which I bought in 2013, and I saw my future self, which looked much like I do today. I knew that I had been a widow for at least seven years, and that I was a watchman. I saw several visions where I was standing by my windows watching over the valley and the skies. I was also intently watching what was happening in the world through the news media, and seeking the Lord's guidance in a challenging environment.

The events I saw then are coming together now before everyone's eyes. Hardly a day goes by that we don't hear or see threats of World War III. It has now progressed from heated rhetoric to a hot war in Ukraine and continual "war games" being practiced by China, Russia, India, North and South Korea, NATO, and other countries. The world's military titans are rehearsing with live-fire ammunition and test-firing ICBMs, for the big one—nuclear war!

As I am finishing this book in 2024, war has also erupted in the Middle East. It started on October 7, 2023 with a heinous attack by Hamas upon Israeli civilians, and rockets raining down upon Israeli cities. Ironically, Israel's hyper-vigilant military, the IDF, were all "out to lunch" on the Saturday morning when the attack came, and they inexplicably didn't mount much of a defense for about seven hours. This, together with the strange and anomalous "coincidences" and apparent breakdown in Israel's state-of-the-art surveillance and defense systems, allowed "the perfect storm" to play out. The bizarre nature of the attacks and the murder, mayhem, and chaos that occurred were beyond belief—as if scripted and orchestrated by the evilest entities on Earth. And it managed to elicit the outrage of the world!

The whole world is now reacting with extreme anger, ironically directed toward Israel more than Hamas. Why? Because it appears to the world that the Israeli government leaders were complicit in the attacks upon their own people! Then, Israel quickly seized this event as an excuse to carry out revenge and genocide upon Gaza—attacking Hamas and more than a million innocent Palestinian civilians. But sadly, there is another group of innocent people who are suffering the blame for this government's actions—the Israeli people themselves—who have also been rebelling against their overbearing rulers and trying to oust them for the past few years. But now, the whole world sees this controversial

Netanyahu government as intolerable—an evil that must be eliminated. Will this be the catalyst that ignites World War III—or will the nations of the world unite to remove this regime?

Whether the trigger is Israel, Russia, China, Iran, or something else, the world is now on the precipice of World War III. This is what God showed Dumitru Duduman, Henry Gruver, and to me in several open visions, revelations, and prophetic dreams over the last forty years. "In the Wings of an Eagle" was the first of these visions. The fact that the Lord began by showing me Psalm 91 speaks to His compassion and love toward us. The first thing He showed me was hope and salvation—in the wings of a giant divine eagle, who would rescue those who love Him from the calamities.

Nuclear war is the kind of horrifying message that nobody wants to hear or have to deliver. But it is the reality of the world we are now living in, and God wants His people to be informed and prepared. However, the "powers that be" have done an amazing job of gaslighting Americans, keeping us in the dark and distracting us with frivolous games, gossip, and political theater. And most people are unwittingly enabling the con game because they refuse to hear anything "negative." They just want to enjoy today, and believe things are getting better. And that may be so in the future, for those who agree to join the kingdom of "the Beast." But first, I believe the world will suffer much destruction of what now exists—so they can "build back better!"

However, Christians are not to be like the world. Jesus commands us to be sober-minded, always watching, and recognize the signs of the prophetic times and seasons. He specifically warns us to be aware and alert, so we won't be caught in the snare that will suddenly come upon the world in the end-days.

"But take heed to yourselves, lest your hearts be weighed down with carousing, drunkenness, and cares of this life, and that Day come on you unexpectedly. For it will come as a snare on all those

who dwell on the face of the whole earth. Watch therefore, and
pray always that you may be counted worthy to escape all these
things that will come to pass, and to stand before the Son of Man."
(Luke 21: 34-36)

We are to trust in Christ Jesus, remember His promises, and obey whatever He commands us. Those who do will see the promises of Psalm 91 and other scriptures fulfilled in their lives. The only thing we are to fear is God Himself—and obey Him!

"And I say to you, My friends, do not be afraid of those who kill the
body, and after that have no more that they can do. But I will show
you whom you should fear: Fear Him who, after He has killed, has
power to cast into hell; yes, I say to you, fear Him!" (Luke 12: 4-5)

As mentioned earlier, as I have seen prophecies being fulfilled, I've realized that I must share what God has shown me. But in all honesty, I didn't want to. So, I asked the Lord for confirmation through two, three, or more persons whom He had shown the same things that I had seen. The Bible says that two or three witnesses are required to establish the validity of a matter. I was hoping I wouldn't get the validation, but that didn't happen—the Lord soon brought me multiple confirmations. Then, He did so again when I asked for confirming witnesses of Rhett's testimonies about Heaven and Hell.

Many of the things Dumitru, Henry, and I were shown are being fulfilled right now, as you will see in the testimonies that follow.

The Train Cloud

A *few minutes after my eagle's wings vision,* I was given another vision of myself in my seventies. I was standing in my current home overlooking Salt Lake Valley, thinking about how the world had changed. It seemed like we were entering into a golden age of peace, safety, and prosperity, and everyone was feeling secure and optimistic about the future. The world had gone through a difficult time but we had emerged, and it felt like we were on the cusp of a new utopia!

As I was gazing out my living room window, amazed at how quickly things had changed, a white cloud in the southwest corner of the valley caught my eye. It was billowing and expanding northward like a long train. I was captivated, wondering what was causing it to move in such an unusual fashion. Then suddenly, I was viewing this train cloud in Heaven, watching many heavenly beings coming together inside the cloud. There was a lot of excitement about what they were getting ready to do—return to Earth with Jesus as His supernatural heavenly army!

Vision partially fulfilled:
On a quiet day in late August 2019, I was gazing out my living room window, reflecting on how President Trump had been boasting about how well our country was doing and what a bright future the United

States was about to experience. The stock market had been going up nonstop for three years and the economy was booming. Companies were struggling to find enough workers for all their jobs! Trump was launching his new Space Force, and was extolling the amazing high-tech world it would open up for us!

The United States was enjoying peace and prosperity and I was amazed at how he had turned things around so quickly. We had finally recovered from "The Great Recession" that lasted seven years from 2008 until 2015. I was thinking that he would certainly be reelected because the Democrats had no one who could compete with him.

Then I noticed a white cloud at the southwest end of Salt Lake valley that was rapidly expanding northward, in the shape of a long train. I was curious about its unusual shape and movement, but I didn't immediately connect it with my 1983 vision. Then, a few months later our nation's prosperity took a sudden U-turn that seemed to mark the end of America's golden age.

Now, here we are five years later in 2024. Trillions of additional dollars have been created to fund Covid and the Ukraine War and prop up the US financial system. As these multi-trillions of new dollars are finding their way into our economy, America is experiencing serious inflation that is eroding our purchasing power and standard of living. Will our economy collapse under hyperinflation? Or, is our current monetary system being revamped in "The Great Reset" that has been promised by the World Economic Forum? Will that result in utopia for all—or dystopia for those who do not comply with its dictates? We will soon find out.

Vision about to be fulfilled:

Scripture tells us that when Jesus comes for His church, the world will be saying "peace and safety." Is that time just around the corner, as they settle the world wars and "build back better" into their vision of a new world system? Or are we already near the end of peace and safety? Either way, I believe the Train Cloud will arrive before much longer!

+ *For when they say, "Peace and safety!" then sudden destruction comes upon them, as labor pains upon a pregnant woman. And they shall not escape. (1 Thessalonians 5:3)*

+ *Then the sign of the Son of Man will appear in heaven, and then all the tribes of the earth will mourn, and they will see the Son of Man coming on the clouds of heaven with power and great glory. (Matthew 24:30)*

+ *And the armies in heaven, clothed in fine linen, white and clean, followed Him on white horses. (Revelation 19:14)*

Judgment of the Wicked

A *few nights after I experienced The Visitation in 1983*, I had my first prophetic dream. In this dream, it was a delightful summer day and I decided to take my son, Greg (three years old at that time), and walk down to the 7-Eleven about a half mile from our home. It felt like a time of peace and safety with no worries or concerns. On our way home, as we were approaching our cul-de-sac, everything dramatically changed! Missiles began shooting down over the mountains from the southeast. But when the missiles hit Earth, heavenly beings dressed in white appeared and began pulling certain people out of their houses and attacked them with fire!

What was really shocking to me was who they were going after. They seemed to be targeting the Mormons in my neighborhood. And the more religious the person (like the bishop and his wife), the greater their vengeance toward them. I watched in disbelief and horror as this was happening, aghast that these people couldn't seem to die!

Then suddenly, Greg and I were caught up in the air by two angels and whisked away into our home. Jesus was standing there in my living room, and we were deposited directly in front of Him. He was standing behind me with His hands on my shoulders, and Greg was standing in front of me. Together, the three of us watched

through a glass door, as the angels carried out their judgment on
the wicked!

I knew that we were saved from this horrific event because we were
behind the Door, under the saving arms of Jesus!

Vision partially fulfilled in scripture:

+ *. . . the harvest is the end of the age, and the reapers are the angels.
  Therefore, as the tares are gathered and burned in the fire, so it will be
  at the end of this age. The Son of Man will send out His angels, and
  they will gather out of His kingdom all things that offend, and those
  who practice lawlessness, and will cast them into the furnace of fire . . .*
  (Matthew 13:39-43)

+ *For He shall give His angels charge over you, to keep you in all your
  ways. In their hands they shall bear you up, lest you dash your foot
  against a stone.* (Psalm 91: 11-12)

+ *"Let both grow together until the harvest, and at the time of harvest
  I will say to the reapers, "First gather together the tares and bind
  them in bundles to burn them, but gather the wheat into my barn.""*
  (Matthew 13:30)

These prophetic scriptures will soon be fulfilled when Jesus returns!

The Eagle in the Cloud

On *September 16, 2011,* God gave me a very unusual vision. This vision took place in a supernatural way, but using the physical realm instead of the spiritual realm. It was a beautiful autumn day, my favorite time of the year. I was doing my morning exercise routine when I glanced out the glass door onto my deck. A very unusual cloud grabbed my attention. It was quite low and positioned right in front of my window, as if facing me. There were actually two clouds: a flat white cloud that looked like a round piece of paper, and a charcoal-gray cumulous cloud positioned on top. The gray cloud was perfectly shaped in the form of a large, flying eagle.

I was stunned and mesmerized by this extraordinary picture displayed in the things of nature. As I studied the cloud, the flying eagle started to move slightly, as it began shedding large chunks of cloud from its body. Chunks of gray cloud were continually falling from the eagle's body as it was flying, but amazingly it didn't diminish in size or shape.

Although the eagle was struggling to fly, it managed to keep going much longer than seemed possible. As I watched, transfixed on this amazing phenomenon for about ten minutes, the eagle's head suddenly disappeared. It was just gone, but you wouldn't notice unless you were looking for it because of the way the eagle was flying. The body continued to fly without a head for another two to three minutes.

Suddenly, the eagle's body morphed into two swirling black circles of equal size. I understood the US government had collapsed into vitriolic groups of people who were adamantly divided in ideology. This continued for about two minutes, as the black circles contended against each other. Then they unexpectedly melted into one amorphous mass of total destruction.

Astounded at what I had just watched, I pondered this supernatural display as I went back to exercising for a few minutes. Then, I looked back toward the window. It was still there—the flat white cloud with a dark cumulous cloud in the center. But the dark cloud had changed shape again. It was no longer a mass; it was perfectly shaped as a large eagle's head. It didn't have a body; only this large head, cocked upward toward Heaven, as if mocking God!

Amazed, I continued watching it for about two more minutes until the head collapsed and it began mixing in with the white cloud. The show was over, and the whole cloud began moving away.

I realized this had to be a message from God, and that I should record what I had just witnessed. So, I grabbed my little digital recorder and began describing the entire vision. After I finished, I played it back and was shocked at what I heard. In the middle of my narration, an eerie screech is heard in the background! I still have this recording today, and everyone who hears it is freaked out by this sound. It is not of this world—it sounds like the screech of a demon, gleeful about this destructive future event they want to happen.

What is the meaning of this strange vision?

This vision occurred about three years into the "Great Recession," and I think it depicts what will happen to America going forward. I believe the eagle represents the United States. The body and wings represent the people and society, and the head represents the government, or the power that controls the eagle. The large chunks continuously falling off the eagle's body are enormous amounts of money being wasted or stolen from the US Treasury and the people. But the eagle's body doesn't seem to diminish because the Federal Reserve is pumping as much fiat money into the system as necessary to keep the eagle flying.

There are a few scenarios that could cause the eagle to implode into a civil war. And if or when it does, I believe the US will descend into social, political, and economic dissolution, as the vision depicted.

Although this is a very disturbing message that nobody wants to hear, the Lord always shows His watchmen what is coming ahead of time. He tells them to warn His people to repent and be prepared mentally, physically, and spiritually to make it through the storm!

In-process fulfillment of this vision:

I believe this vision is currently being fulfilled as described below:

The eagle was seriously wounded in the 2008 financial debacle and looting of the US Treasury, which plunged us into "the Great Recession" for the next seven years. But unfortunately, it didn't stop there. The US economy has continued to be systematically manipulated and drained with "quantitative easing" and financial maneuvers, ripping off huge chunks of money from the eagle's body.

Such a scheme was revealed in 2018, when Catherine Austin Fitts, former Assistant Secretary of the Department of Housing and Urban Development ("HUD"), together with economist Dr. Mark Skidmore and a team of PhD candidates at Michigan State University uncovered and documented at least $21 trillion that had gone missing from just two US government bureaucracies—HUD and the Department of Defense. Since then, Dr. Skidmore's team and other people investigating the US government's missing money mysteries have estimated the amount to be over $100 trillion! No wonder the eagle has been struggling to fly all these years!

In 2020 the eagle lost its head, in my opinion. It was a stealth operation that most people didn't notice, just as the vision had indicated. I believe this happened on March 13, 2020, when President Trump declared the United States to be in a "National Emergency" due to Covid-19, and relinquished much of his authority to a small group of quasi-government virologists. Such a declaration by the president of the United States can carry with it some alarming effects, like suspending certain constitutional rights of the people and relinquishing much of the president's authority to other entities.

When this happened, I believe the decapitation began, as those new authorities proceeded to lead our country through a controversial crisis that resulted in a lot of confusion, misinformation, social division, death, disease, and great damage to the US economy—especially small businesses. Then a few months later, in November 2020, the decapitation was confirmed when the presidential head was officially severed. Since then, the Eagle has been floundering as the social, economic, and political dissolution intensifies.

On February 24, 2022, the Covid campaign was upstaged by international war, as Russia unleashed its "special military operation" on Ukraine. The US and NATO immediately responded by declaring economic war and sanctions against Russia. Within a few months tensions ratcheted up—and now the world sits on the brink of World War III, as nuclear weapons are brandished on the world stage by several countries.

Then on September 1, 2022, President Biden tried to incite civil discord among American citizens. In the most shocking speech ever given by a US president, Biden stood in front of a dramatic background designed to look like "the gates of Hell," in my opinion. And, in Hitleresque fashion he essentially declared civil war on "MAGA" Republicans—his political opponents that represent half of the voting American people!

Sadly, it looks like the events depicted in this vision are playing out now. If it continues, I believe we will soon see the collapse of the eagle and civil war, followed by the complete destruction of the United States of America!

Out of the Blue

On May 5, 2014, I was given a prophetic dream. Until this point, the Lord usually showed me open visions rather than dreams. However, He tells us in the Bible: "Your young men shall see visions, your old men shall dream dreams" (Acts 2:17; Joel 2:28). I guess I am seeing more dreams now because of my age. But what was also unusual about this experience was that this dream occurred within thirty minutes after I went to bed, almost as soon as my head hit the pillow!

The dream:

> On a sunny morning in the middle of summer, I was in my home visiting with my daughter and her husband. People were enjoying life and going on vacation. Everything seemed to be getting better and there was a feeling of optimism in society.
>
> It was about noon when I got up from my sofa to get something and happened to glance out my patio door. Instantly, I froze—a huge missile was speeding straight at me from the west! The Lord enabled me to see it up close, and its design seemed odd to me. It was a hybrid—constructed by a high-tech nation (represented by a precision red ring around the nose) and a

low-tech nation (represented by a lot of green painted around the lower half of the missile in an imprecise manner). I felt that these colors somehow represented specific nations. The green also indicated that the low-tech nation was supplying a lot of money to fund the project, while the other nation provided the technology.

I didn't have time to move or react, but in a split second my mind was flooded with questions in disbelief: *What enemy is due west of Salt Lake City?* I wondered.

The world seemed to be at peace, so who would want to ambush us like this?

Why would they attack Utah, of all places?

I couldn't believe this was how I would leave this world—but thankfully, I didn't! The missile whizzed just over my right shoulder, and I breathed a deep sigh of relief.

I turned to see where it was going, and suddenly I was no longer in my living room, but standing on a huge map covering the United States. I watched as the missile continued at hypersonic speed until it was over the Midwest, just south of Des Moines, Iowa. It abruptly made a ninety-degree vertical turn, soaring straight above the Earth into the black starlit sky of outer space!

The missile exploded with the loudest boom imaginable—I felt the reverberations in every cell of my body! When it exploded, a white cloud of powder-like debris filled the black sky like an umbrella over the United States, and began raining down on the earth.

I suddenly woke up—as I was falling out of my bed to the floor. It seemed that the tremendous power of the explosion had literally blown me out of bed, even though it was a dream!

Partial fulfillment of the dream:

This dream was confirmed in what I believe was a harbinger, two months later on July 17, 2014. It was the event where an Indonesian airliner with several hundred passengers was shot down by a missile over Ukraine. The Western news media were quick to identify the Russians as the culprits, claiming it was a deliberate war crime.

As soon as I heard the story on TV, this dream flashed in my mind and the Holy Spirit showed me that the missile had come from the west. It was a war crime on many levels, but the culprit was not Russia—it was the West!

I felt this dream was also showing that retribution will come against the United States. Nations will return judgment in like manner, for the egregious acts of those who perpetrated this war crime, among others. I believe this dream was foretelling an EMP type of attack on the US that will come when no one is expecting it. It will come from west of the United States—just like what happened to those people on the airliner!

Israel Is Alone

On *may 8, 2014*, three days after the missile dream, I had another prophetic dream that again was very unusual. It also occurred about thirty minutes after I went to bed, around 10 p.m. In this dream, two angels came and woke me up as I was sleeping. They said that they had been ordered to take me someplace to show me something. I didn't want to go because I was sleeping well, but they were adamant that I must go with them.

They picked me up and we rose straight up into the sky, then we were transported across the globe to the Middle East. It didn't take long—we just ascended above the Earth and were suddenly on the other side of the world!

The angels were extremely strong and powerful, and they surrounded me like a helicopter. We were hovering in the night sky over the Mediterranean, just off the coast of Gaza. It was very dark, and a heavy gloom filled the atmosphere, as thousands of black evil birds swirled furiously over the dark sea and coastline. The angels were very concerned about what was happening and the evil that these spirits were stirring up between Gaza and Israel.

Gaza was burning! The intense orange, red, and yellow flames were a dramatic contrast to the blackness surrounding the city, as the whole coastline seemed to be engulfed in fire. I could see missiles being launched in a northeast direction, as Gaza made a feeble attempt to fight against this overwhelming attack by Israel. They appeared to be suffering the brunt of the conflict, and I felt the angels were concerned for them as well as for Israel. These angels had been given great responsibility to minister God's will in this region. Their hearts cried for Gaza, but I sensed their greatest responsibility had to do with Israel.

Israel will be alone, on its own against a hostile world. The United States will no longer be able to help them, and their enemies will begin attacking like wolves. Although they will have powerful weapons, Israel's only help will be from God. But Israel is not innocent. They have also done evil in the world and to their neighbors. I believe the Lord will bring judgment upon them as well as Hamas in Gaza.

Dream partially fulfilled:

This dream was also partly fulfilled two months later. On the morning of July 18, 2014 (one day after the Indonesian airplane carnage), I turned on my TV and the vision that I had seen in my dream of Gaza burning was filling the screen! The night before, Israel had launched an overwhelming attack on Gaza and apparently spared almost no one. The whole coastline was burning, just as I had seen. Once again, I felt this attack was a harbinger of a future time when America is taken out; and retribution will come to Israel, in a manner similar to how they were treating Gaza.

In this 2014 attack upon Gaza, residences, businesses, and civilians were targeted, along with military installations. Over 2,500 people, including women and children, died, and more than 17,000 were injured in Israel's indiscriminate nighttime attacks!

Why weren't they charged with war crimes for these heinous deliberate murders? The media has been silent on this. But the Lord is a God of justice, and He *will* judge them for such atrocities—at a time when America cannot help them!

Israel suffered fewer than one hundred deaths and about 2,500 injured in this skirmish. Thanks to their Iron Dome military defense technology, their cities were far less impacted than Gaza in this conflict.

And now, here we are ten years later in 2024—and Israel has effectively destroyed Gaza! On October 7, 2023, Hamas somehow managed to pull off an astonishing surprise attack on Israel. The slaughter and mayhem went on for hours before the Israeli military raised a meaningful response. Thousands of Israelis were killed, maimed, and terrorized. More than a hundred Israelis were kidnapped and held as hostages by Hamas for months. The whole thing was shocking and unbelievable!

Attack of the Masked Men

In early 2018, I began asking the Lord for confirmation regarding the things He had been showing me in visions and dreams for several years about the future of America. I needed to know if my understanding was correct and what He wanted me to do with the information I was given.

A few weeks later, I was listening to a geopolitical discussion between two men on YouTube, when one of them made an off-hand comment that suddenly grabbed me! He named three men and said if those guys were right, then specific events would soon happen. I don't remember now what specific events they were referring to, but when I heard the name "Dumitru Duduman," I experienced a God Moment! I knew the Lord was telling me that there was something about this man that I needed to know.

So, I googled his name and found a book he published in 1992, titled *Through the Fire Without Burning.* Luckily, it was still available on Amazon, so I ordered it. And there were my answers! The Lord had revealed many of the same things to Dumitru that He had shown me about America. We had both been given three visions that were virtually the same message regarding missile attacks and judgment upon America. But the Lord also gave Dumitru information that I was not given. I encourage the reader to read Dumitru's book and additional information he shared, which may still be available on the internet.

Who was Dumitru Duduman?

Dumitru was a faithful pastor of a small country church in Romania, whom the Lord used from the 1970s through 1983 to smuggle hundreds of thousands of Bibles into the Soviet Union. Dumitru paid a heavy price for his brave sacrifice. He was caught and detained several times and brutally tortured. Then, in 1984, the Communists gave him an ultimatum: a mental institution, life in prison, or expulsion to the United States. He and his immediate family reluctantly chose America, and left Romania with nothing. The Communists refused to let them take extra clothing or any personal items (pictures, etc.) with them. They came to America penniless and empty-handed!

But it was actually God who brought Dumitru to the United States, so He faithfully provided for them. He took them to Fullerton, California and connected them with a Christian congregation who helped them with housing, basic necessities, and to learn the language and skills needed to work in the US. But life was not easy, and they suffered much for the first few years.

The Lord brought them to America because he had another important mission for Dumitru to accomplish, which He revealed to him shortly after they settled in California. Dumitru was to deliver a prophetic message to the United States—a warning from Almighty God about America's future. It was an urgent call to repentance, and a warning of specific judgments that would come if America continued down its wicked path!

Mystery Babylon

God sent an angel to tell Dumitru why He was to warn America. The angel said that America was going to burn if she didn't repent soon. He showed him California, New York, Florida, and Las Vegas—saying that they were "Sodom and Gomorrah and would all burn."

He also told him that America is "Mystery Babylon" because she was established as a Christian nation, but we allowed immigrants to bring their false gods into our country. Then, the people began to follow the strange gods and turned their backs on the God Who had built and prospered this country.

For scriptural proof of the things the angel said, he told Dumitru to read Jeremiah 51:8-15; Revelation chapter 18; and Zechariah chapter 14. (See Chapter 12: "Messages from God" in Dumitru Duduman's book, *Through the Fire Without Burning*). I strongly advise reading the above referenced scriptures. They are prophecies we all need to know!

For the next several years Dumitru was taken to various churches throughout the US, to deliver God's warnings. During this time, the Lord gave him several more prophetic dreams, angelic messages, and visions regarding America. One of those messages was about the attack of the masked men, which he described in his vision, "America, the Falling Star," on page 175 of his book.

This dream was a forewarning about an increasing number of nations that would begin turning against the United States. Dumitru first saw a very large star with crooked tips high in the sky. Then, he heard hoofbeats and saw four horses pulling an old-fashioned chariot with four world leaders inside. These men had been conspiring to bring down America, and now they were going into action. The chariot abruptly stopped and they all took aim and shot at the star, using heavy artillery. The star caught fire and burned, then fell to the ground. But before long, it recovered its position in the sky.

So, later they launched another attack. In this attack, the group had grown to six world leaders sitting in a chariot pulled by six horses. *But this time, they were all wearing masks!* As they shot at the star with even greater weapons, it caught fire and crashed to the ground. But once again, the star regained its position in the sky.

Dumitru woke up, disturbed by the dream. After praying for a while, he went back to bed and the dream resumed. This time he heard a very loud noise, much greater than the previous two incidents. Now, there were eight world leaders and eight horses pulling a chariot. Once again, they all shot at the star with even greater weapons. The star caught fire and fell to the ground again, but this time it blew up. Their third attack finally destroyed America!

Then, in the same place high in the sky where the star used to be, Dumitru saw a man dressed in white. The man said, "The star represents America. The reason the tips are crooked is because America has fallen away from the Truth, and the Way of God. The eight horses and the men in the chariot represent eight kings that will rise up against America and will overcome her." Then the dream ended.

In another prophetic dream in his book titled *The Star*, on page 166, Dumitru saw the star fall and blow up sixteen times. Then a voice told him, "Do you see this star? It represents America. This is how fast the fall of America will be! As fast as that star fell!"

The Bible sometimes uses the metaphor "a time" to represent a one-year period. Was the voice indicating the takedown of America would be accomplished in sixteen times—sixteen years?

Then, the voice said: "There will be a time of preparation for the people. The ones who need to repent should do it now, before it is too late. The time without trouble will last until the total number of the chosen is fulfilled."

My understanding of Dumitru's star dreams:

I believe that Dumitru's vision, "America, the Falling Star," foretells a time when America will become hated by other nations who will conspire to destroy her. They will attack and wound America in their first two attempts but not succeed until their third attack. Strangely, they will all be wearing masks in their second attack. I believe this indicates 2020—the year when everyone throughout the world was required to wear masks!

I think their first attack was the September 2008/2009 financial debacle and bank heist that drained the US Treasury and catapulted the whole world into the "Great Recession." The US economy was devastated for the next seven years, with millions losing their jobs, homes, and businesses and going bankrupt. America suffered a hard blow, but thankfully, the star managed to retain its position as world hegemon!

Although the second attack (Covid) was even more devastating, America can print the world's reserve currency, so the star managed to regain its place in the sky once again. But that is now changing, as many nations have turned against the United States, just as Dumitru was shown. The BRICS nations (Russia, China, India, Brazil, and South Africa) have designed an economic system to bypass using the dollar as their international medium of exchange—and several more nations are now joining them. Saudi Arabia, Iran, United Arab Emirates, Egypt, Ethiopia, and Argentina were just admitted into BRICS in January 2024, and more than twenty additional nations have also applied for membership.

This is threatening to destroy the petrodollar that has enabled America to become the world's greatest superpower. Saudi Arabia has effectively canceled their agreement to only sell oil in dollars, thus undermining America's economic and political dominance. In addition, our allies are showing signs of disaffection with America. French President Macron is proposing that France and the EU decouple from America's dominance over them and become a "third superpower." They reportedly want to reduce Europe's dependence on America, and avoid getting dragged into a confrontation between the US and China over Taiwan.

Have all eight world leaders now turned against America?

When China "Frees" Taiwan

This is another vision given to Dumitru that is critical for everyone to know about. He was shown this vision on April 22, 1996, one year before he died. Several visions Dumitru saw regarding China and Russia corroborate what the Lord has also shown me in visions and dreams.

In his book *Midnight Strikes*, on page 248, author Daniel Holdings shares one of Dumitru's most important prophetic messages. An angel showed Dumitru a vision of the future presidents of Russia and China, conspiring to destroy America by having China take back Taiwan. In the vision, a holy "man" said, "When America goes to war with China, the Russians will strike without warning." He then told Dumitru, "You must tell them what is being planned against America. Then, when it comes to pass, the people will remember the words the Lord has spoken."

The "man" then said: "America's sin has reached God. He will allow this destruction, for He can no longer stand such wickedness. **God, however, still has people that worship Him with a clean heart as they do His work. He has prepared a heavenly army to save these people.**" Dumitru then stated, "a great army, well-armed and dressed in white, appeared before me."

Around the time America goes to war with China, civil war will break out in America. On page 161 of his book *Through the Fire Without Burning*, Dumitru writes: "When the Americans will think that it is peace and safety—from the middle of the country, some of the people will start fighting against the government. The government will be busy with internal problems. Then from the ocean, from Cuba, Nicaragua, Mexico (and two other countries he couldn't remember), they will bomb the nuclear warehouses. When they explode, America will burn."

Dumitru then asks, "What will you do with the Church of the Lord? How will you save the ones who will turn to you?" The holy man said, "Tell them this: 'how I saved the three young ones from the furnace of fire, and how I saved Daniel in the lions' den, is the same way I will save them."

My understanding of this vision:

Dumitru's visions are being fulfilled right now!

China, Russia, and other countries have entered into political/economic pacts to exclude and destroy America economically. They are also holding military exercises in the Pacific, practicing tactics to destroy the United States, and saying they will use nukes if necessary. And, China recently stated they will soon take back Taiwan.

Russia and China will execute their plan when civil war gets going in the United States. We will be greatly weakened—divided socially and politically and distracted, fighting two wars at the same time.

China will start war with the US around Taiwan and hit us with an EMP. Then, Russia et al. will attack with their devastating nuclear missiles that are now surrounding the United States.

When these events start happening, the Lord will send a Heavenly army to rescue His people who are living righteous lives. I believe this is the Heavenly army I saw in "The Train Cloud" vision.

Dumitru's visions confirm numerous things that God showed me in the following testimonies:

+ In the Wings of an Eagle

+ The Train Cloud

+ Come Away with Me

+ Judgment of the Wicked

+ The Eagle in the Cloud

+ Out of the Blue

I believe many of those rescued from the coming calamities will be taken to a place on Earth where they will dwell in the presence of Jesus until it is time for the rapture. This was the understanding I had in my vision "Come Away with Me."

Dumitru was given a similar understanding in his vision, "The Camp of God," on page 169 in his book. He saw a vision of a very large "man" who placed the sun, moon, and stars into a tent. Then he was shown a huge tent with a bright light shining through the cracks of the door. Inside was Jesus with a large group of His people. A voice proclaimed, "These are all my redeemed which are on the earth who have a clean life and who are washed in my blood."

Russian Submarines

In 2019, *God led me to another watchman* in response to my requests to confirm the visions I was shown. The Lord soon brought a man named Henry Gruver to my awareness. I shared some of the miracles God did in Henry's life earlier, at the end of Part I. But it was Henry's vision of Russian submarines described below that was the primary reason the Lord led me to him.

Henry Gruver was an electrical engineer by profession, but his first love and priority was to be an evangelist. This remarkable man had a unique ministry of "prayer walking" the nations of the world. He would go to the nations and cities the Lord led him to, and walk up and down the streets (as the Lord led), praying for the nation and the people in those places. He did this for many years and covered numerous countries prayer walking, leading people to Jesus, and performing astounding miracles. There are several videos of Henry Gruver on the internet and on the website www.stevequayle.com where Steve is interviewing Henry that are well worth watching.

In 1986, while Henry was prayer walking the streets of Wales, God showed him a profound vision. As he was going down to the bay to pray one morning, the Lord told Henry to go across the bridge and into Caernarvon Castle, where Prince Charles had been coronated as the Prince of Wales. Then, the Lord instructed him to go to the top of a tower (the Eagle Tower). Once there, Henry began to pray and was looking over the sea and islands below, when instantly he was caught up into the heavens in a vision. He saw a big-picture view of Earth, and it looked like a beautiful blue globe.

As Henry gazed down in awe at the beauty of Earth, he noticed a massive military operation of Russian submarines coming through the oceans from above Finland, down into the North Sea around England. The submarines continued stealthily into the Atlantic Ocean, Gulf of Mexico, and Pacific Ocean, where their torpedoes were strategically positioned just off the shores of America to launch a devastating attack from all directions at a future time.

Next, Henry saw all of America's communication towers hit with some kind of EMF technology, turning them to "dust that was sprinkling to the ground." Then, suddenly, nuclear missiles began shooting out of the oceans, striking New York City and major coastal cities all around the shores of the United States. Huge cities were instantly vaporized!

Henry's descriptions were further confirmation of the nuclear missile attacks that I had also been shown. I believe the EMP I saw explode high over the middle of the United States is probably why the communication towers turned to dust in Henry's vision. Then, Henry saw the Russian submarines go into action and launch powerful nukes. I also saw what I believed to be Russian nukes coming from unexpected directions that vaporized *interior* cities in the United States!

I am sorry to say that Henry's vision of Russian submarines is being fulfilled right now! In September 2022, Russia reportedly launched their Belgorod submarines into the White Sea, in response to their Nordstream pipelines being blown up. The submarine fleet is believed to have proceeded north of Scandinavia into the Norwegian Sea and down into the Atlantic Ocean. Several military analysts believe they have now deposited numerous Poseidon nuclear torpedoes around all the shores of the United States.

The Poseidon missiles are unique—only Russia has such weapons. They are capable of creating 1,600-foot tsunamis full of nuclear contamination that can wipe out entire nations. Russian spokespersons have boasted that two could destroy Great Britain, and six would devastate the United States!

It looks like Henry's vision is playing out exactly as he saw it.

I wish I didn't have to report this kind of information; however, I must. But do not fear—prepare—mentally, physically, and spiritually. Remember the promises of Psalm 91—and get ready to stand before Jesus!

"But take heed to yourselves, lest your hearts be weighed down with carousing, drunkenness, and cares of this life, and that Day come on you unexpectedly. For it will come as a snare on all those who dwell on the face of the whole earth. Watch therefore, and pray always that you may be counted worthy to escape all these things that will come to pass, and to stand before the Son of Man." (Luke 21:34-36)

The Strange New Society

During the first week of January 2023, the Lord gave me another dream. It was vivid, followed a storyline, and was spiritually impacting. I also remembered every detail and understood its meaning.

But I didn't want to believe it was prophetic because it was very disturbing to me. I tried to push it to the back of my mind, telling myself it was just a message dream about some attitudes developing in society but not actually prophetic. Then, a few weeks later the Lord suddenly brought it to my mind again, and I knew the message was prophetic and I should share it.

My dream:

> In this dream I was in my late fifties and had just been hired for a corporate position working in a large, modern office building. There were a number of different companies housed in this upscale professional complex. But I had been self-employed for several years, so I was perplexed that I would want to return to that type of work environment.

As I entered the building on my first day, I was impressed by how everyone seemed to be very focused on their own business and didn't interact much with others in the hallways or common areas. There wasn't the comradery that you normally see among people whose paths cross on a regular basis, with polite greetings and casual joking or comments. It felt overly businesslike, lacking in personality.

I walked into the office of my new employer and encountered the same type of environment. It was devoid of the relaxed, lighthearted relationships, interactions, and office buzz that are common in a healthy company—the kind of environment I remembered from years before when I worked in the corporate world.

A young woman came into the front lobby when I entered and told me to sit down and wait a few minutes, so I did. As I looked around, I could see into the back-office area where several employees sat at desks a few feet apart in a common office area that wasn't very well-lit. There were no cubicles or offices for these people, just a common area where each person was intensely focused on their computer, as if immersed in their own world. They all looked about the same age—late twenties to early thirties. I was hoping I wouldn't be the only older person in the office.

After several minutes the woman came out and took me to the office of the corporate executive who had hired me. He wasn't there, so I was told to sit down and wait for him. After several minutes he came in and barely acknowledged me. He retrieved something from his desk and left without comment. He appeared to be a man in his fifties, professionally dressed and very self-absorbed. After an hour or so, I went back into the main office hoping to get some basic information from the woman about where the restroom was and when and where to get lunch. She gave me very matter-of-fact answers, which felt cold and dismissive. Then, she went back to her desk.

Several minutes later the woman suddenly directed everyone to gather together around a few desks in the middle of the office space. It was lunchtime, and the workers began to come to life, eating and talking as if they were all best of friends. But again, I was ignored. The woman's lack of common social grace and etiquette toward me felt deliberate. But why? Did they dislike older people that much?

As I sat there observing them, I could hear parts of their lively conversation. They were excitedly talking about the latest and greatest technology and different aspects of their jobs. Each seemed to boast about their achievements and the exciting cutting-edge things they were doing. They bragged about their new devices, programs, skills, and knowledge, like people would brag about their latest vacation—when I was that age.

They seemed to have abnormally close relationships with each other, like a cult centered around a common value system. They didn't talk about their personal lives, families, politics, and things going on in the world. They seemed to be focused on their careers, technology, and their group.

Lunchtime ended, and they all agreed to meet after work at the club. Something about that reference bothered me. But I brushed it off, assuming it was a nightclub where techies gathered to relax and have some fun after work, which sounded refreshingly normal to me. Maybe they were typical young adults after all, I thought.

But their devotion to their jobs and technology didn't seem normal to me. It was as if those were the most important things in the world to them and what defined their value in the world. Their identity and value system appeared to revolve around technology, and they seemed to judge the value of others through that lens.

They all disbursed back to their desks. The young woman saw me sitting in the lobby area and approached me almost with disgust as if to say, "What are you still doing here?" She picked up some papers from her desk and shoved them in front of me. "If you're wondering why nobody wants to associate with you, this is why," she stated haughtily. "I can't believe they even hired you," she continued. "Look at this! You have a back-score in the 900s! I have never heard of someone with such a high back-score!" she exclaimed.

What is a "back-score" and how does she know that kind of information about me? I wondered. I hadn't taken any test for this job. I had the distinct feeling that if my back-score were 1,000 I would be officially declared a dinosaur, or worse—maybe even a racist! She and her cohorts clearly had no tolerance for someone so yesterday and out of alignment with their societal values. I was deplorable to them, a social pariah.

Then it struck me, why I had such an eerie feeling about the people in this building and the way they behaved. They weren't really human. They were roboticized humans whose minds were influenced by some kind of technology, like a supercomputer. An entity that made them love technology rather than God and other human beings. *Are they cyborgs or AI synthetic robots?* I wondered.

I also understood why their interactions with each other during lunchtime as well as their emphasis on meeting at the club had bothered me. I felt like I had just encountered the society depicted in the book *Brave New World*!

Then, the dream ended and I woke up.

Is this where the controllers of this world are trying to take us? Is this what the "Great Reset" is really about? This cold, soulless society was horrifying to me, and I hope that we won't have to live in that dystopian world!

The Watchmen's Summary

The testimonies shared in "Warnings of the Watchmen" present strong evidence that we have entered the perilous times Jesus and the apostles said would come in the end-days. This will involve nuclear war, among other disasters. Although this realization is sobering, the Lord has created and equipped His people "for such a time as this." We are commanded to watch and not cower in fear, but to rise up in faith and obedience to His word, and "fight the good fight of faith!"

> He who overcomes shall inherit all things, and I will be his God and he shall be My son. But the cowardly, unbelieving, abominable, murderers, sexually immoral, sorcerers, idolaters, and all liars shall have their part in the lake which burns with fire and brimstone, which is the second death." (Revelation 21: 7-8)

It is imperative that we stay close to Jesus, remembering that He forewarns us through scripture, His prophets, watchmen, and personally through the Holy Spirit, to know what to expect and do. He has also given us prophecies and strong promises throughout the Bible, including Psalms 23 and 91—to build our faith and give us comfort and hope.

Spiritual warfare is a battle between fear and faith. Fear is the power of evil. Faith is the power of God. If you are a born-again Christian living in obedience to Jesus, you have authority over every demon, evil spirit, and Satan himself. Do not give up your power by acquiescing to fear and surrendering to evil. Stand in faith with Jesus! The one you obey is the one you love—and will be with for eternity!

How the Watchmen testimonies apply to our time

We are on the brink of World War III. It will be a nuclear-type war that Russia and China have been collaborating to bring against America. Other nations will join them; most are enemies of the United States but some will be former allies.

Americans will be blindsided when this happens. My perception was that Americans will have a false sense of security, peace, and safety regarding foreign enemies at the time the missiles come. It will come as a shock to most everyone.

But unfortunately, a civil war will be unfolding in America at that same time. The Eagle will finally collapse into two factions pushing against each other. Then, America's enemies will take advantage of our dysfunction; and China will move upon Taiwan, triggering war between the United States and China. America will be distracted and weakened, fighting China and a civil war at the same time. That's when China, Russia, et al. will launch their attack on the United States. God will allow it to come as judgment on "Mystery Babylon." However, Jesus will protect and rescue His *righteous* people from the catastrophies!

The kingdom of the Beast will emerge:

After the devastation of WWIII, I believe the Antichrist will be revealed and they will "build back better" into a global society with amazing technologies—a utopian world that is increasingly non-human. As I saw in my vision "A Strange New Society," I believe it will include human hybrids (Cyborgs) and sentient robots who worship technology and hate any Christians who remain. There may also be "alien" and AI entities who control civilization and purport to be Christ and/or demigods.

But it will really be the kingdom of the Beast, and most will worship the Antichrist—until the day he/it arrogantly stands "in God's temple," and Jesus Christ returns to judge them all!

+ *And then the lawless one will be revealed, whom the Lord will consume with the breath of His mouth and destroy with the brightness of His coming. (2 Thessalonians 2:8)*

+ *"Therefore when you see the 'abomination of desolation,' spoken of by Daniel the prophet, standing in the holy place" (whoever reads, let him understand) (Matthew 24:15)*

+ *For at that time there will be great tribulation, unmatched from the beginning of the world until now, and never to be seen again. If those days had not been cut short, nobody would be saved. But for the sake of the elect, those days will be cut short. (Matthew 24:21-22 BSB)*

PART III

HEAVEN IS FOR REAL
AND SO IS HELL

*For God so loved the world that He gave His
only begotten Son, that whoever believes in Him
should not perish but have everlasting life.*

John 3:16

Have You Been Saved?

Why did the Son of God have to leave Heaven, become a man, and suffer an excruciating death to save you? What was He saving you from?

God the Father sent His Son, God the Word, to save mankind from death and Hell—the abode of Satan and his demons. Their realm is the epitome of evil and far worse than anything we can imagine. Hell is the antithesis of God and everything good. The demons thrive on fear, hatred, and doing evil, especially to the souls who become their victims. They hate God and love torturing those who were made in His image—humans. Hell is a massive prison inside the earth that was created to restrain Satan, his fallen angels, and his demons. The environment is a palpable, oppressive darkness filled with the spirit of fear. As Jesus said, it is a place of suffering—weeping, wailing, hopelessness, and demonic torture in the midst of unquenchable fire. Hell is so horrid that even the demons hate to be there, and are trying to get out!

Unfortunately, Hell became the default destination of human beings when they die. Satan acquired claim to the souls of humanity when Adam and Eve gave their allegiance and authority over Earth to him. When Satan took over, sin entered with him, corrupting humanity and separating us from God.

But the good news is that "with God all things are possible," as Jesus stated. Satan had used his most ingenious diabolic plan to deceive Adam and Eve. But the Father had an ace up His sleeve—Jesus!

For God so loved the world that He gave His only
begotten Son, that whoever believes in Him should
not perish but have everlasting life. (John 3:16)

God created humanity to become His children, and He was not about to let Satan have them. He would send His Son, Jesus, to defeat the devil, rescue His children, and deliver them to Him in Heaven. But Satan had obtained legal claim over them, so a ransom had to be paid to get them back. And, Satan's price was high—the sum total of all their sins—and he wanted his "pound of flesh" for each one!

The Father had a solution for that problem, as well. He would provide a proxy to pay the price for His captured children. But the value of that proxy's life had to be sufficient to pay for all the sins of humanity, which meant that it had to be a sinless life of tremendous value. And that is exactly what Jesus is—the perfect Son of God, whose life and blood are of utmost value.

Now, those who ask Jesus to become their Lord and Savior are released from Hell and demonic torture. The punishment for their sins was paid by the Word of God Himself! But there is something each person must do for His payment to be appropriated to them. They must believe in Jesus, confess their sins, and ask Him to save them. Then, they must follow and obey Him for the rest of their lives.

Hopefully, this book can help you believe and come (or return) to Jesus Christ to be saved. But don't procrastinate—we cannot presume upon tomorrow in today's crazy world!

In Part III, I present several testimonies of persons whom God has taken to both Heaven and Hell in recent years. The first testimony is that of my late husband, Rhett. I share the transcript from my interview with him about his experience. Although I tried to keep it as concise as possible, it is somewhat lengthy because he experienced a complete tour of Heaven. He was given the kind of experience that Christians will have when they leave this world and are taken to Heaven by angels. He describes his trip through the heavens and its awesome beauty—then he describes what Heaven looks like from outer space, as one is approaching it. Next, he talks about what takes place at the gate of Heaven, where Jesus accepts or rejects those who are brought to Him. Then, he describes what those who are able to enter through the gate will experience once they are in Heaven!

As I mentioned earlier, when I began writing this book in 2019, I felt that God wanted me to share Rhett's testimonies as well. So, I asked the Lord to give me confirmation through at least two or three witnesses whom He had given similar experiences. He actually gave me six other witnesses. I didn't go looking for them—God brought them to me in serendipitous ways. I was secretly hoping I wouldn't get validation about his experience in Hell, because I didn't want to talk about that horrible reality. But the Lord gave me overwhelming confirmation, and quickly. God wants me to share both—the good news about Heaven and the bad news about Hell!

After Rhett's testimonies, I share the testimonies of the corroborating witnesses that the Lord provided me. I am now grateful He did so, especially with regard to testimonies about Hell, because I don't remember most of the details that Rhett told me about his experience there. When he shared his experience in Hell, there were some things he described that were so dreadful, the Lord wiped them from my memory. I couldn't be happy knowing such horrible things were going on beneath my feet. So, three days after Rhett shared his testimony, I asked the Lord to remove those memories from my mind—and He did.

If you haven't been saved or have backslidden in your walk with Jesus, I hope these testimonies will motivate you to get right with Him now!

Rhett's Experience
in Heaven

Recorded January 16, 2014

In may 2012, my husband, Rhett, had one of the most fantastic supernatural experiences I have ever heard. I had led him through the "Sinner's Prayer" about six months earlier, upon his request. Although he had prayed such a prayer twice before over a thirty-year period, his belief didn't become as transformational as it should have been. He attended church regularly but his lifestyle and behavior never seemed to change much. After about twenty years, he started falling back into the world and began living a sinful lifestyle—resulting in our divorce in 2005. However, thanks to the Lord, we reconciled five years later and were remarried in 2010.

Soon after he had asked the Lord for forgiveness, Rhett's life became much different. He began showing the fruits of the Holy Spirit almost immediately. He quickly developed a very close personal relationship with Jesus, and began spending hours every day on our patio (his "secret place") praying and talking to God.

Then, on a beautiful spring day in May 2012, Rhett was home alone on our patio, praying and asking the Lord about something he was confused and upset about. He had asked me earlier that morning if we would be together (married) in Heaven. I told him what Jesus said about that subject: "You are mistaken, not knowing the Scriptures nor the power of God. For in the resurrection, they neither marry nor are given in marriage, but are like angels of God in heaven." (Matthew 22:29-30)

I was not at home that day, but Rhett said he had been praying for about two hours when he suddenly found himself transformed into a different reality. He was no longer in this world, but was being ushered by two angels through the heavens. After a beautiful and breathtaking cosmic journey, he suddenly found himself standing in a group of people who had just died and were gathered before the gate of Heaven. Was he physically taken or was this an experiential vision? I don't know but he felt like he was physically taken. The apostle Paul also described having a similar experience himself, and stated that he didn't know if it was actually in the body (physical) or out of the body (in the spirit). (2 Corinthians 12:2-4)

As I shared earlier in this book, Rhett wasn't going to tell me about his experience because he was afraid that I would think he had lost his mind. The way I found out was by pinning him down about his extraordinary spiritual and Biblical knowledge and insight. After expressing several highly astute comments and opinions during our morning Bible studies, I knew it was more than just God giving him understanding. Then, he divulged how he had suddenly gained such supernatural knowledge and wisdom.

Transcript of Rhett's testimony:

So, tell me, what happened when you were taken to Heaven, Rhett?

Well, it was like I was transformed, rapidly traveling through space, then boom—I was standing with a group of people before the gate of Heaven.

Heaven is like a big city with a big wall all around it and there were large groupings of angels all around on the outside of the wall. The wall around Heaven was awesome and beautiful and shined and sparkled. It was made of a substance that looked like different beautiful translucent gemstones. It was translucent because light shined through it, but you couldn't see through the wall into Heaven.

Jesus was there surrounded by angels. He was standing at the gate, and he was like the door of Heaven. Nobody got through the gate unless He welcomed them in. There was a large group of people standing outside the gate waiting to get in. They were the souls of people who had just died and were brought to the gate of Heaven by their angels.

What did they look like? Did their souls look like they did in this world?

Their souls resembled them but were a whitish color and made of a different substance. They had the same general form as their earthly bodies, and they had individual characteristics. They were all wearing the same kind of robes, not earthly clothing.

Was everyone who died brought to the gate?

No, these people all claimed to believe in Jesus. There were no unbelievers or obviously sinful people in this group. Many of these people were Christian leaders like pastors, evangelists, and Sunday school teachers as well as regular Christians. There were several people whose names you would recognize or were in respected leadership positions in the Church.

I was able to read their thoughts and minds, as they were waiting to stand before Jesus. Many of them were anticipating great rewards for all the good works they had done for God. They would each go up when it was their turn, eager to enter the gate into Heaven. Jesus would look at them, and examine their mind and heart. He then either welcomed them through the gate, or He would say, "I don't know you." You should have seen their faces when He said that to them! They were expecting praise and great rewards for all their service and leading others to Him. They never thought He would reject them!

If He knew them and their heart was right, He would put his arms around them and welcome them into Heaven. But if their heart wasn't right, He would say, "I don't know you." Then immediately, Satan's dark angels would swoop down and grab the person and fly away with them.

Did people say anything or react to being taken away? Could you hear them?

Yes. They started crying and pleading, begging and saying things like, "Please, Jesus, I love you, I love you . . . I did this for you or that for you." Some would start saying all the good works they had done, miracles and all kinds of service they had done for Him. Many of them were leaders in the church, like pastors, televangelists, Sunday school teachers, theologians, and well-known Christians.

But their heart wasn't right for some reason, or they had been following a false Christ. In many cases with those in Church positions, their motives for all the Christian works they did were not right. They didn't do them out of love for God and His people. They did it for themselves—for money or to build their own reputation, or to be respected by other people. Many were hypocrites who harbored sin in their heart or were committing secret sins. Sins like unforgiveness and hatred were also a big reason that many people were rejected.

There were a lot of things that disqualified people, but the reason was because their heart wasn't right. Some actually believed in a fake or fantasy Jesus, not the real Jesus of the Bible. Many were rejected because they thought they could sin and still get into Heaven, so they did. This is what the "once-saved-always-saved" doctrine leads people to believe. But if there is anything in your heart that would offend the Father, Jesus will not let you into Heaven!

When it was your turn, what happened?

I was actually advanced rapidly to the gate, and it was made known to me and everyone there that I was on a special mission—I hadn't died. I was in my human body and clothing, so I stood out. I didn't look like everyone else.

Jesus greeted me, put his arms around me, and took me through the gate. My welcoming committee was there to meet me. After I talked with them, Jesus took me through The City to meet His Father in the Throne Room!

Then He gave me to my welcoming committee who were waiting for me. Your dad was there and my mother and Verl were there. There was also a woman that I didn't know but I was introduced to her as your sister, who had been miscarried by your mother, so none of you ever knew her. But she was beautiful.

Everybody (except me) had a spiritual body that was made of a spiritual substance. It looked like different colored gemstones that light shined through and sparkled. But some people shined brighter than others. This was one of the rewards of Christians— the glory of their spiritual body. The degree of the brightness and shining and sparkling of their spiritual body was in accordance with their faith, love, and the Christian works and deeds they did in this world. The greater the rewards a person was given, the brighter they shined and sparkled!

Everyone's appearance was like they were around age twenty-five to thirty, when they were in their prime. We look similar to how we looked in this world, except perfect. For example, your dad had a full head of black curly hair and didn't wear glasses. And nobody was fat or deformed or had any ailments or physical or mental problems. People had the same size and basic facial features as in this world, and our hair and eyes were the same as in this world. But we don't have flesh. Our bodies were a spiritual material like different transparent gemstones that shined and radiated the love, joy, peace, and beauty that everything in Heaven radiates.

What was Jesus like?

Oh, wow! He is the most beautiful and shines the brightest of all. And His eyes . . . they are really beautiful. They are the most beautiful color of blue . . . and they just grab you, like tractor beams. His eyes are deep and mesmerizing. And oh, man it is just wonderful! There is no more wonderful feeling than looking into His eyes . . . they just melt you with the most penetrating love, compassion, joy, peace, understanding, wisdom, and holiness you can ever imagine. They are captivating, almost like you're hypnotized. I felt like He was my best friend who knew everything about me and still loved me completely . . . and He is my Savior, my hero. I was just . . . oh, man . . . He was like *everything* to me!

So, what did He look like physically? Did he have a spiritual body like the rest of us?

Yes, but he shined and sparkled much brighter than anyone else and His presence was very powerful. But He wasn't an outstanding specimen of a man, like Mr. Universe, for example. He didn't stand six-two and 180 pounds. He was just an ordinary-looking kind of person, a little shorter than me (six feet), and His face is different from how the world's artists depict Him. He has dark brown, shoulder-length, wavy hair with beautiful blue eyes.

You can really tell He is in charge in Heaven. He has such power and command, and He generates such love, peace, joy, and brightness. He is very special spiritually, especially His eyes and His speech.

What about His speech?

He spoke mostly through mental telepathy, so I heard Him in my mind. And everything He spoke was amazing and you knew it was the truth and wisdom and perfect and you could feel it—it was powerful. I can't really describe it.

Did everyone speak or communicate this way, through mental telepathy?

Yes. Everyone communicated mostly through mental telepathy. You could read each other's thoughts, so there wasn't a need to speak with your mouth. But you could speak with your mouth if you wanted to—it was, like, more personal.

What was Jesus like personally with you? Did you have any type of spiritual or emotional experience that you hadn't had before?

I just felt complete love and compassion, like He was my best friend, like He was my Savior. He was just everything to me. I've never felt so loved and relaxed, so full of joy and at peace. It was like I just wanted to kneel down and kiss His feet.

What was Jesus's main purpose or activity in Heaven? Was there any particular thing that He was really focused on? What was He all about there?

He was the love of Heaven and the peace and joy and happiness of Heaven. He was like the head guardian and commander-in-chief, and He was like the personal secretary to God the Father. He was the Gatekeeper; you didn't get through the gate unless He let you in.

And you didn't get to the Father unless He took you. You couldn't enter the Father's presence unless He was with you. The power and responsibility and glory and everything He had . . . was just indescribable!

It sounds like Jesus was the central attraction and focus in Heaven.

Well, you don't get to the Father except through the Son.

And all the children just love Him, and they are always with Him, like following Him around. He really loves the children and they really love Him!

Why are there children in Heaven? Do they grow up or remain as children?

They are people who died as babies, miscarried, or died as children. They do grow up to adults in Heaven.

So, it sounds like it's all about Jesus in Heaven, right?

No, it's all about God—the Trinity—the Father, the Son, and the Holy Spirit. It's about all of them. But especially the Father. I mean—He is the ultimate. He's the final word. He's everything! He is, "I AM!" And He is so holy—that's why Jesus had to be with me in the Father's presence.

The Father can't have anything in His presence that isn't holy and perfect. Jesus protects the Father from that. He loves the Father so much that He won't do anything that might offend the Father. That's one of the reasons people who harbor negative character traits like hate, bitterness, unforgiveness in their hearts don't get through the gate. It would be a great offense to the Father for any such traits to be in His presence. Jesus insulates the Father from you and you from the Father. He's like a buffer. That's why you have to go through Jesus.

After Jesus welcomed you into Heaven, then what happened?

Then, after I visited with my welcoming committee and walked and talked with everybody, Jesus took me into the Throne Room where God the Father is.

So, was that some distance from the gate? Did you walk there?

Yeah, I guess it was, but it didn't seem like it. I was just looking around at all the marvels inside the gate, and all the buildings and everything and how beautiful everything was. There are a lot more colors in Heaven than in this world. It's really beautiful. I was just in so much awe that it didn't seem like it took very long to get to the Throne Room.

You were looking at all the buildings—was it like a city?

It was like a city . . . but everything was made out of transparent gold and gemstones, and they are alive. Everything is alive, even the streets and the buildings. And light shines through everything! Everything radiates love, joy, and peace and other wonderful feelings and powers. I don't know how to explain it . . . It was just beautiful and everything is perfect!

We were walking on streets of transparent gold, but it didn't feel like you were walking . . . kind of like you're floating. There is no night there, either. And there isn't a sun. It is full of light because God is there, and Jesus is the light of Heaven. Light radiates out from Him.

Was the Throne Room a building?

Sort of. There was like a big courtyard, with a building; and then the building had a courtyard inside it. When you are inside the building, you feel like you are in a courtyard also. In the center of the Throne Room was a huge chair for the Father to sit in—it was huge. The Father is huge, enormous! He was kind of a blur to me. I could see His form but not His face. He was in a white robe with a gold sash around his chest and waist. His hair is either white or light blonde. I couldn't see him clearly because I wasn't staying in Heaven. You can't see him clearly or see His face until you are accepted into the kingdom by Him and given your spiritual body and your new name.

On the right hand of the Father was an empty chair for Jesus. It was empty because Jesus was standing next to me before the Father. Then, on the right side of Jesus's chair was Michael the archangel. And on the left side of the Father was Gabriel the archangel. He was in a white robe with a gold sash, and had long, flowing, whitish hair. He resembled the Father.

Were you able to see Gabriel's face? What did he look like?

He looked like a nice, beautiful person; you could tell he was a male, masculine. His wings were white. He was a love type of being. He and Michael are very large, maybe thirteen feet tall.

What did Michael look like?

He looked like a warrior with a big breastplate and armor. He had a large sword, about eight feet long that was like on fire, but not really on fire—it glowed. He was the same size as Gabriel. He had somewhat darker wings and long, dark hair. He was the commander of the armies of warrior angels.

What was the reason you were taken into the Throne Room—did you know?

Just to see it. I was being given a tour of Heaven. I wasn't going to be staying there, and that's the reason I wasn't able to really see the Father. That's why He was blurred to me.

What is the reason for going to the Throne Room and standing before God for most people—those who would be staying there?

The Father would give them their blessings and rewards—and make Himself appear to them and give them their new name. They would be transformed into their spiritual body. Afterward, they were sent on their way and released to their welcoming committee, to be taken to their dwelling place or mansion, depending on their rewards. I wasn't able to have all that because I wouldn't be staying.

But while I was up there, I was allowed to walk wherever I wanted to go. So, after the Throne Room, Jesus released me to your dad, my mother, and my welcoming committee. We walked all up and down through the streets, and they showed me different things, like where my dwelling place would probably be located. It was an area where most people's dwelling places were at—not on the Mountain but in the City.

So, everybody in Heaven knew these things ahead of time?

Right. In Heaven everyone has supernatural knowledge and understanding. You know everyone's thoughts and read their minds. Most communication is by mental telepathy. You have supernatural knowledge, intelligence, and understanding about everything.

My welcoming committee also showed me many of the wonders of Heaven. They showed me how to transform and do—something like a hologram. So, for example, if you wanted to remember things from this world, you just close your eyes and think about it. Then when you open your eyes, you're there! You are able to actually create your dreams and desires with your thoughts, and make them into a virtual reality. You can talk and interact with whomever you want in your hologram, just like it is actually happening. But you can only remember or create good things; you cannot think, remember, or do anything negative or evil.

So, if I wanted to go fishing with you, for example, I would just close my eyes and think about it and when I opened my eyes, we would be in the mountains together. There would be beautiful trees, a lake, and everything would just be perfect. I could talk with you and we could fish and do different things. It would be like being on a perfect Earth. And you can do that anytime you want to!

What is the purpose of people in Heaven? Is there any work or activity going on in Heaven, or is everyone just sitting around creating holograms?

People do whatever they want to do. There is a lot of singing and praising God going on all the time. It is really gratifying to just do that, because He—God (Father, Son, and Holy Spirit)—is so awesome and wonderful, and you're so full of love and happiness and gratitude to the Lord. And it fills you with even more love, joy, and good feelings whenever you worship and praise God.

You are also constantly meeting new people and visiting and getting to know others. Everyone loves each other so much and is eager to meet you. Everyone gives and receives love from each other.

Everything you want or can imagine is there for you. If you feel like working—you can go out and chop wood, for example—and it's all beautiful and perfect. You can also learn about things and gain knowledge and wisdom if you want. Anything you want or can imagine is there for you—as long as it's good and not evil!

Did you see or experience the Holy Spirit? What is His presence like?

I can't remember if I saw Him, but I felt Him inside of me; I felt Him everywhere. And Jesus everywhere, and the Father everywhere. Everything was just full of love and joy and peace everywhere—it was just perfect. I can't really explain it.

They—the Father, Jesus, and the Holy Spirit—were all in everything. All of Heaven radiates their presence and their character traits. And yet, you could feel each of them separately in everything! They were all radiating in everything and it was all based on perfect love, joy, peace, and other wonderful feelings.

Did you have a sense that there is a hierarchy in Heaven, between the Father, Son, and Holy Spirit?

Oh yeah. The Father is definitely in charge—He is greater than all. He is the power, like He is the CEO. Jesus is under the Father, but not by much. They are very closely connected to each other. It's like Jesus is in the Father and the Father is in Jesus. They are a combination of everything, or everything is a combination of them. I can't explain it, but the Father was definitely in charge.

What was the Holy Spirit's relationship with the Father and the Son?

He intermingled with both of them and He is such peace. He radiates from both of them. But mostly from the Father.

Did the Lord answer your question about marriage in Heaven?

Yes, and I experienced the answer myself. There is no need for marriage in Heaven because the love we have for one another is far greater than marital love. And we give and receive that love from everyone!

Did you see me or our children in Heaven?

I was given a glimpse into the future, and I saw when you show up there. Your dad was like a little kid with a brand-new toy—I've never seen your dad so happy or so proud. He was just so happy and joyful when you arrived!

You arrived as an older person. Jesus took you into the Throne Room and you were given your new name and spiritual body. Then, He turned you over to us, your welcoming committee, and we all went up to where your place is on the Hill. Everyone has a different size and kind of dwelling place. It is a big part of your rewards. It is based upon what you did on Earth . . . your faith and your love and your works. But it's mainly your faith and your love. Your works aren't really that much of it—it is mainly your faith and your love. But if your works were really acts of faith or love, they are rewarded.

Your rewards also result in different kinds and sizes of dwelling places and mansions. The higher up you are on the Mountain, the greater your rewards and the closer you are to God, the Father. He dwells at the top of the Mountain.

It is a huge mountain . . . but compared to the size of Heaven, it looks like a hill in comparison. Most people's dwelling places were not on the Mountain; they were down at the base or in the city. But they are still beautiful and wonderful.

Do we have the same senses we have in this world like taste, smell, touch?

We have more senses, such as mental telepathy, instant knowledge, and the ability to absorb love, joy, peace as well as other wonderful things.

Do we have any supernatural powers ourselves?

Oh yes. In addition to being able to create holograms and mental telepathy, you can actually spend personal time with God whenever you want to. For example, you can have long, peaceful walks with God the Father and Jesus, ask them questions and learn wonderful truths and wisdom from them whenever you wish. You also have supernatural knowledge in Heaven. You automatically understand things and the reasons behind them.

Do we eat or sleep?

> If you want to, but you don't need to. You can do anything you
> want to do!

What do the angels do in Heaven? Are there a lot of angels there?

> Yes, there are a lot of angels and they're everywhere. There are
> different kinds and sizes of angels and they have different traits
> and jobs or purposes. Some are warrior angels; they are Michael's
> army. They fly around and protect Heaven. There are also lots
> of servant angels, whose purpose is to serve us, God's children.
> They are actually there at our service whenever we hail them, to
> do whatever we want them to do for us. There are also a lot of
> guardian angels. We each have our own guardian angel.

Why do we need guardian angels in Heaven?

> Because Satan's out there always trying to get in, to take over.
> He and his army of angels are always trying to get in to disrupt
> Heaven. That's what Michael's job is—to protect Heaven. He
> has warrior angels stationed throughout Heaven and outside of
> Heaven, and all throughout the stars. Satan has a lot of evil angels
> out there and they're always fighting, trying to get into Heaven.
> The battle is constant. It will go on until God the Father finally
> binds Satan.

Earlier, you said that there were a lot of people who thought they were
Christians and would get into Heaven, but they were turned away, and
even rebuked by Jesus at the gate. You said that they were surprised
they weren't getting in. Did you have any understanding as to why they

assumed they were going to Heaven, and what exactly was preventing them from getting in?

There were several reasons people didn't get in, but it mainly was because of such things as:

> They were believing in a false Christ or a false gospel. Their heart wasn't right. They harbored things like unforgiveness, hatred, bitterness, lust, covetousness. They didn't really love God first and foremost or didn't love others, especially other Christians.
>
> Many people did things in Jesus's name for self-serving reasons, like to be admired by other people, or to promote themselves—or for money. Some people loved the things of this world more than God. Jesus wasn't their "first love." Some may have believed in Jesus but they didn't obey Him. If you love God, you will obey Him.
>
> The bottom-line reason they were rejected was because their heart wasn't right. It's all about what is in your heart—the love of God—or something else?

Why do you think you were permitted to go there and experience these things, but not allowed to stay?

> I think it was to seal my faith and let me know that I was on the right path and to answer my questions about marriage in Heaven. Until I went there and experienced what Heaven is really like, I couldn't imagine Heaven being that great if we couldn't be married.
>
> I think it was also to share my experience with others—to help them believe and be saved.
>
> But I wasn't meant to stay because I hadn't died. I was there on a special mission. It wasn't my time yet. The Lord Jesus told me that I have more work to do here. I need to learn some important

things, repent and overcome some things, like smoking and negative character traits.

I also need to help others who have gone down the wrong path and fallen into sin. I need to do what I can to help them see and follow the truth before it's too late! They can lose their salvation if they don't repent. Satan is trying to destroy them in this world and steal their salvation. They need to wake up now!

So, you are saying that a born-again person can lose their salvation?

Oh, yes—you can lose your salvation. After you are born-again you must follow Jesus and obey Him. You must learn His word, the Bible, and grow in love for Jesus and the Father and love others, especially other Christians. You must stop sinning and grow in the likeness of the life that Jesus lived.

It sounds like what you are saying is that the doctrine "once-saved-always-saved," which is believed by so many Christians, is not correct. Our salvation very much depends on how we live after we receive God's gift of grace. Is that right?

Well, let me put it this way: You have two choices. You can believe and obey the things of Satan; or you can believe and obey the things of Christ. Which one is going to get you to Heaven? The one you obey is the one you love!

Did God tell you to quit smoking for some reason? Is smoking a sin?

It's not a sin that keeps you out of Heaven, but God hates it because it hurts His temple, your body. He wants me to overcome it.

What are the three most important things that you learned from this experience, that you would want other people to know?

1. Just to love everybody, don't hate anybody, and forgive everyone who has hurt you or offended you. Don't hold any grudges or remember the offenses of other people. Be quick to forgive and be gracious to others, just like God is gracious to you. Forgiveness is a *decision*, not just a feeling. Make sure there's no hate or unforgiveness in your heart or mind toward anyone. You won't get into Heaven if you hold hatred or unforgiveness in your heart!

   Also, be a loving person. Love is the main way you get into Heaven—and it's the biggest factor in your rewards. Look for ways to bless others and give love. If you can't give love, you're not going to receive love!

2. Love God and put Him first in your life. He must be number one and the most important thing in your life. You must be obedient to God and know His word. Obey His word. Learn all of Jesus's teachings and obey them. This is how you get to know Him. You grow in love for God just like you do a person—by spending time with Him in prayer and reading His word, the Bible. The more you do, the more He will reveal Himself to you—and when He does, you can't help but love Him because He is so wonderful and awesome!

   Also, make sure you don't have any other "gods" in your life. And by that, I mean don't put anything before God. I mean anything—not your job, money, people. Don't lust for things in this world, and don't covet anything in this world. Everything in this world is like junk and garbage compared to the things in Heaven. Don't trade something so fantastic for the trash of this world. Set your mind and heart on Heaven and knowing God!

3. But first you have to be born-again. That is step number one. Jesus said that you cannot see the kingdom of Heaven unless you are born-again (John 3:3). After that, you must follow Jesus and obey Him. You cannot live like the rest of the world; you must start transforming to be more like Jesus.

Okay. So, you didn't know any of these things you have talked about before you went to Heaven? I mean, like you hadn't read the Bible or heard them taught before, right?

Right. I hadn't really heard it or read the Bible before. I learned it there. Even though I believed and thought I was a Chirstian for the last thirty years, my heart wasn't really in it and I didn't learn much. Everything I have said in this testimony I saw, experienced, and learned in Heaven.

This is an amazing testimony, Rhett. As far as I can tell, all that you have said is Biblical, and you have given new insight on some important things that many of us have misunderstood or been taught incorrectly. As your wife for over forty years, I know that there is no other way you could suddenly know these Biblical truths and have the in-depth understanding you have. It had to be God!

Many Christians today believe that grace means "once-saved-always-saved" and that a born-again believer cannot lose their salvation, even if they practice sin! They are also told that striving to live a righteous, obedient life is practicing "legalism" and "works righteousness," which they demonize as heresy. They call good evil and evil good! This doctrine is a blatant contradiction of the teachings of Jesus and His apostles, as recorded in the Bible. To say these doctrines have brought confusion and division into the body of Christ is an understatement. They have also produced an abundance of evil fruit, in my humble opinion.

And this is what you are also saying, Rhett. Those who ignore the teachings of Jesus and engage in sin will absolutely not enter Heaven. They are believing doctrines of demons and practicing iniquity—those are the very people Jesus rejects!

Christians need to wake up, study God's word for themselves, and obey the Jesus of the Bible, not the false doctrines of men. He commands His people to "make disciples" and teach them to obey everything He has commanded (Matthew 28:19-20). We enter Heaven through the narrow gate, not the broad, live-as-you-please gate!

> *"Enter by the narrow gate; for wide is the gate and broad is the way that leads to destruction, and there are many who go in by it. Because narrow is the gate and difficult is the way which leads to life and there are few who find it. (Matthew 7:13-14).*

End of Interview

In the two years between this interview and Rhett's passing, he often shared additional information with me about Heaven. Following are some of those things:

Rhett's Journey Through the Universe

+ In talking about his trip to Heaven, Rhett described how he had been on our patio praying one beautiful spring morning in May 2012. Suddenly, two angels appeared saying they had been sent to take him to Heaven. They picked him up and began ascending into the sky, then they entered into a light tunnel and began traveling at tremendous speed into outer space. Rhett was awestruck with the beauty and vastness of the Milky Way and its billions of stars and planets. But that was just the beginning, as they continued deep into the universe.

Billions of stars and galaxies turned into streaks of light, as they sped through the blackness of outer space. Occasionally, the angels would slow down or stop along the way, to view certain galaxies, constellations, and supernovas. It was as if they were in reverence or awe of their beauty or greatness.

After resuming their journey through the vast universe for some time, a beautiful white light appeared at a distance. As they continued toward it, Rhett could see that it was the most enormous galaxy of all. And it shined and sparkled with the most brilliant light and beautiful colors he had ever seen. As they got closer, he could see that there was a big wall around a city, and the glorious light shined through the wall into the universe. He could also see heavenly beings, like angels, all around it!

He was then taken to the gate of Heaven, where Jesus was judging those who had been brought there by the angels, as described earlier. Please refer back to that testimony for the subsequent details. Rhett couldn't stop raving about how beautiful Heaven is with a "thousand" more colors than we see on Earth; and how everything is alive and radiates love, joy, and peace. He was especially enthusiastic about The City of God with its transparent gold streets, gemstone walls that sparkling light shined through, exciting festivals, and worship services that were the best experience of all. This was surprising because on Earth he didn't like cities—he loved doing things in nature, and he didn't like crowds and festivals.

+ He said there are certain buildings scattered throughout The City where one can utilize special devices to view specific people on Earth, and pray for them.

+ He also raved about the people in Heaven, the perfect love they have for each other, and how everyone is excited to meet each other. He also said that people are always doing exciting and enjoyable activities

with each other. For example, if they want to go golfing, they can—
and the grass, surroundings, and their skill would all be fantastic!

+ He was really impressed with the Throne Room and the courtyards
around it. He described the design, materials, colors of the linens,
and curtains that hung over the doorways, and construction of
the courtyards. His description was very much like the tabernacle
that God instructed Moses to build in the book of Exodus. He
said there was an outer courtyard where most of the people were
at, and he described certain protocols people had to go through
to enter the courtyards. He said the people in the inner courtyard
were like priests who were focused on reading or doing something
with tablets they carried.

+ Then, he described a doorway covered with colorful draperies in the
inner court that looked like the entryway to a small room. But it
was a paradox, because when you went through it, it opened up into
something huge—another dimension or reality. The Father, Jesus,
and Holy Spirit were there, along with millions of heavenly creatures
and wonders. He said it seemed like another realm of eternity!

+ I asked him who the most honored and revered people in Heaven
were, expecting him to rattle off names like the apostles, Moses,
and prophets of the Old Testament. He answered without hesita-
tion, stating emphatically that the most important and honored of
all are the children. Jesus really loves the children and they really
love Him. The angels diligently attend to the children, as if that
is the most important job in Heaven. The children are honored by
everyone in Heaven, and they follow Jesus everywhere He goes.

But the Lord loves all of His people uniquely. He sees deep into
our spirit and soul and exults over each of us as His wonderful,
special child!

+ Rhett said that there are many different kinds of heavenly beings, and he described three types of angels: Warrior angels are the largest, and make up Michael's army. Ministering angels that are created to serve humans are the smallest in size. Guardian angels are mid-sized and assigned to protect each human being individually. Humans are the most honored creatures, because they are God's children.

+ There is no sun, moon, or night in Heaven. Brilliant light radiates out from Jesus, filling all of Heaven with glorious sparkling light that shines through everything. There is no need to eat or sleep, and your spiritual body does not get tired or have to rest. And, there is a lot going on in Heaven all of the time for you to enjoy!

+ Rhett described beautiful landscapes full of exquisite flowers, foliage, colors, and creations that fill Heaven outside of the City of God. Everything is filled with life, its own personality, and praises God—including things that are not sentient on Earth. Jim Woodford confirmed this phenomenon in his testimony stating, "The flowers sing to you, and every sound and every color flows toward the Throne of God, as praise." The Bible also verifies such wonders in the following scriptures:

> But He answered and said to them, "I tell you that if these should keep silent, the stones would immediately cry out." (Luke 19:40)

> You will go out in joy and be led forth in peace; the mountains and hills will burst into song before you, and all the trees of the field will clap their hands. (Isaiah 55:12)

+ He talked about the festivals and worship services where people, angels, and heavenly beings gather to socialize and worship God, and what ecstasy it is to do so. He said that sometimes you will hear a trumpet sound, to announce different occasions and events—and when very honorable people arrive in Heaven.

+ He also raved about the Mountain of God and how magnificent and special it is. He said that the Father dwells at the top, which I think he said is covered in clouds, if I remember correctly. It is a mountain of holiness where different kinds and sizes of mansions are located at different levels. The mansions are rewards for those people whose lives demonstrated great love or faith on Earth. The greater your rewards are, the higher your mansion is placed on the Mountain and the closer you are to the Father and His holy presence. The size of your mansion seems to be determined by the number of people you will be entertaining in your house. I imagine that may be relative to how many people you helped or led to the Lord on Earth.

+ Speaking of helping people on Earth, Rhett said that persons like doctors, nurses, teachers, and those who operated out of love, compassion, and a desire to help others are very honored when they arrive in Heaven. He said that the angels and others gather to greet and honor such persons. Are they some of those announced by the trumpets?

+ But the number one thing that Rhett raved about most of all was Jesus—sitting at His feet listening to Him speak, and gazing into His beautiful, mesmerizing eyes. He said there is no better feeling than that! Jesus has such spiritual power, authority, and wisdom; and everything He says is powerful—it resonates inside you, and you know it is absolute truth.

+ And Jesus's eyes . . . they are the most beautiful blue eyes—filled with love, wisdom, compassion, and you are overcome by how much he values you! It is very humbling. But His eyes are also mesmer-izing, as they draw you deeper and deeper into His soul, and you experience how awesome and wonderful He really is!

After his tour of Heaven was complete, Jesus told Rhett that he must return to Earth. He said that it wasn't his time yet, and there were some things he had to learn and do before he would be ready to enter Heaven. Jesus didn't tell him what those things were. Rhett had to seek for those answers himself. And he did. As I have shared previously, Rhett gained the Biblical knowledge he needed and repented of his sins—especially unforgiveness.

Other Christians Who Were
Shown Heaven and Hell

Following are the testimonies of persons the Lord led me to for confirmation of Rhett's testimonies about Heaven and Hell. I have summarized each of their testimonies in this book, but I also give details as to where you can obtain their books and videos for more information.

The first person is a man named Ivan Tuttle, who was also given extensive experiences in both Heaven and Hell. But God actually commanded Ivan not to tell anyone about his experiences until he was given permission at some point in the future. That time turned out to be thirty-five years later!

It's interesting that the Lord also held me back for thirty years before I was told about my calling as a watchman, and to share my testimonies at this point in time. We must always follow God's timing because if we release prophetic information too early, people often judge it as false prophecy. But the Lord is moving upon many of His watchmen with a strong feeling of urgency to share our stories now.

You can read Ivan's full testimonies of Heaven and Hell in his book *A Journey to Hell, Heaven and Back*, which is available on Amazon.com. Following is a synopsis of his experience in Heaven:

Ivan Tuttle's Testimony of Heaven

In his book, Ivan describes how in 1978, he died from a blood clot when he was only twenty-six years old. Ivan had been suffering with extreme cramps in his left leg for several weeks that he tried to ignore, thinking it was a pulled muscle. But they continued to get worse, finally sending him to the hospital, where he was diagnosed with a blood clot in his left leg. After receiving powerful blood thinners for several days, he was sent home—but things got worse!

After falling asleep early that night, he was suddenly awakened when something evil grabbed him, yanking his soul from his body, and dragged him through what seemed like outer space at hyper-speed, straight into Hell. (I share Ivan's detailed experience there in the next section, "Hell Is for Real.")

But God quickly intervened, and commanded Hell to release Ivan!

After describing a terrifying experience in Hell, Ivan heard "a voice, like a mighty roar of thunder that said, 'It is not his time yet. His mother has been praying for him since he was a little boy. You must release him now; I made a promise.'"

Immediately, Ivan was released and his soul flew out of Hell, into outer space and straight to the gate of Heaven. He then found himself standing outside a wonderful place, surrounded by a bright, glowing light that penetrated his entire being, filling him with indescribable ecstasy.

As Ivan proceeded toward the gate, he was stopped by an angel who told him he could not stay there. He was only to observe and then return to Earth and tell others what he had seen, but not until God gave him the okay to do so. He talks about how he had instant knowledge about everything in Heaven, but he was only allowed to view things from just inside the gate. The angel stayed with him, acting as his guide. He was not allowed to explore Heaven freely on his own.

Then he talks about his experiences and things the angel revealed to him:

As Ivan stood there with the angel, he experienced a bright light radiating from the center of Heaven that felt like pure love. But he wasn't allowed to move closer to the light because he had not yet done what he needed to do on Earth. Ivan said that this holy light fills all of Heaven, and there is no night there.

He also describes different kinds of angels: Helper angels that are about the size of humans; guardian angels that are larger and assigned to each person; messenger angels; winged angels; and archangels like Michael and Gabriel.

Ivan describes how exquisite and perfect everything is in Heaven. He raves about the beautiful ethereal music, and how singing and praising God is the most euphoric "high" one can experience. He describes how bright, vibrant, and shiny the colors are, how the streets are made out of pure gold, and how magnificent homes are made out of something like white marble.

Ivan's angel also showed him disturbing visions of things happening on Earth. He saw how generational curses are destroying lives and families, and that these curses must be broken.

Another disturbing thing he saw was homosexuality gaining acceptance in society, with an agenda to normalize pedophilia. He also saw horrifying things being done to children.

The angel also told Ivan about the seriousness of "hidden intentional sin" that many believers are practicing in their lives. Such persons are hypocrites. He stated that if you are looking at porn, treating your family badly, using drugs, abusing alcohol, committing sexual sins, lusting, aggravating your children, etc., while purporting to be a Christian, these are "hidden intentional sins." He said that those who do not repent, God will judge, and their sins will soon be exposed for everyone to see. Scripture also predicts that this will happen!

Ivan was also shown prophetic visions of events that are now taking place on Earth:

+ He saw people all over the world communicating on personal computers and cell phones, facilitated through a net that enveloped the whole world. He said Satan would use these devices to isolate people and hamper normal human relationships, connecting people with devices rather than each other. We are now seeing these visions being fulfilled.

+ He said there would be spirits of delusion and false hope possessing certain people. Their mission is to corrupt leaders and convince the people to trust them, and everything will be fine. Again, we are seeing these prophecies being fulfilled today.

+ Ivan then describes a sound like nothing heard on Earth before that will start happening. It is the earth moaning, and it will travel all around the world. This prophecy is also being fulfilled. There are YouTube video recordings of this disturbing sound that has occurred in Russia, Norway, Sweden, the UK, Africa, Europe, Asia, the Middle East, South America, Central America, the United States, Australia, India, and other countries.

+ In 2013, Ivan was given permission to start talking about these visions that occurred in 1978. However, there were certain visions that he has not yet been given permission to disclose. So, he will have more to share when that time comes, which will likely be soon.

Earth's timeline

At the end of his book, Ivan describes some astonishing things that the angel showed him about Earth's timeline. Here are a few highlights:

"While in Heaven, the angel told me to turn and look, and as I turned, I saw the earth. It was like . . . in a timeline, from the beginning to way into the future. I saw the earth being formed. It looked like a ball of water—no clouds and no land. It was very dark, but I was able to see everything because it was my spirit and not my physical eyes."

Ivan goes on to describe how he watched and heard God speak and create the earth, heavens, land, vegetation, and animals much as it is described in the book of Genesis. Then, He created man differently—not by speaking, but with His hands—forming him out of the dust of the earth. He breathed life into his nostrils, and man became a living, intelligent being, created in the image of God!

He said that Adam communicated with God and the animals telepathically, and they all spoke one heavenly language.

He watched many scenes from the Old Testament unfold, such as the tower of Babel, where God confused mankind's language and they lost the ability to communicate with animals. He talks about the amazing faith David had when he killed Goliath, and how terrified the Philistines were of the Israelites and their God.

Ivan then moves to the New Testament and talks about Jesus. He says there were possibly millions more miracles He performed that were not recorded, and He cast out far more demons as well. "Everything Jesus touched was changed, and when He spoke His words had such power!"

He described the compassion in Jesus's eyes, and how with one look from Him, you felt such profound love! He talks about how Jesus would deny Himself sleep and rest, to serve the multitudes of people who needed healing and miracles. Ivan also describes Peter in such a human, relatable way that you really get an understanding of his personality and passionate love for Jesus.

He also talks about Jesus's crucifixion and how astonishing it was, the way they turned the crowd against Him. Many of them were people who had been healed by Jesus. He said the crucifixion was much worse than we imagine, and he remarks about how the guards seemed to get pleasure from torturing Him.

Ivan then watched as Jesus was raised from the dead, and said that His resurrected body did not look exactly like His previous body. He said that the way people recognized it was Jesus was through the compassion in His eyes!

Future world events:

Some of the things Ivan is not yet authorized to relate have to do with future events that are coming. However, here are some highlights of the things he was allowed to share in 2013:

+ Great storms, earthquakes, and natural disasters will occur throughout the world—as a wake-up call to repent.

The world has been experiencing these anomalous natural disasters in the past few years, especially since Covid hit in 2020!

+ There are going to be great volcanic eruptions in the earth, many in places that have lain dormant for thousands of years. "Some of these volcanos will be so great that they will tear apart whole areas of a country."

Again, anomalous volcanic eruptions have been occurring recently. In fact, a super-volcano in Italy and another in the Pacific are awakening, and expected to erupt soon.

+ There will be earthquakes so strong, they will be recorded at 9.5 to 12.5. Whole cities will be flattened, especially in Asia. Europe will also have many strong earthquakes that destroy buildings and structures that have been around for many centuries. Dams and bridges will be destroyed by earthquakes and floods. There will be times of extreme drought followed by extreme rain, floods, and natural disasters throughout all of Europe.

The extreme drought/rain/floods/natural disasters throughout all of Europe have begun happening in the past few years.

+ Strange things will happen over the skies of Russia that will cause people to repent because these things are so unusual. The earth will also shake in Russia and huge holes will open up deep into the ground.

Huge holes have been opening up in Russia in the past few years also. The other events may have also begun to happen; but because of political fighting with the West, we may not have received that news.

+ Great earthquakes and volcanoes will occur all over the world, including the United States. Yellowstone will eventually erupt, devastating the US, and changing the global climate. Ivan offers some comfort by stating that he didn't see it happening in the near future. However, he says that *a sign that it is imminent, will be when the big geysers like Old Faithful, start to erupt with unusual timing, or maybe stop erupting for days.*

In conclusion, Ivan believes God will soon pour out grace upon people all over the world, and the Holy Spirit will randomly come upon individuals, as God chooses. He encourages believers to keep praying for others, reminding us of his mother's effective prayers for him.

Ivan ends his testimony with one last reminder to *repent of your hidden intentional sins,* stating that God sternly warned him that it is necessary to save one's life.

Jesus is compassionate and He doesn't want your sins to be revealed to everyone, any more than you do. *Remember, what you confess and repent of Jesus will remove from you as if you never did it!*

> *If we confess our sins, He is faithful and just to forgive us our sins and to cleanse us from all unrighteousness. (1 John 1:9)*

Laurie Ditto's Testimony about Heaven

Laurie Ditto was given a brief but wonderful experience in Heaven, which I detail below. Then, a few years later, God gave her a profound experience in Hell. But unlike Ivan, she did not die first. Laurie, like Rhett and a few other people, was supernaturally transported into these spiritual realms as a tour, to reveal some profound spiritual truths for herself, and that God wanted her to tell others.

In her book *The Hell Conspiracy*, Laurie describes how she was given a magical vision of Heaven in the early 2000s, while attending a Christian Women's Conference at the International House of Prayer in Kansas City. She became born-again during that vision encounter, and was radically transformed into an on-fire Christian.

In her vision, Laurie suddenly found herself in a grand castle in Heaven, standing about a hundred yards from Jesus Christ. She knew He was the King of Heaven and that He was the Creator, the most powerful being ever. He was also the source of light. He looked as if he were made out of diamonds and was sparkly, transparent, shiny. He was filled with brilliant light that he could modulate for a person to see Him, depending on the level of light they can endure and their unique relationship with Him. She also understood that obedience to Him is considered love.

As Jesus began drawing closer to her, she was invited to gaze into His supernatural body of light, as if it were a television. She saw him dancing with a woman, His bride, who had made herself special for Him. After admiring this wonderful scene and wishing it could be her, Laurie was suddenly transformed into that bride, enveloped in the amazing love of Jesus as she danced with Him and gazed into His mesmerizing eyes! She describes the exquisite light-filled clothing that Jesus dresses all of His people in, and how every color in Heaven shines through this supernatural covering.

After their wedding dance, Jesus touched His forehead to hers and immediately changed her self-image, from low self-esteem to Christ-esteem. She became a new creation in Christ!

In love and gratitude, after their dance Laurie asked Him, "Is there anything I can do for You?" Jesus replied, "Go, tell others about Me." So, she did—and has never stopped!

Suddenly, she was back on Earth sitting in the prayer room. But Laurie was a different person. Now, she was happy! The depression she had struggled with for years was gone, and she was on-fire for Jesus! She began raving about Him constantly, telling her family about Heaven until they became so annoyed, they accused her of being a religious fanatic and began to avoid her. So, she told everyone else about Jesus. Meanwhile, God began working on her family, and within a few years her husband and their two daughters were also radically transformed into Jesus-lovers!

Laurie and her husband Mike became active members of their church and a few years later moved to Kansas City, where they joined the ministry at IHOPKC—International House of Prayer Kansas City. Both Laurie and Mike were involved in ministry and passionately serving the Lord for the next few years. Then, God did something very unexpected in Laurie's life. He gave her another vision—but this time it was an experience in Hell!

I share a synopsis of Laurie's experience in Hell in the next section: "Hell Is for Real."

Randy Kay's Testimony of Heaven

Randy Kay had been a successful biotech CEO and businessman, when he unexpectedly died and encountered the reality of God, Heaven, and—evil entities! You can find several videos where Randy shares his spiritual experiences and those of others he interviews on the internet and on his website, randykay.org. He has also written some wonderful books, including *Revelations from Heaven* and his most recent book *Heaven Stormed*, available on Amazon.com.

Randy's experience began at his home in Southern California. He had just returned home after a long flight from New York City when he suddenly developed blood clots in his legs and was rushed to the hospital. His condition quickly went from bad to worse, as he contracted a MRSA blood infection, leading to sepsis. A short time later, he went into cardiac arrest and died. Randy was clinically dead for thirty-one minutes—but not spiritually dead!

He didn't experience any sensation of dying, except that a glorious golden light began pulling his soul out of his body, into the spiritual realm. He immediately went into an ethereal environment (the "second Heaven") in which he saw two groups of very large beings that were fighting over his soul. The entourage on his right side were glorious warrior angels dressed in armor with swords and covered by a golden light. The beings on his left side were also very large and strong, but gangly, hideous-looking creatures that he identified as Satan's "fallen angels." In the midst of this frightening encounter, he realized that he needed to cry out the name of "Jesus," so he did. Instantly, he felt soft whiskers against his cheek, as Jesus embraced him, and profound love penetrated every part of his being.

Jesus then gave Randy a tour of Heaven in a dynamic, interactive vision. He saw God the Father, Whom he describes as having flowing white hair, sitting on a huge throne. He describes people in Heaven as having spirit bodies that are made out of light, and that the brightness to which they glow or shine reflects their spiritual status in Heaven. He also talks about how you have instant knowledge and that most communication is through mental telepathy. Then he raves about all the vibrant colors and fragrances in Heaven, stating that they are maybe a thousand times greater than what is on Earth. He marvels at how the streets and paths are made out of translucent gold, and how everything in Heaven is alive and filled with love!

He saw people in Heaven who were aware of the lives of people on Earth, and were praying for them. And he describes how Jesus is always interceding for Christians on Earth, and how He mourns over those who are lost or have left Him, because He doesn't want anyone to go to Hell.

After a glorious experience in Heaven, Jesus told Randy that he must return to Earth because he needed to do some things. Immediately his soul returned to his body lying in the hospital bed, and he awoke to hear a couple sitting by his bedside, singing a prayer for him. It was the same glorious song that the angels in Heaven were singing, as he departed to return to Earth!

In one of his video interviews, Randy talks about "postcards from Heaven," which he says are a special way God enables those in Heaven to communicate messages to people on Earth. Was my testimony, "The Hummingbird," that I shared earlier a postcard from Heaven?

Since returning to Earth, God has also blessed Randy with prophetic gifts in visions and dreams that bring great blessing and insight for Christians in today's challenging and confusing world. I encourage everyone to check out Randy's website, where he shares the things that God is showing him, along with many interviews of other people who have also been given supernatural experiences with God in recent years. These testimonies really help us understand the time we are living in, and build our faith!

Jim Woodford's Testimony of Heaven and His Brush with Hell

Jim Woodford was a career airline pilot for many years, then retired and became a very successful and wealthy businessman. Jim was living the good life, enjoying the fruits of his labors and financial success in this world. However, he was not a Christian and didn't really believe in God.

But "Diamond Jim's" idyllic life began to change in 2010, when he was diagnosed with a rare and very painful nerve disease that came with creeping paralysis. After suffering for a few years as the disease progressed, his doctor finally found a medication developed in France that provided some relief and enabled him to regain some function and mobility. This enabled him to live a more normal lifestyle.

Then, on a spring day in April 2014, as Jim was in his pickup truck surveying some of his property, he accidentally took too much of his medication. Suddenly, he couldn't breathe, his body began shaking violently, and he knew he was dying. But something very unexpected happened next. Jim was overcome with a profound feeling of remorse for the self-centered, Godless, and unthankful way he had lived his life. From deep within his soul, Jim was profoundly convicted of his sins and ingratitude. In broken-hearted regret, he raised his shaking hands toward Heaven and cried out, "God, forgive me!" He was profoundly ashamed and sorry for the way he had wasted the life and blessings God had so graciously given him.

Jim passed out and collapsed over the steering wheel. A short time later he regained consciousness. He slipped out of his truck and felt great! Then, he looked back and saw his body inside the truck. He couldn't understand how that was possible, but knew he had to get back into his body immediately! He desperately tried to get back to the truck, but his efforts were futile. He had no ability to move around or interact with physical things in this world.

Suddenly, he began rising up into "a tunnel of light." He describes traveling through the universe in this golden light-filled tunnel at warp-speed through the universe, with stars streaking past him. Then, his trip ended and he stepped out of the tunnel onto a field of beautiful light-filled green grass, flowers, and rolling hills in Heaven. But as he was gazing over this stunning landscape, he couldn't find the sun. As a pilot, he had always used the sun to gain his sense of direction—but there was no sun in Heaven!

Suddenly, a dark vertical line hung down from the sky, dividing the landscape. On the right side were the beautiful vistas of Heaven, but on the left side the perfect grass of Heaven began changing from green to brown to black—then the ground abruptly fell off a cliff into a crevasse. He walked over to the crevasse and looked down into a deep pit. The walls of the crevasse were shiny black, like coal; and at the bottom of the pit, he could see a faint red light.

As he stood there gazing into the pit, he heard two metal doors creek open, and a very large (about sixty-foot) hideous shape-shifting monster began lumbering out from the bottom of the pit, clawing its way up the walls toward him. The foul demon reeked with an unbearable sewer/death stench. It began speaking in a raspy hiss, "Jim, it is now your time with us." He turned to get away from the crevasse; but suddenly, he felt the monster's claws on his back and cried out, "God help me!" Then, he looked up and saw three points of light at a far-off distance in the sky, moving toward him. *Is that God?* he thought. Then, he remembered that he didn't believe in God—and lost hope.

But the Lord heard his cry and sent three angels, preceded by a beautiful golden light to save Jim from the demons coming to claim his soul. The golden light washed over Jim and struck the demonic creature. It shrieked, screamed, and scrambled back down into the pit, as God's angels moved quickly toward him. He was in awe of these huge, magnificent angels with violet eyes. He described their clothing as made out of light, and he was stunned by the drastic contrast of their beauty, compared to the grotesque creature from Hell.

The winged angels ranged from ten to fifteen feet tall. But most astonishing of all was how these magnificent, powerful beings honored Jim and deeply bowed before him. They had the strength of a warrior, yet were gentle and filled with love. Why did they so honor him? Because we humans are the children of God, made in His image, and they see the light of God in us!

Then the fifteen-foot angel invited Jim to walk with them, and they proceeded to take him on a stroll through Heaven. He struggles to describe the beautiful landscape in Heaven, and says it is a place like Earth but 100,000 x 100,000 times more magnificent. A beautiful pearlescent light comes out of everything in Heaven. There are no shadows there, and he had 360-degree vision, without turning his head. He also had telescopic vision and could automatically see things in detail.

Jim also talks about how you can manifest your own reality in Heaven—and suddenly, you are there! This is what Rhett also described. There is no boredom, only an incredible nowness, where you enjoy and live in every moment!

He says the flowers in Heaven are stunning and wonderful! They look like they are made of stained glass. The petals are transparent and translucent with a fragrance that is the most wonderful smell ever. The angel told Jim, "That is the scent of sanctity." Color has sound, and sound has color in Heaven. The flowers sing to you, and every sound and every color flows toward the Throne of God, as praise!

He describes beautiful horses in Heaven who, like the angels, are made out of light. Jim loves horses, so this was a real blessing for him to see.

The angels then told Jim how important prayer is, and that our generation is losing the ability to pray. They said that our devices and electronic communication are distracting and interfering in our connection with God. God speaks to us in silence. "Be still and know that I am God" (Proverbs 46:10). Then Jim exclaims, "Do you want to see prayer work? Pray for someone else!"

One of the angels took Jim's hand and they began to rise up, effortlessly flying (like floating) over God's golden City. It is huge and colossal, yet it feels like country roads, full of peace and beauty. The streets are paved in pure gold, and The City is thousands of miles across. Huge buildings of magnificent architecture, carved out of blocks of light, radiate with warmth and beauty. And, the most magnificent building of all was "the nursery," which was filled with joy and peace. He remarks about how the children are the most revered of all beings in Heaven. He also says that our spiritual bodies are made out of light, and everyone looks like the perfect version of themselves, around the age of thirty.

Then, Jim saw Jesus standing a short distance away. He was the most light-filled being of all, and he was standing there, about to open a small and very slim book. It was Jim's personal Book of Life! The angel then turned to him and asked, "Jim, what did you do for my Master?" It was devastating to realize that his Book of Life was so small and insignificant.

He then looked into Jesus's beautiful eyes of love and compassion—and saw eternity.

Jesus held up His right hand before Jim, as if to stop him from proceeding any further into Heaven, and said, "James, My son, this is not yet your time. Go back and tell your brothers and sisters what we have shown you."

Two angels then picked up his arms and escorted him back to the tunnel, and he returned to his body in the hospital bed. As soon as he came back to life, he turned to his wife, who was sitting at his bedside, and exclaimed, "Lorraine, I saw Jesus, and He has horses!"

Since returning from Heaven, Jim Woodford has become a passionate witness for Jesus, Heaven, and warning people about Hell. And, his Book of Life is now destined to be a BIG one!

For more information about Jim and his ministry go to: jimwoodfordministries.com. His book *Heaven . . . An Unexpected Journey* is also available on Amazon.com.

Howard Storm's Testimony of Heaven and a Horde from Hell

In June 1985, Howard Storm was an atheist art professor, teaching at a university in Kentucky. He had just spent several days with a group of his students on a tour of the art museums in Paris. As they were about to return to the United States, Howard suddenly experienced a medical crisis and he was rushed to the hospital. His duodenum had been perforated, catapulting him into acute pain and danger of infection. But unfortunately, it was a Saturday, and no doctors were on duty.

After lying in the hospital for several hours in intense pain and no medical care, Howard knew he was about to die, so he said an emotional goodbye to his distraught wife at his bedside. He closed his eyes and lost consciousness.

Then, he awoke and suddenly felt better than he ever had. No pain. Howard tried to tell his wife, but she didn't seem to hear him. So, he tried to tell a guy in a bed close by, but he didn't hear him either. Howard was dead, but didn't know it.

A group of people suddenly appeared outside his hospital room, urgently beckoning him to go with them. He thought they must be hospital staff, so he agreed to go with them. They proceeded to take him on a long journey that led to a place of abject, palpable darkness. When Howard refused to go any farther with them, this horde from Hell attacked him, and began tearing his soul-body apart with their fingernails and teeth. He felt all the pain and trauma, as if he were in his physical body!

From deep inside himself, he heard a voice say, "Pray to God." But he didn't know how to pray; he didn't believe in God. Finally, he began remembering bits and pieces of Psalms 23 and the Lord's Prayer, which he had heard during his lifetime, so he began speaking phrases that came to his mind. This greatly angered the horde of demons attacking him, and they began cursing and departing from him. They couldn't stand to hear the Word of God. Then, Howard blurted out, "Jesus, please save me!" Instantly, a light appeared and he was embraced with pure, liquid love. It was Jesus!

They began moving swiftly away from Hell, through outer space, until he saw what looked like the most enormous galaxy of light imaginable—it was Heaven! As they arrived outside the gate of Heaven, a group of angels joined Jesus and Howard for his "life review." But it didn't go well. He was devastated when he realized his sins—especially his indifference. Most of his sins were indifference; he just didn't really care about anyone but himself. And, he realized that the sin of indifference is as bad as violence and abuse in God's eyes—maybe even worse.

After completing his "life review," Jesus took Howard on a tour of Heaven. Howard said that Heaven is full of everything one could ever want. "Everything that is good is there for you." He also stated that the most important people in Heaven are the children. These are the very same experiences and statements that my husband, Rhett, shared from his tour of Heaven!

Jesus answered all of Howard's questions and even took him to different places in Heaven to show him the answers. Finally, Howard asked Him, "What is the whole point of this life on Earth?" Jesus replied, "It's like a garden. We are each part of God's Garden, and have been put here to bloom. Some of us don't—for whatever reason, we choose not to. And, some of us do. But God wants all of His children to bloom; and we are to use the gifts and talents He has given us to the best of our ability—to bloom!"

At the end of his tour, Jesus told Howard that he must return to Earth. That was the last thing he wanted to hear, so he tried to persuade Him to let him stay in Heaven. But Jesus told him, "No, you don't have the character, you won't fit in. You must go back to Earth and develop the character to fit into Heaven."

After accepting Jesus's decision, Howard was instantly back in the hospital bed and the painful reality of life in this world. His body had become septic due to a lack of proper care in France, and his only chance for survival was to be transported back to the United States for care. After a grueling journey back to the US, the doctors said it was a miracle that he had survived the trip. But God had a plan for Howard's life, so He survived!

Howard's recovery required surgery and three months in US hospitals. But he finally made it, and returned to his profession as a professor. However, he was now a different person, and passionate about keeping people from going to Hell. He started sharing his experience with his medical staff, family, and friends. They needed to know that the demons in Hell are trying to bring everyone there, and those who reject Jesus Christ will go there—it's not optional!

All of his friends and colleagues began shunning him. He was no longer a member of their elitist academic clique—who enjoyed mocking and belittling Christians. Soon after that, Howard was ordered by his university dean to stop talking to his students about Jesus. But he could talk about every other religion. Howard was being persecuted for his belief in Christianity. But that didn't deter him; his faith and devotion to Jesus only grew stronger.

A few years later, Howard had lost his wife and most of his family and friends due to his passionate belief in Jesus Christ. So, he went all-in for Jesus and decided to change his profession. He attended seminary and obtained a theology degree; and for the last thirty years, Howard has served as an ordained pastor for several congregations!

I am sure that Howard now has the character to enter Heaven!

To learn more about Howard Storm's inspiring testimony and ministry, search for his videos on the internet or go to his website: www.howardstorm.com.

Hell Is for Real!

Why do people need to know about the awful realities in Hell? Because that is the destination of those who do not obey God—they will spend eternity with Satan in his kingdom, Hell. But if they knew what Hell is really like, they would do everything possible to make sure they don't go there. Most people are more motivated by fear than anything else. I believe that is why God is moving upon so many people in these last days, to show them the terrifying realities of Hell. He is granting them grace to repent and giving them astounding testimonies to share, so that others may do the same!

In the previous chapter I shared several testimonies about the magnificent reality of Heaven; and many people will be motivated to do whatever is necessary to attain that glorious eternal life. However, most people just want to live in this world. They assume they are decent people who don't deserve Hell, if there is such a place. But many believe it doesn't exist. Or, they reason that if it does exist, a good God would never send decent people there.

But that is not what God says—He vehemently warns us about Hell and our need to repent. Jesus actually talks more about Hell in the Bible than He does about Heaven, because the primary purpose of His mission was to save people from going to Hell. He paid the high price to ransom humanity from Satan's dominion. And God the Father made that transfer as simple as possible: Just believe in Jesus, confess your sins, and repent!

Jesus said that those who enjoy their sins don't want to give them up, so they choose not to believe (John 3:19-20). How tragic! No pleasure of sin in this world can compare to the fantastic ecstasies of Heaven—and they certainly won't enjoy their sins in Hell. Quite the opposite—they will suffer endless torture for each sin, at the hand of ruthless demons, in the steaming cesspool called Hell!

As we are nearing the end of this age, God is turning up the volume on His megaphone, hoping people will hear and repent. He is sending His watchmen and many witnesses to share all the details about the glories of Heaven and the horrible realities of Hell. And He is doing so in as many ways as possible—the internet, books, movies, personal testimonies, and webinars. He is even pouring out dreams and visions on people in every nation and every religious system all over the world. Hindus, Muslims, Buddhists, Christians, atheists, and all types of people are suddenly meeting Jesus in their dreams or in open visions! He is reaching out to all humanity, beckoning them to come to Him and be saved, before God the Father brings this evil age to an abrupt end!

"In the last days, God says, I will pour out my Spirit on all people. Your sons and daughters will prophesy, your young men will see visions, your old men will dream dreams. (Acts 2:17 NIV)

Jesus is coming soon for His righteous Bride, but most Christians are not ready. Many are practicing sin and need to hear the truth loud and clear: "Hell is for real and it's much worse than you can imagine. Backsliders, hypocrites, and those who love the things of this world more than Him do not get into Heaven. Repent now while you still can!" When God sends the "strong delusion" as a judgment upon humanity, the Bible indicates that most professing Christians will believe "the lie," fall away from the faith, and no longer be able to repent. Only the "remnant" will be saved. (2 Thessalonians 2:9-12; Romans 9:27; Matthew 7:22-23)

Hopefully, the testimonies shared in Part III will help you see the truth, build your faith, and give you the resolve to do whatever is necessary to attain Heaven, and not end up in Hell!

Four Profound Testimonies of Hell

In *late February 2015,* Rhett had a medical emergency and was taken to the VA hospital in Salt Lake City. He had chronic heart failure and his oxygen level had gotten out of balance, creating a CO_2 problem. He had been recovering in the hospital about three days, and I was expecting him to be released on the morning that I received a phone call from one of his physicians.

But that wasn't the reason he was calling. His doctor was upset and asked me to come to the hospital immediately because they were afraid that he might die at any moment! He said that Rhett was not in a coma and was fine when he went to sleep the night before. But inexplicably, they couldn't get him to wake up the next morning. They had tried everything they could think of, even poking him with needles, but there was no response. He said they had never seen anything like it before and the specialists didn't understand what was happening with him.

I arrived about forty-five minutes later, and the doctor came out to meet me at the reception desk. He began apologizing, but not because Rhett had died. No, he was somewhat embarrassed and apologized for calling me like he did because soon after he called me, Rhett suddenly opened his eyes and sat up—he was coherent and seemed just fine! When I followed the doctor into Rhett's room, several more doctors were standing around his bed with puzzled looks on their faces. Nobody could explain what had happened. But Rhett did.

As soon as the doctors left the room, Rhett began telling me why they couldn't wake him up—he wasn't there. His soul was on a tour of Hell! Just as God had allowed him to experience what happens when a person dies and goes to Heaven, now He was allowing Rhett to experience what happens when a person dies and goes to Hell. But someone was with him for this tour. He didn't know if it was Jesus or an angel, but he was aware of a supernatural Guardian by his side protecting him. Nonetheless, God allowed Rhett to experience the following scenario for what must have been at least four hours, according to the doctors.

+ Dark demon spirits suddenly appeared and grabbed Rhett (his soul), rapidly dragging him away, as if they were flying. They finally came to a large pit (like a volcano) and threw him in! He fell through this bottomless abyss, tumbling for what must have been many miles. His soul-body was ricocheting off jagged walls of rock, as he fell helplessly in total blackness. It was terrifying!

+ Then somehow, he was standing on solid ground, like a ledge inside a volcano. From there he began his tour of Hell, as he was led from one level to the next in downward progression. Whoever was leading him wanted to make sure he had a good understanding of what Hell is really like!

The way Rhett described the structure and overall environment of Hell reminded me of "Dante's Inferno," as described in the classic poem *The Divine Comedy*. It is like being on the inside of a volcano whose jagged walls encase a labyrinth of ledges, tunnels, and caverns, punctuated by volcanos, descending to the bottom of the pit. These tiers are in the mantle of rock beneath Earth's crust, winding for millions of miles throughout the earth's voluminous interior. It is the habitation of grotesque demons, evil creatures, and the human souls who are their victims.

+ Just as on Earth, various locations in Hell display different characteristics. None are good, but some are worse than others. Each tier or level represents the severity of different kinds of sin and the type of penalty demons can carry out as punishment. Like Jesus said, these are "the tormentors," and they enjoy their job! But the penalty must fit the crime—so, not all sin is punished the same.

+ The levels closer to Earth's surface are where those guilty of less severe sins would be, and their experience would be less severe than someone who had committed the worst sins. But their experience would still be dreadful! And, the worst sins may surprise most people. God doesn't see things like we do in many cases, so some of those judged most harshly may look like decent people to us.

   For example, those who are wealthy, respected professionals, celebrities, church leaders, or in prominent positions may be guilty of some of the worst sins in God's eyes. What are those sins? Such things as pride, arrogance, hatred, unforgiveness, false doctrine, lying, greed, covetousness, slander, gossip, betrayal, blasphemy, and hypocrisy. These sins are prevalent among many people who are respected in society.

+ A revelation that really shocked Rhett was how harshly Jesus judges unrighteous and self-serving Church leaders. Those who do many good works in His name, but not out of love for Him and His people. They are hirelings motivated by money or self-promotion. Also, those who taught or tolerated false doctrine. Christ's shepherds must share His character, His heart, and the truth!

✦ Those who mistreat or mislead children will also receive the harshest judgment.

"But whoever causes one of these little ones who believe in Me to stumble, it would be better for him if a millstone were hung around his neck, and he were thrown into the sea. (Mark 9:42)

Rhett was amazed at how much Jesus loves the children and how much they love Him in Heaven. He said that "they are always with Him, following Him around wherever He goes." He said that the children are the most important and honored people in Heaven. So, it makes sense that those who mistreat children will receive the harshest punishment in Hell.

Those who abuse or mislead a child, especially one who believes in Jesus, will receive extreme judgment. This could include parents who are irresponsible and allow His children to believe whatever they want, and fall away from Him; and obviously those who have physically, emotionally, or sexually abused one of His children. But even they can be forgiven, if they truly repent and apologize to those they offended.

The Environment of Hell

Satan and his kingdom are the antithesis of Jesus and Heaven. As the polar opposite of Heaven, Hell is filled with hatred, fear, torment, and whatever offends God the most.

As Jesus described in scripture, your soul-body retains the same faculties, memories, feelings, and senses that your physical body has, but even more intensely. You can think, remember, have emotions, speak, and feel pain just like your physical body does. Those who have been there say that the pain you feel is throughout your entire body; whereas your physical body only feels pain in specific locations. For example, if a demon brutally gouges your arm, that pain radiates throughout your soul-body. You also retain your sense of smell, taste, temperature, sight, and hearing.

All suffering is intensified and, unfortunately, the soul is immortal and cannot die. So, in a sense those souls "die a thousand deaths" every day for eternity, as demons relentlessly torture them. Evil spirits enjoy making humans who were "created in the image of God" suffer!

Following are some of the things Rhett described:

+ The stench that fills the "air" in Hell is worse than anything anyone has ever smelled on Earth! It is an intense concentration of everything that has seeped into the ground: sewage, decaying flesh, garbage, chemicals, sulfur, and noxious gases. It's hard to breathe because of the smells and because there is very little air in that enclosed environment!

+ It's really hot! At the bottom of the chasm is a lake of fire—molten rock and hot gasses, the birthplace of volcanos. Souls suffer from the extreme heat and many burn in flames as their punishment.

+ It is very dark—blackness infused with extreme fear. The presence of demons is palpable; you can feel them approaching you. Their strength and hateful, malevolent intentions keep souls in constant terror. Intense fear fills the environment of Hell.

+ The only time Rhett could see anything with his natural eyes was when a volcano erupted, casting a glow. Then he could see the demons, souls, and activity that was constantly taking place in the darkness.

+ The sounds were horrendous. Deafening screams, yelling, and crying echoed throughout the chambers of Hell.

+ Rhett only told me about one type of demon he saw; however, other witnesses say there are many different kinds of demons in Hell. What Rhett described had a large human-like body, combined with non-human characteristics. It sounded to me like the infamous "Baphomet" demon that is depicted in drawings by people who are Satanists.

+ By the time Rhett reached the seventh level, he couldn't take any more! There was at least one and possibly two levels beneath him, and then the lake of fire. The seventh level was where the demons punish sexual sins. He could hear loud, clanking, metallic sounds coming from the eighth level below, and felt that the tortures there were really awful.

+ The intensity of evil taking place as each tier descended was more than Rhett could endure, so he cried out "Jesus save me!" as he felt the hot breath of a demon on the back of his neck! Instantly, he saw a bright flash of light and was back in his body in the hospital bed. That is when his eyes popped open and he startled the doctors!

Rhett said that all kinds of torture were taking place—everything depicted in horror movies and much worse. Unfortunately, I cannot describe most of the details he told me. As I mentioned earlier, three days after he shared his testimony with me, I was so distressed that I was sinking into a state of depression. How could I ever be happy and enjoy life again, knowing the horrifying things taking place beneath my feet? So, I asked God to remove those memories from my mind—and He did. I do remember a few of the less horrific things, as mentioned above; but the nightmarish details are gone, wiped clean!

Ivan Tuttle's Testimony of Hell

As I shared earlier in Ivan's testimony about Heaven, in 1978 at the age of twenty-six, Ivan suddenly died from a blood clot in his left leg. But before going to Heaven, his soul was first taken to Hell. Following is a summary of his experience in Hell:

Ivan was finally back home lying in bed, after spending two weeks in a hospital where he was receiving intense therapy to dissolve life-threatening blood clots in his legs. He was sleeping peacefully around 9:00 p.m. when something jolted him awake. A large, grotesque demon had a tight grip on his wrist, and yanked his soul out of his body. They passed through walls and into the spiritual realm, where they began flying at hyper-speed through time and space straight into Hell!

The Reality of Hell

"The evil spirit that had hold of me had begun laughing at me. It was incredibly grotesque looking and had the strength of a hundred men." Then, they began falling through a pit of utter darkness as they entered Hell. Deafening screams and bloodcurdling shrieks echoed throughout the caverns of Hell, penetrating his entire being. He could actually feel the pain of the souls being tortured by fiendish demons as he passed by them. "The pain and anguish there is beyond any suffering you have ever known; it literally engulfs your whole being. Kind of like the worst toothache or headache you have ever had times a thousand and throughout your whole being."

The soul body has all the faculties of a physical body, but even greater. "It's difficult to explain in words. You feel pain, and you see and hear everything with perfect vision and hearing. But the pain in Hell is unbelievably worse than anything on Earth . . . If you get a cut in the flesh, it only hurts where you got cut, but in Hell if you cut your finger it hurts throughout your whole being."

"People down there seemed to be chained up in little areas, but there were no chains or bars to prohibit them from moving; they just couldn't get out of their assigned areas." He then tries to better describe the horrid existence of billions of souls restrained in this agonizing prison.

"Imagine solid, jagged rock walls with people attached by some invisible force, like being chained up, and these walls go on forever—over a million miles in every direction. It is dark, it stinks—the smell of rotten flesh and garbage mixed with a sulfur smell and heat so hot that your flesh would melt off its bones—that is just a little idea of what hell is like." And it never gets better. The palpable darkness is filled with an overwhelming spirit of fear. Souls are in a constant state of intense anxiety, as they anticipate even worse things coming upon them. "The sense of hopelessness I felt in this place was totally overwhelming . . . all hope and expectation of life was gone."

The Demons in Hell

"I'm sure I have not adequately described the creatures in hell—what they looked like, smelled like, and what they did. There were some creatures that were very big, about ten or twelve feet tall and they were very grotesque with rotted flesh and a smell that matched. Many of them had long, disfigured arms and legs and they were so strong that they could rip you in half. There were others that seemed to just slither around like huge snakes."

Ivan describes how much the demons enjoy torture and that they fight over who gets to torture someone. These evil spirits are there to torture you and they get such pleasure out of it. "The demons are tearing you apart, but you don't come apart; you only rip and tear but stay together. This pain is horrible."

But the demons' greatest pleasure is when they can torture someone who fell for their lies while on Earth. They delight in deceiving people, especially in obvious ways that demonstrate how stupid humans are. Their favorite victims to humiliate are former Christians, whom they hate most of all. These evil, twisted creatures love to taunt and mock them for their foolishness, adding insult to injury. The intense regret these poor souls feel as demons remind them of what they traded greatly increases their suffering.

Souls in Hell

The Bible tells us that the vast majority of people on Earth are wicked in God's eyes and will, therefore, go to the default destination in Hades. But Ivan also talks about seeing many former Christians in Hell. "I saw so many people there who never thought they would end up in Hell. These were good people—some were even former pastors of churches, deacons, Sunday school teachers, some familiar men and women from our past—very good people, but they were doomed to Hell forever."

He doesn't say why they were there, but later he expounds upon the "fake Christians" in Hell. "I call them 'fake Christians' because they claim to be a Christian, but their walk with God is nothing like Christ. They were only satisfied with pleasing themselves." He describes them as worldly, self-serving people who think they can live however they want, as long as they "believe" in Jesus. So, they live like hypocrites, bringing shame to the name of Jesus Christ—and damnation to themselves. Ivan talks about how these people were deceived by false doctrines of men that have infiltrated Christianity, especially the "once-saved-always-saved" teaching.

Demonic Strategies

He goes on to describe how he was made privy to the tactics demons are planning to use to deceive people on Earth; and he issues a vehement warning to parents about the tactics they would use to target children. In 1978 he saw these things in Hell, before some of them were even invented. They include using the occult and subliminal technology through movies, music, and video games with which demons can gain access into humans. "There are millions of types of demons of numerous sizes, shapes, and assignments, but they all have the same overall mission, and that is to destroy your relationship with God any possible way they can," he writes.

Sex is one of the most powerful doorways for demonic possession. In 1978, Ivan saw that a type of new technology would greatly increase video porn. He said that "in the near future this technology will even produce human-like forms that will be part of the worst lust the world has ever seen." Was he describing AI sex-robots?

He also states that "Hidden intentional sin" is rampant with people who claim to be Christians, and this greatly displeases God. He states, "If you are looking at porn, treating your family badly (abuse), cheating on your spouse, are into violent or graphic gaming, use illegal drugs, abuse drugs, daily drinking alcohol—these are examples of hidden intentional sin." He said that he was sent to warn the Church: "either you repent and change your ways, or it will be exposed."

He emphasizes that parents and believing Christians must fight against these evil spirits, by praying and "pleading the blood of Jesus" over ourselves, children, and others. Ivan describes how he understood all the different tactics that evil spirits use to deceive people on Earth, and get them to sin or believe lies. He then states that "the biggest lies are 'once-saved-always-saved' and 'extreme grace.' These lies are sending more people to Hell than atheism."

Jesus Rescues Ivan from Hell

Then, Ivan heard a voice of thunder command Hell to release him! Jesus proclaimed that it was not his time yet, and that He had made a promise to Ivan's mother! Instantly, he was released and his soul flew out of Hell, through the universe, and straight to the gate of Heaven—where he experienced his glorious tour of Heaven, described earlier.

But why did Ivan go to Hell when he died? After all, he had been a born-again believer most of his life, loved the Lord, and even attended Bible college for a few years.

He went to Hell because he wasn't walking with Jesus at the time he died. He was living like the world, drinking, partying, doing drugs, and not obeying the gospel. Ivan also believed the OSAS doctrine and thought he was fine. He wasn't motivated to change his wicked ways—so he died in his sins! Ivan's testimony is similar to what happened with my son, Greg. I shared his story in my testimony "Back From the Dead" in Part I.

The Bible says that your past righteousness will not save you in the day you give in to sin! (Ezekiel 18:24)

Laurie Ditto's Vision of Hell

On August 28, 2008, Laurie Ditto's spiritual life took an abrupt turn. She had been an on-fire Christian for several years, after being radically saved and blessed with a vision experience in Heaven, as I shared earlier. She was head-over-heels in love with Jesus, and passionate about serving Him with her whole life. Laurie was working with a large ministry when suddenly, the Lord gave her a life-changing vision of Hell! But why—what did she do to deserve such a thing?

The short answer is: unforgiveness. Laurie, like so many believers, was harboring unforgiveness in her heart. She had read the scriptures and knew that Jesus said:

> *For if you forgive other people when they sin against you, your heavenly Father will also forgive you. But if you do not forgive others their sins, your Father will not forgive your sins. (Matthew 6:14-15 NIV)*

So, why did Laurie choose to ignore the Word of God and disobey such an important commandment? She assumed God would never send a believer like her to Hell. She was in full-time ministry, doing many good works for Jesus and leading others to Him. She also believed that the "once-saved-always-saved" doctrine guaranteed her salvation, so she wasn't worried about unforgiveness.

Following is a summary of the things she experienced in Hell:

+ Laurie went to Hell for unforgiveness. But once there, all other sins done in her lifetime were piled on and were also to be punished. These included: unkindness, harshness, impatience, and many other sins of the heart.

+ Everyone in Hell is there because they are guilty—they would not love and obey God. She saw many Christians there who didn't believe or obey the truth. Everyone in Hell understands and agrees that they deserve to be there—because they have instant understanding of God's righteous judgment.

+ Laurie was still herself with the same personality and mental and physical characteristics, but everything was more intense. Especially the pain of regret for disobeying God. There is also extreme distress from watching others suffering in agony and the constant sound of screams, wailing, and weeping. All of this could have been avoided by just obeying Jesus's words!

+ She describes the environment of Hell as oppressive fear and darkness comprised of multiple layers of blackness. There is no light in Hell. You are isolated and cannot associate with anyone else because that would be a form of comfort, which you are not allowed. Everything is filled with hatred, especially self-hatred. There is no mercy or compassion.

+ There is no water, creating a desperate and painful thirst. You are engulfed in flames that are dark, not colorful—and you cannot die. There is no sleep or rest allowed. You can't really breathe, only short gasps because the air is so hot and noxious.

+ Hell is huge and always expanding to contain all the souls constantly coming there!

After learning the dire consequences of disobeying God's written word, Laurie says that what really sends a person to Hell is unbelief and rebellion. They disobeyed or disrespected God by refusing to believe and obey His words, commandments, and precepts. She then compares her sins of unforgiveness to the parable Jesus taught about the unmerciful servant in Matthew 18: 21-35. In that parable, Jesus shows us how God will treat Christians who refuse to forgive others. He will rescind His grace from the unforgiving person—and throw them into prison (Hell). And that is where Laurie said she would have gone, if she did not repent of her unforgiveness and other sins!

Laurie states that after her experience in Hell, she no longer believed the OSAS doctrine. So, she conducted her own in-depth research into that teaching, and found that it is not Biblical. It is a false doctrine!

You can read more about Laurie's riveting experience in her book, *The Hell Conspiracy*, available on Amazon.com.

Bill Weise's Testimony of Hell

In 1998, a Christian man named Bill Weise was given a profound spiritual experience in which he was taken to Hell and then rescued by Jesus. There are several videos on YouTube and the internet in which he shares his horrifying experience, titled "23 Minutes in Hell."

In the middle of the night on November 24, 1998, Bill awoke around 3 a.m., needing some water. As he was walking from his bedroom through the living room, he suddenly collapsed on the floor. Then, something grabbed his arm, yanking his soul out of his body. A powerful demon with tremendous strength began flying with him at lightning speed across the earth, then hurled him into a large opening that descended like a tunnel into Hell. After a terrifying fall through pitch-black darkness, he came to an abrupt landing on a hard surface. Everything was dark and smoky and the heat was unbearable—it didn't seem possible to live in such extreme heat. A putrid stench filled what little air there was, making it even harder to breathe. He had no strength whatsoever in his body; he couldn't even stand up. Though difficult to see through the darkness, he soon realized that he was in a dungeon—a filthy chamber with solid rock walls and bars across a gateway.

Two grotesque demons about thirteen feet tall began pacing in front of him. Suddenly, a reptilian-looking demon picked him up and hurled him against the wall with tremendous force. It felt like every bone in his body broke; but strangely, he had no bones. The second demon then dug his twelve-inch claws into Bill's chest, ripping him open. The pain was excruciating, but there was no blood. He couldn't understand how he could survive such trauma, but he did. He also couldn't understand why these entities hated him so much. It seemed personal.

Bill then found himself sitting in a very large cavern on the edge of a deep, mile-wide pit filled with fire. The flames were raging high, providing just enough light in the deep darkness to make out shadowy figures of souls and demons that were filling the space. He could see demons all along the cavern walls; some were huge spiders, snakes, frogs, twisted half-human creatures, and maggots that covered the floor.

Many agonizing souls were burning in flames, and they looked like skeletons with flesh hanging from their bones. It was the most awful sight imaginable. Other souls were being tortured by demons, and their deafening screams and wails were unbearable to hear. There was also no rest or sleep in Hell, even though you desperately crave it, as well as other bodily needs. You are constantly hungry and thirsty, but there is no relief. Nor is there any relief for your constant pain, as every cell in your body hurts. There is no social or emotional comfort either. Souls dwell in isolated darkness and have no interaction with others.

Different levels of punishment are carried out in the myriad chambers throughout Hell, some worse than others. But the most awful experience of all is the palpable darkness that penetrates your entire being with intense fear, as your soul is consumed with terror and fearful expectation of what is coming next.

As Bill was languishing in Hell, the finality and hopelessness of his situation began to sink in. He was overcome with regret as he realized how serious the consequences of sin really are—and that there is no escape from Hell. Bill didn't remember that he had previously been a Christian; that knowledge seemed to be taken from him. He believed that Hell was his destination and what he deserved, and the hopelessness of his situation became the most agonizing experience of all.

Then, something unusual happened. Bill began ascending upward through a black tunnel—until suddenly, he saw a bright white light with the figure of a man in it. Instantly, his soul cried out "Jesus!" and a booming voice replied, "I am!" At that moment Bill fell at Jesus's feet, unconscious. But Jesus lovingly reached down and touched him, restoring Bill to consciousness and fellowship with Himself. At that moment, Bill became profoundly aware that if Jesus had not gone to the cross and paid for his sins, he would have spent eternity in Hell with no hope. His soul was so overwhelmed with gratitude that all he could do was exclaim, "Thank you, Jesus! Thank you, Jesus!" over and over again!

He continued ascending out of Hell, and began rising into the heavens high above the earth. Looking down upon the earth, he was in profound awe of its beauty and the ordered manner of its position and turning. As he lifted his eyes to look out into the universe, Bill was overwhelmed by its vastness, and mesmerized by its amazing beauty and intelligent design. He was astonished at the billions of worlds, stars, and galaxies filling the blackness of outer space with glorious light. He states that there is no way anyone who sees such things would not believe in the reality of God. Beholding the awesome universe is a profoundly religious experience. Bill then recalls how as a child, he wanted to become an astronaut. He felt that the Lord had finally answered the desires of his heart with this extraordinary experience.

Gazing down upon the earth, Bill was astounded by what he saw next—an opening into the pit of Hell. As he watched in horror, he witnessed many people falling into it, one after another. Jesus was also watching as He stood there beside him, and Bill felt the Lord's profound anguish for every individual descending into the pit. His heartbreak for each person was far greater than anything we can comprehend as humans.

As Bill stood there, reflecting on his experience when he was in that awful place, questions began coming into his mind. So, he asked Jesus why He had sent him there, and why didn't he remember that he was a Christian when he was in Hell. Jesus told him that He had sent him there to be an eyewitness. Many people, including Christians, no longer believe that Hell is real. So, they are not motivated to repent and live righteous lives to avoid going there. And, other Christians believe false doctrines about the nature of Hell, thinking it is just a state of "soul sleep" or annihilation where the soul ceases to exist. But nothing could be further from the truth. Hell is more real than life in this world; its consequences are horrendous and they are for eternity. It is the abode of Satan and his demons, and those who go there become their victims!

He then asked Jesus why the demons hated him so much, as if it were personal. Jesus replied, "They hate you because they hate Me, and you are made in my image." The Lord proceeded to tell Bill that He had purposely blocked his knowledge that he was a Christian while he was in Hell. Why? Jesus wanted Bill to experience the *hopelessness* and *regret* that people have in Hell, because this torture of the mind is the worst experience of all. If Bill had remembered that he was a Christian, he may have had hope of rescue because he didn't deserve to be there. But Jesus wanted him to experience the utter hopelessness of those who are not saved, and passionately communicate that reality to others.

Bill's soul was then returned to Earth, and reentered his body lying on the living room floor. As he came into consciousness, memories of Hell were running through his mind—and he began screaming, as if he were still there. His wife was suddenly awakened and rushed to his side. She realized that he was having a terrifying and traumatic spiritual experience, so she began earnestly praying over him. As he came to his senses, he shared his horrific experience with her. She never doubted what had happened. She knew her husband and how out of character this behavior was for him. She understood that the Lord had given Bill this supernatural experience for an important reason.

A few weeks later, Bill mustered the nerve to tell his best friend what had happened. Then, word began to spread and he was asked to share his testimony with others in his church community. But it took seven years for Bill to finally agree to share his experience with a larger audience. He talks about a conversation he had with the Lord, in which he told Jesus that he wasn't comfortable talking about his experience in Hell, because people would think he was a kook. He explained to the Lord that he had built up a respected business, and had a reputation to maintain for the sake of his family. But the Lord replied, "Bill, it's not about you being comfortable; it's about you being obedient." That launched Bill into full-time ministry, sharing his story with thousands of people!

Since then, Bill has traveled all over the United States, speaking before large audiences, doing broadcast interviews, and speaking in numerous videos on YouTube and other online platforms. He is an excellent speaker who delivers a profound and convincing testimony with sincerity, humility, and a professionalism that is above reproach. The Lord has been using Bill to lead multitudes of people into a born-again relationship with Jesus Christ and salvation. But perhaps even more importantly, He is using Bill to inform many professing Christians about the reality of Hell and the requirement that we live a righteous lifestyle, uncompromised by sin and hypocrisy.

In recent years, Bill has also been led by the Lord to warn about the danger of the "once-saved-always-saved" teaching. He and his wife, Annette, have produced two excellent YouTube videos examining this doctrine, which are well worth watching. You can find his videos, book, and interviews at his website: soulchoiceministries.org.

The Great Deception
and Strong Delusion

*T*hroughout history, supernatural works and miracles have represented the manifestation of God in this world. Only He can perform true miracles and the greatest supernatural acts, like the parting of the Red Sea, sustaining the Israelites for forty years in the desert, and their miraculous military victories over giants and formidable armies, as illustrated throughout the Old Testament. It was also through the miraculous and supernatural that Jesus proved to the world that He was the Son of God:

"If I do not do the works of My Father, do not believe Me; but if I do, though you do not believe Me, believe the works, that you may know and believe that the Father is in Me, and I in Him." (John 10: 37-38)

The Holy Spirit also led the apostle Paul to take the gospel to the Gentiles, first and foremost, through the demonstration of God's supernatural power. Why? To build strong belief and faith in God and Jesus. Our faith is to be in the power of God—and not in the doctrines of men!

And my speech and my preaching were not with persuasive words of human wisdom, but in demonstration of the Spirit and of power, that your faith should not be in the wisdom of men but in the power of God. (1 Corinthians 2: 4-5)

Satan and evil entities also have supernatural power but to a lesser degree, as demonstrated in the showdown between Moses and Pharoah's sorcerers in Genesis chapters 7-12. In that contest, the workers of evil could only mimic three of the ten supernatural works performed by the Holy Spirit. However, the Bible says that in the end-days, God will purposely allow Satan and his minions the ability to do greater supernatural works than ever before—even bringing the dead back to life and calling down fire from Heaven!

+ *I saw one of his heads as if it had been slain, and his fatal wound was healed. And the whole earth was amazed and followed after the beast . . . (Revelation 13:3 NASB 1995)*

+ *Then I saw another beast coming up out of the earth; and he had two horns like a lamb and he spoke as a dragon. He exercises all the authority of the first beast in his presence. And he makes the earth and those who dwell in it to worship the first beast, whose fatal wound was healed. He performs great signs, so that he even makes fire come down out of heaven to the earth in the presence of men. And he deceives those who dwell on the earth because of the signs which it was given him to perform in the presence of the beast . . . (Revelation 13:11-14 NASB 1995)*

Why would the Lord grant the forces of evil such power? To fulfill prophecy and accomplish God's will. I think it may be to fulfill prophecy concerning the great deception, and the "strong delusion" that God will send upon the unrepentant and wicked in the end-days. The Bible says that everyone except a small remnant of devout Christians called "the elect" (Matthew 24:31) will fall under a delusion that is either the result of a great "falling away" or causes the falling away, (2 Thessalonians 2:3). The Antichrist "Beast" will then be revealed and the whole world (except the elect) will worship him. He will not likely come looking and acting like the devil, but more like a man of peace with solutions to the world's many problems. Satan will give him his authority and supernatural power to carry out his mission. The False Prophet will promote the Antichrist and cause the whole world to worship the Beast, as he performs miracles and all the lying wonders of Satan in the Beast's presence. This great deception will lead people to worship the Antichrist.

> *The coming of the lawless one is according to the working of Satan, with all power, signs, and lying wonders, and with all unrighteous deception among those who perish, because they did not receive the love of the truth, that they might be saved. And for this reason, God will send them strong delusion, that they should believe the lie, that they all may be condemned who did not believe the truth but had pleasure in unrighteousness. (2 Thessalonians 2: 9-12)*

But what exactly is the strong delusion that causes people to believe "the lie," and will it come upon professing Christians? Does it cause the great falling away or simply add to it?

The Bible doesn't tell us exactly what it is, but the Lord apparently sends it as preliminary judgment just before the Antichrist is revealed, to seal the fate of all those who "did not receive the love of the truth." Those professing Christians who are living worldly lives or disobedient lives, or love a false doctrine, will likely fall under the delusion because they did not love and obey the truth.

I have a theory about something the delusion may entail, based on an experience that happened to someone I know as well as certain scriptures that seem to support my theory. This theory may only be one aspect of the delusion, but I think it is something worth considering.

Doug's story:

Doug, a man I have known for many years, recently told me about something he experienced a few years ago that instantly changed his religious beliefs. Doug had been an intellectual believer in Jesus Christ most of his life and had been quite active in his church. Then, one day in 2010, everything suddenly changed when he had a very unusual spiritual encounter.

As he was shopping on a Saturday morning at his local Costco store, he looked up across an open space and noticed someone staring at him, a short distance away. It was Linda, a coworker he had been good friends with for a long time. But he had really missed her for the last few years, since she suddenly left unexpectedly. Linda had died, and Doug was devastated. He spoke at her funeral and gave money to a charity in remembrance of her. He had kept her picture on the wall in his office ever since, and often looked at it in fond memory of their fun and engaging relationship, muttering, "I sure wish I could see you again, Linda."

But now, there she was—intently watching him, and smiling!

He quickly approached her and breathlessly exclaimed, "Linda, what are you doing here? You're supposed to be dead—I went to your funeral!" She kindly replied, "Yes, I saw you there, and thank you for all the nice things you said about me and the money you gave."

They continued to talk for several minutes, in what he described as a surreal bubble in which they seemed to be the only people in that busy store. Linda proceeded to tell him about the spirit world and how people go into this perfect reality when they die. She described an existence different from what the Bible teaches, with no judgment—an idyllic existence in love, peace, and harmony with others.

But most convincing of all was Linda herself. She was transformed into this beautiful, luminescent, perfect version of herself. She was around fifty years old when she died, but now she looked like she was thirty—and she spoke such wisdom and mesmerizing truth. Doug felt so good—so loved, at peace, and valued in her presence that he wanted it to last forever. He couldn't wait to join her on the other side!

Then she said, "I have to go now. My husband is here today and I need to go see him also." She turned and began walking away down the aisle—then suddenly disappeared.

Doug was very emotional when he was sharing his story, and I felt that it really did happen. But he complained that nobody would believe him. He had been telling everyone for over ten years about his experience and the "truth" about what happens when we die—but they all thought he was crazy! It was very upsetting and frustrating to him, that he wasn't believed.

I told him that I believed him, and tried to share the Biblical scriptures that speak about such encounters. But he wouldn't have any of it! He no longer believed in the Bible or Christianity—he *knew* what the truth is and adamantly refused to hear anything different. He said that he didn't care what the Bible said, and nothing could change his mind. He actually became angry if I spoke anything from the Bible—as if it were a lie!

That night, I prayed and asked the Lord what had really happened in Doug's experience. As I was waking up the next morning, the Holy Spirit was speaking into my mind, answering my questions. I was impressed that Doug was approached by a "familiar spirit" (Leviticus 19:31) and was drawn into another dimension in which he experienced his interaction with "Linda." I also felt that this type of supernatural encounter may become prevalent in the near future.

The Bible teaches that most people throughout the world will be deceived by the strong delusion that is coming, and only a remnant of faithful Christians will be spared. I believe that in the end-time spiritual beings like familiar spirits and Satan's fallen angels will be allowed to come upon humanity—and most people will have the same reaction that Doug had. Their religious beliefs will instantly change when they see the beauty and experience the love and blissful feelings emanating from these luminescent beings. And, when they hear their pleasing new doctrines full of "wisdom" and Heaven without judgment—that's all it takes! They have experienced the "truth" for themselves. Their belief in Christianity and all other religions goes out the window, as they wholeheartedly embrace the seductive delusion!

But does the Bible support my theory that the "strong delusion" may involve fallen angels and demonic spirits that God sends upon humanity? I think it does. Revelation chapter 12 states the following:

+ *And war broke out in heaven: Michael and his angels fought with the dragon; and the dragon and his angels fought, but they did not prevail, nor was a place found for them in heaven any longer. So, the great dragon was cast out, that serpent of old, called the Devil and Satan, who deceives the whole world; he was cast to the earth, and his angels were cast out with him. (Revelation 12:7-9)*

+ *"Therefore rejoice, O heavens, and you who dwell in them! Woe to the inhabitants of the earth and the sea! For the devil has come down to you, having great wrath, because he knows that he has a short time." (Revelation 12:12)*

The apostle Paul also describes the deceptive tactics these entities will use in the end-time:

+ *And no wonder! For Satan himself transforms himself into an angel of light. Therefore, it is no great thing if his ministers also transform themselves into ministers of righteousness, whose end will be according to their works. (2 Corinthians 11:14-15)*

+ *Now the Spirit expressly says that in latter times some will depart from the faith, giving heed to deceiving spirits and doctrines of demons . . . (1 Timothy 4:1)*

I believe these scriptures are saying that when Michael and his angels defeat Satan, God will cast him and his entourage down to Earth. Satan and his angels are master transformers able to manifest themselves in whatever manner they desire, even as angels of light with counterfeit love, joy, and peace! Demons can also impersonate our deceased loved ones as "familiar spirits." Satan will undoubtedly utilize all of his minions, both "good" and evil, to carry out his end-time strategies!

Regard not them that have familiar spirits, neither seek after wizards, to be defiled by them: I am the LORD your God. (Leviticus 19:31 KJV)

These luminescent deceivers will cause people to feel blissful in their presence, and may even heal people. Some may claim to be gods themselves and mankind's creators. Others will manifest as deceased loved ones who have returned to teach us the "truth" in new doctrines that contradict Christianity. And, they may even come up with artifacts and historical evidence to support their new teachings!

So, beware and be on guard!

PART IV

CONNECTING THE DOTS

Do the Dots Connect?

If you have made it this far, you probably have a lot of information churning around in your head and a ton of questions. You have read some amazing things, some unsettling things, and some confusing things—and you're not sure what to make of all this. Most likely, some of this information is challenging your beliefs, whether you are a Christian or not. But you can't quite see it yet—how all of this comes together and what picture it paints. And most importantly, how it applies to you.

In this chapter I will try to bring everything into a cohesive picture that you can get your head around. I hope to help the reader see how all of these stories and information connect, and clearly see the picture that emerges. We will look at the evidence and proof that has been presented to determine if it confirms the premise of this book: *God is for real and so are Heaven and Hell.* And if so, what that means for all of us.

In order to make a lot of information as concise as possible, I am organizing the evidence for each testimony according to the Part or category it was first presented in. Then the testimony is grouped according to its stage of fulfillment: (1) already fulfilled, (2) currently in-process of fulfillment, or (3) yet to be fulfilled. For the testimonies already fulfilled, I ask the reader to refer back to the original testimony, where its fulfillment details are given at the end of the story. However, for the testimonies that are currently in-process of fulfillment, I will briefly give those details within this chapter.

At the end of this chapter, I will try to connect the dots between all the testimonies and information presented. What are the common threads and what is all of this saying? Would the evidence presented be sufficient to convince any honest jury that God is for real and so are Heaven and Hell? What about honest scientists—is it sufficient to convince them also? After intelligently weighing all of the evidence, which side would you bet your life on—the God of the Bible, or something else?

My Fulfilled Visions and Supernatural Events
(from Part I)

Visions and Premonitions fulfilled in the physical world
Please refer back to the original testimony for details of the fulfilment

1. Premonition of Imminent Disaster

2. I Feel Your Pain

3. Salvation of my Extended Family

4. Blessed to Help Others

5. It's a Girl

6. Rhett's Greater Purpose

7. Back from the Dead

8. Kelli's Winter Camp

9. The Golden Spear

10. Connect the Dots

11. Demonic Vultures

What is the significance of these supernatural events for other Christians—how do they apply to you?

+ They prove God's existence and that He still does supernatural works and miracles in the lives of His people, which strengthens our faith!

+ They prove that God is fulfilling prophecy in today's world—the prophetic messages given to His watchmen, as well as prophecies recorded in the Bible.

+ They show that God is fulfilling His promises *to pour out His spirit on all kinds of people in the last days*—with visions, dreams, revelations, and prophetic messages.

+ Many of these supernatural events prove the power of faith and prayer, especially when we pray in agreement with others for a specific issue.

+ These testimonies also prove the reliability of Christian precepts. For example:
  + The supernatural power of forgiveness, compassion, and love toward those who have wronged us. Showing how God uses our obedience to turn things around.
  + The power of the Holy Spirit continues to supernaturally heal and work miracles in the lives of His people.
  + God blesses us, so we can help others. Then, He blesses again... and so it goes.

My Visions that were fulfilled or confirmed through Scripture

1. I Am That I Am

2. Be Still and Know That I Am God

3. The White Light

4. The Fear of the Lord

5. The Dark Cloud

6. Follow Me

7. The Things of Earth or the Things of Heaven

8. Our Exciting Future in Heaven

9. Baptism of the Holy Spirit

How do these experiential visions of Biblical scripture apply to other Christians?

+ They validate the veracity of the Bible, and show that many scriptures we thought were metaphors will be fulfilled literally.

+ They confirm the validity of fundamental doctrines: God is light; He is "I Am;" *The Fear of the Lord* is essential for Christians; *Baptism of the Holy Spirit* is absolutely for us today; and that Jesus's statement *"Follow Me"* is not a request—it is a commandment.

+ They reveal profound mysteries and insights into the nature and person of God—and His desire to have a personal relationship with us.

+ They verify the fact that God still manifests Himself to people—literally and through scripture.

+ They demonstrate the power and gifts of the Holy Spirit, proving that He never ceased working in the lives of believers. His gifts and powers have only ceased with those who suppress and reject Him.

+ They reveal wonderful truths about Heaven that give us hope, and eager anticipation for the glorious life that awaits us.

My Visions In-process of Fulfillment

1. The Glory Clouds

2. Follow Me

3. I Will Rejoice Over You with Singing

4. Come Away with Me

5. In the Wings of an Eagle

6. The Bride and the Kingdom

How are these visions playing out now, and how do they pertain to all Christians?

+ *The Glory Clouds:* This vision depicts our catching up in the clouds to meet Jesus, as promised in First and Second Thessalonians and other scriptures throughout the New Testament! This prophetic event is also referred to by many as "the rapture." Although I wasn't familiar with this Biblical prophecy at the time of my vision, I later realized that the Lord had enabled me to experience this event supernaturally. I believe it was to confirm this event will happen, and also that I will experience it within my lifetime. If so, that time is coming *soon*—and we can now see those signs coming together!

+ *Follow Me:* Jesus spoke this iconic command to every believer. It is only by following Him on a daily basis that we can stay on the right path, as we live out our lives in this dangerous and wicked world. Jesus said that His disciples *follow* Him—and those who do He gives eternal life, and no one can take them out of His hand. But to follow Him, we must stay very close, so as to hear and obey His every command. He is beckoning to us through the things shared in this book and through scripture, to return to Him and follow closely in these last days.

+ *I Will Rejoice Over You with Singing:* This was one of the most blessed visions of all! In this vision I experienced how much the Lord Jesus loves and appreciates each of us uniquely and personally. He rejoices and sings over each of us, as if we are His long-lost best friend! I was awe-struck, deeply humbled, and filled with immense love and gratitude that He valued me so.

   It is mind-boggling how *He can love each of us, as if we are the most important person to Him ever!* But the Bible says we are fearfully and wonderfully made, and He even numbers the hairs on our head to fashion each of us into His ideal unique creation. Only Almighty God can love like that! Each of His people will soon experience His amazing personal love—as He is returning soon!

+ *Come Away with Me:* This vision revealed how Jesus will rescue His faithful followers in the time of trouble. Those who are watching and preparing to be with Him will be supernaturally taken to a place of refuge when calamity comes to them. They will be in a safe place in the presence of Jesus until it is time for the catching up, or rapture, described in First and Second Thessalonians. Dumitru Duduman saw this place as "the Camp of God," which he describes in his book *Through the Fire Without Burning*. The things I saw in this vision are playing out now. Our daily headlines are filled with rumors of nuclear war and tribulation ahead. This vision is about to be fulfilled, so please make sure you are right with the Lord!

+ *In the Wings of an Eagle:* This is wonderful news for Christians! This vision illustrates God's fulfillment of Psalm 91, and shows us how He will rescue His people described in this Psalm. As the world grows darker and end-time events unfold, we can have peace, hope, and assurance that God will fulfill the promises of Psalm 91. Make sure your life fits the description of "He who dwells in the secret place of the Most High."

+ *The Bride and the Kingdom:* In this vision, God revealed some fundamental truths about how Christianity is to be lived out in this world. But these Biblical truths have been largely usurped and nullified by erroneous doctrines of men; especially the permissive "once-saved-always-saved" doctrine that many Christians have been taught. In this vision, Jesus revealed OSAS as a false doctrine. He then revealed that the correct model for living out the Christian life is demonstrated in "the Bride and the Kingdom."

"The bride" represents Christ's people who will join Him in Heaven; and "the kingdom" is referring to His Church or kingdom on Earth, as illustrated in the parables Jesus taught. They lay out God's righteous precepts and examples of a godly life; and they illustrate what the Church in this world actually looks like—the good, the bad, and the ugly. Not every citizen of the kingdom (those born-again) lives the righteous life that is required to become the bride, attend the wedding, and enter the kingdom of Heaven. They show that many kingdom citizens on Earth are rejected because of sin, wrong beliefs, and failing to prepare for the wedding.

It is also important to remember that Lucifer, God's most glorious angel, was cast out of Heaven because sin was found in his heart. Confess your sins and repent now, while you can. Jesus will not allow anyone to enter Heaven who has anything in their heart that would offend the Father!

Miracles, Wonders, and Supernatural Acts

Following is a recap of the supernatural events shared in Part I:

1. Several miracles in the explosion of my father's business

2. My premonition of the above event

3. Rhett's supernatural protection in an explosion, three helicopter crashes, and several dangerous missions in the Viet Nam War

4. Our family's salvation—independently of each other, within a short timeframe

5. Supernatural gifts given to heal, deliver, and prophesy

6. Sean's miraculous shield of protection in a serious car accident

7. Greg's resurrection from the dead

8. Kelli's premonition of Greg's event

9. God's audible voice of warning to Michelle in Hawaii

10. Kelli's miraculous, instant recovery from a near-death injury—following intense prayer by many Christians

11. My premonition of Kelli's event

12. God's sudden, miraculous healing of my psoriasis—after forty years of suffering

13. My recovery from multiple life-threatening conditions in 2013

14. The Holy Spirit using Rhett, Michelle, and me to deliver someone of demons on Rosh Hashanah 2012

15. Rhett's profound experiences in Heaven and Hell

16. Rhett's advanced spiritual knowledge of Biblical truths following his tour of Heaven in 2012

17. The numerous astounding "coincidences" surrounding Rhett's funeral

18. The wonders of the amazing little hummingbird

19. The obstructive tree and precision tornado

20. The astonishing thunder on New Year's Day 2020—prophetically revealed to be a lion-angel sent by God to guard my home!

The Amazing Miracles of Henry Gruver

I also shared some of the amazing miracles of an evangelist named Henry Gruver, whom the Lord led me to for confirmation of certain visions He had shown me. Although God performed many additional miracles in Henry's life, the ones I shared included:

1. Several supernatural healings, restorations to life, supernatural words of knowledge, and revelations

2. Henry's miraculous death experience in a serious car accident that took him into outer space—and subsequent collaboration with preeminent astronomers at NASA

3. Numerous miracles of gold flakes and precious jewels raining down from Heaven on his audiences

4. Eradication of plagues, as detailed in the following testimonies:
   - *The Dragonfly Miracle*, ending a deadly mosquito plague in southern Taiwan
   - *The Curse of Habu Island*, where Henry cast out millions of deadly Habu snakes that had plagued the island for thousands of years. Habu Island was then quickly transformed into a fruitful land and thriving community, as Henry prophesied would happen

The numerous miracles shared above were witnessed by many people, documented in news stories, medical records, scientific data, and other physical evidence.

The abundance of evidence presented in these testimonies is more than enough to convince most people that God exists and Jesus Christ is our savior. But Henry Gruver and I are only two of possibly millions of Christians who have similar or even greater testimonies. And, when the multitude of fulfilled prophecies and miracles recorded in the Bible are added to those of today, the evidence that the God of the Bible is for real is irrefutable!

Status of the Watchmen Visions, Dreams, and Messages

Fulfilled Visions and Prophecies

+ *Attack of the Masked Men:* I believe this vision given to Dumitru Duduman, of six world leaders who would attack America while all were wearing masks, was fulfilled in the Covid attack of 2020. That virus is now believed to be a bioweapon that was developed and released on America and the whole world. It did serious damage to the United States economically, socially, and physically. During this attack all world leaders and everyone else were required to wear a mask!

In-Process Visions and Prophecies

1. The Train Cloud

2. The Eagle in the Cloud

3. I Have Made You a Watchman

4. Russian Submarines

5. When China Frees Taiwan

6. The Strange New Society

How these visions are being fulfilled:

+ *The Train Cloud:* Part 1 of this vision was fulfilled as a harbinger in August 2019, as I watched a train-like cloud expanding across the valley from my living room window. At the same time, I was marveling at the prosperity and optimistic future that was unfolding under President Trump.

America was respected or feared by the nations of the world again, and Trump was making peace with our adversaries. It felt like we were on the cusp of a new golden age of peace and prosperity. This also marked the pinnacle of America's reign as world hegemon. Then, we were hit with a "black swan" event (Covid) and it has been downhill from there. The second part of this vision will be fulfilled when God sends His heavenly army in the train cloud to Earth. I believe that will be much sooner than most Christians would expect.

+ *The Eagle in the Cloud:* This vision has been unfolding since 2011 when it was shown to me. The flying eagle representing America demonstrated what our country would endure in the economic, political, geopolitical, and social challenges that have plagued us ever since. The huge chunks being shed from the eagle's body have proven to be enormous amounts of money being stolen from the United States Treasury and thus the American citizens. And now, signs of the collapse of the eagle, civil war, and subsequent destruction of the United States depicted in the vision are rapidly coming together.

+ *I Have Made You a Watchman:* When the Lord revealed my watchman calling in 2013, He began teaching me the things I needed to know and do to fulfill my calling. The visions I saw in 1983 depicting myself as a watchman in my latter years have now been fulfilled. God has also helped me understand how the things He has shown me connect with His word, the Bible, and the world we are now living in. He has led me to write this book to share these things with His people, and I will continue to do so for as long as He leads and permits.

+ *Russian Submarines:* The vision God showed Henry Gruver in 1986 when he was evangelizing in Wales has been partially fulfilled. As I described in this testimony, Russia recently deployed the Belgorod submarines with Poseidon autonomous nuclear torpedoes. They are believed to have followed the path Henry described, proceeding north of Scandinavia into the North Sea, then into the Atlantic Ocean, Gulf of Mexico, and Pacific Ocean. Their formidable Poseidon torpedoes are believed to have been stealthily deployed around the shores of the United States, awaiting activation.

+ *When China Frees Taiwan:* Today, the world is anxiously anticipating war with China over Taiwan—just as the angel told Dumitru Duduman would happen if America did not repent. Well, America didn't repent—her sins continued to get much worse. And now, Dumitru's prophetic visions are coming true. China's attack on Taiwan seems inevitable, as they continually unleash terrifying live-fire "war games" to intimidate Taiwan! The world is holding its breath, knowing that China's games can turn into a full attack on Taiwan at any moment, launching the world into World War III. The missile attacks on the United States will soon follow, as God has shown His watchmen!

+ *The Strange New Society:* In early January 2023, I experienced a prophetic dream about a frightening future society of cyborgs and sentient robots, and augmented humans that seemed to worship technology. Certain aspects of the dream also felt like the shocking civilization depicted in the book *Brave New World*—a post-Christian and post-human world devoid of God and traditional values.

 Within a few weeks, my prophetic dream was confirmed. America was suddenly made aware of AI (Artificial Intelligence) and the AI revolution that was being unleashed upon the world. It was aggressively promoted throughout the media. Everyone was talking about

ChatGPT and extoling the fantastic new sci-fi world that AI was taking us into! And now in 2024, we are all stunned at how quickly AI is transforming our world, as large corporations are shedding tens of thousands of employees at a time and replacing them with AI.

The world also began talking about trans-humans and sentient robots replacing Humanity 1.0—those of us who were created in God's image. Humanity 2.0 (the humanoids) will be much smarter, faster, cheaper, and easier for the "powers that be" to manage. For a while, this sci-fi technology may create a fantastic new utopia for the "elite"; but I believe it will become a nightmare for the humans who remain. I hope and pray that Christians will not have to live very long in this dystopian new society!

Watchmen Visions Not Yet Fulfilled

These visions are still pending. However, they are all visible on the horizon and could come together very quickly in today's world.

+ *Out of the Blue:* I believe this vision was depicting an EMP that will be launched upon America at a time we do not expect.

+ *Judgment of the Wicked:* In this vision I saw the Russian et al. missile attack upon the United States. I believe it will also be fulfillment of Biblical prophecy that God will send His angels to judge the wicked with fire, just before Jesus returns.

+ *In the Wings of an Eagle:* This vision will be fulfilled when Russia, China, and others launch a devastating attack on the United States.

+ *Israel Is Alone:* When the United States is no longer able to help Israel, her enemies will begin attacking. She will have no friends or allies in the world, and only God will be able to help her.

Part III: Heaven Is for Real and So Is Hell

In Part III, I shared the compelling testimonies of seven people including my late husband, Rhett, whom the Lord took to Heaven, Hell, or both. They are all devout Christians now, but several were atheists, agnostics, backsliders, and worldly unbelievers until the day they suddenly found themselves in Heaven or in Hell! They came from a variety of backgrounds, ages, lifestyles, and professions, yet they all give stunningly similar testimonies of what they saw and experienced. Multiple eyewitnesses whose testimonies corroborate each other and the testimonies of Jesus—about the reality of Heaven and Hell!

Most of these people died first, but not all. A few were suddenly transported into another dimension and taken to Heaven or Hell without dying. Those who went to Heaven testified of a glorious reality filled with perfect love, joy, peace, and happiness. It is somewhat similar to Earth but much larger, and a million times more beautiful, thrilling, and perfect in every way!

Those who went to Satan's abode reported a very real and terrifying experience in the pitch-black pits of Hell. It is a real place, not a metaphor or ethereal reality, and it is located in the center of the earth, like in a volcano. A place of palpable fear, hatred, intense pain, fire, putrid smells, horrifying sights and sounds, and grotesque demons relentlessly torturing the hopeless souls that are imprisoned there. Just as Satan is the diametric opposite of Jesus, Hell is the polar opposite of Heaven!

Whether the witnesses had gone to Heaven or Hell, they all experienced Jesus as God their Savior, and knew that He had granted them grace for a purpose. It wasn't their time to die yet, and each had a calling or requirement to fulfill on Earth before they could enter Heaven. Part of their calling was to be a witness to others and tell them what they had experienced in Heaven or in Hell. The following is a synopsis of the most profound and frequently reported experiences of these witnesses:

Those who went to Heaven:

Most of these people reported:

1. The City of God is a magnificent city made of pure, transparent gold through which glorious light shines.

2. They raved about how everything in Heaven is alive and radiates exquisite love, joy, peace, wisdom, and other wonderful feelings.

3. They describe Heaven's astonishing beauty, creations, music, fragrances, and wonderful people, angels, and creatures all living in pure ecstasy!

4. Most testified that Jesus is the light of Heaven, and several talked about His amazing, mesmerizing eyes.

5. They give very similar descriptions of our spiritual bodies that are like gemstones made of light—and that the degree they shine and sparkle is in accordance with the person's rewards.

6. Most all said that communication in Heaven is through mental telepathy, and that you have instant knowledge and understanding about everything.

7. Several said that there are many more colors in Heaven than in this world.

8. Several described traveling at hyper-speed through outer space in a light tunnel, and described what the Earth, worlds, and galaxies looked like—and many of their details are very surprising but similar.

9. Most of them said that the "once-saved-always-saved" doctrine is a lie, and that you must repent of your sins and wrong beliefs, or you don't get into Heaven!

10. Some described the different kinds of angels in Heaven, and talked about Michael and his angels fighting against Satan and his angels in the second heaven (outer space).

11. Many witnesses said that the children in Heaven are the most honored people of all.

12. Several testified that people look like they are around age thirty; and they are the perfect version of themselves.

13. They all raved about the love and bliss in Heaven and especially when you are in the presence of Jesus.

14. Several described the awesome Mountain of God, and that the Father dwells at the top. They said there are mansions in different sizes and locations on the Mountain, representing the rewards of people who showed great faith and/or love on Earth.

15. Many testified that no one can enter Heaven if there is serious sin in their heart, such as unforgiveness, hatred, and other specified sins listed in the New Testament. Confess those sins in your life and be cleansed!

16. They were all humbled and amazed at Jesus's compassion and understanding, and how much He loved them.

17. Several talked about the Throne Room and seeing aspects of the Father, but no one could see His face.

18. Several said that obedience is how you prove your love for God.

19. More than one person described how you can do whatever you desire in Heaven—even create your own reality and enjoy

relationships with God, people, places, and activities whenever you wish.

20. Some described how there are special devices for people in Heaven to view loved ones on Earth, and pray for them.

Those Who Went to Hell

Most of these people reported:

1. They described evil spirits, sometimes appearing to be their dead loved ones, coming for them. Several said a very strong demon yanked their soul out of their body and flew with them across the earth to the pit.

2. They describe being thrown into a terrifying pitch-black pit, and falling helplessly for a great distance.

3. Many people describe these demonic entities biting, battering, and tearing their soul-body apart. They felt all the pain, even more intensely than in a physical body, but couldn't die.

4. Most of them complained passionately about the stench in Hell. Putrid smells of everything that goes into the ground—sewage, rotting flesh, garbage, chemicals, noxious gases, sulfur, etc. are intensified in that enclosed, air-deprived environment.

5. They struggle to describe the intense fear and hatred that fills the palpable darkness; it is a heavy and oppressive presence and souls can discern the demons' evil intentions as they approach them.

6. They describe how dreadful it is to hear the gut-wrenching screams, weeping, wailing, crying, yelling, demonic screeches,

and horrendous sounds that echo throughout the chambers of Hell.

7. Anticipation of demonic attacks keeps souls in constant terror and anxiety. There is no place to hide. And there is no rest for these weary souls.

8. Many witnesses describe how unbearably hot it is, and how utterly weak and debilitated they are.

9. They describe having all the feelings, faculties, and memories they had in their physical body—only more intense.

10. Several witnesses talk about seeing numerous Christians in Hell, including Church leaders. Many were arrogant, unforgiving, unloving, self-serving, and worldly people beneath the surface—who practiced secret sins or loved false doctrines.

11. Most of the witnesses testified that the OSAS doctrine and similar lies are sending millions of "believers" to Hell.

12. Some found themselves in a type of prison cell where grotesque demons tortured them.

13. Others experienced the horrid environment of Hell as a tourist—and could feel the pain and anguish of souls they passed by, as if by osmosis.

14. Some found themselves burning in flames, because that was what their punishment would involve if they didn't repent of certain sins.

15. Overwhelming hopelessness is said to be the worst experience of all. Souls dwell in deep remorse and self-hatred over their foolishness.

16. Some of the most accessible doorways for demons to gain control over a person are said to be: illicit sex, pornography, hatred,

unforgiveness, evil speech (slander, gossip, maligning others), drug abuse, and the occult.

17. One of the worst things about Hell is that you are utterly alone, and cannot associate with other souls in Hell. That would be a form of comfort and pleasure that they won't allow.

18. There is no sleep, food, or water in Hell—and your soul body is in constant pain. You suffer, as your physical body would, from a lack of these essential needs being met.

19. At some point, each of the witnesses were delivered from Hell. This never happens. But they had a special calling on their lives, so God gave them exceptional grace. In most cases, they suddenly saw a white light (Jesus) and were instantly rescued from the pits of Hell!

20. Some were then taken to Heaven, and others were returned to their bodies in this world. But all were instantly and passionately transformed into devout Christians!

Pulling It All Together

I have presented a preponderance of evidence in this chapter, showing that most of the testimonies, supernatural events, and prophecies shared in this book have been fulfilled or confirmed. And, those that remain are currently in-process of fulfillment, or can be clearly seen on the horizon. This includes all of my personal testimonies and the Miracles and Supernatural events in Part I; the Watchmen testimonies in Part II; and the witness testimonies of Heaven and Hell in Part III. These supernatural incidents can be verified through an abundance of evidence including: numerous eyewitnesses, affidavits, news reports, official documentation, medical documentation, physical evidence, and biblical validation.

Other compelling evidence to consider:

+ The numerous different watchmen and witnesses whose paths never crossed, yet reported essentially the same supernatural experiences and information. These people come from a variety of backgrounds, age groups, educational levels, professions, lifestyles, and nationalities. Most of their visions and experiences are also corroborated by Biblical scripture.

+ Dramatically changed lives, due to their "God Moment" experience. Several people were instantly transformed from atheists, agnostics, and worldly critics to passionate Christians. And, most of the things they testified or prophesied about are playing out in the world today.

The Bible says that the truth of a matter is validated by the testimony of two or three witnesses. The Lord has brought together an abundance of witnesses in this book, with the same vehement testimonies:

+ God is for real, and so are Heaven and Hell.

+ The "once-saved-always-saved" doctrine is a lie that is sending millions of believers to Hell!

+ The end of this age is rapidly coming upon us—a plethora of signs are everywhere.

+ Repent now and get right with God through Jesus Christ. One second too late—is an eternity in Hell!

With so many witness testimonies saying the same things, as I have stated before, it is like God is taking out His megaphone to urgently warn His people to wake up. Many of us have been deceived by false doctrines of men that have led us to believe doctrines of demons and fall into sin. We must repent and study the Bible for ourselves, asking the Holy Spirit to give us understanding. Then, obey whatever the Lord commands us—that's how we prove that we love Him!

The dots are connecting very fast lately, and two pictures are quickly emerging:

1. Great calamities and a dystopian new world system are coming soon, as described in the book of Revelation.

2. Jesus, God Almighty, our Savior is also coming soon for His people.

Make sure you're ready for both of these events!

> *"Watch therefore, for you do not know what hour your Lord is coming." (Matthew 24:42)*

Take Heed That No One Deceives You

I *tried four times to write* my Conclusion for this book, but the Lord kept telling me I wasn't done—there was something more that He wanted to say. He then began speaking into my mind, and this chapter is what He led me to write. I believe it is probably the most important chapter in this book. But it is not something I would have written on my own, because the overarching message is very uncomfortable for me, my family, and most Christians I know on a personal level. Most of us have been deceived. But the Lord Jesus loves us, and we need to hear this message now—before it's too late!

Jesus warned His end-time Church:

> *"Take heed that no one deceives you. For many will come in My name, saying, 'I am the Christ,' and will deceive many. And you will hear of wars and rumors of wars. See that you are not troubled; for all these things must come to pass, but the end is not yet. For nation will rise against nation, and kingdom against kingdom. And there will be famines, pestilences, and earthquakes in various places. All these are the beginning of sorrows." (Matthew 24:4-8)*

Most of the watchmen and witness testimonies shared in this book are emphatically warning that many Christians are asleep or dangerously deceived, and we need to wake up fast! The end-time signs that Jesus described are happening now, and He is sending His watchmen and witnesses to deliver specific warnings to His people. We need to understand the time and season we are in, and prepare to stand before the Lord!

The witnesses are testifying that multitudes of believers are going to Hell, because they are believing false doctrines that cause them to *love a lie and fall into sin (Revelation 22:15).* And, the "once-saved-always-saved" teaching is identified as the biggest culprit of them all! This popular doctrine is largely attributed to John Calvin and his followers. But Martin Luther taught similar doctrines and created the theological foundation that Calvin based his radical new doctrines upon as well. So, what are the doctrines these men devised, and why are they causing Christians to end up in Hell?

Martin Luther was a Catholic theologian who lived in Germany between 1483 and 1546. He is regarded as the most influential person in the Protestant Reformation that swept throughout Europe in the 1500s and beyond. Luther was a deeply religious Augustinian monk and theologian who devoted himself to Biblical study in search of the truth and understanding God's will. Early in his ecclesiastical career, the Lord poured out His grace upon Luther and he was born-again. His spiritual eyes were opened and he realized that salvation is an act of God's grace through faith—not through works, as the Catholic Church had emphasized.

God continued to give Luther insight into serious false doctrines and abusive practices that the Vatican was perpetrating upon the people. Their egregious abuses against God's word and the people greatly angered Luther— especially their practice of selling *indulgences.* So, he began approaching the Vatican through many essays and treatises, detailing their violations of Biblical doctrine, in an effort to get them to see their errors and repent. He also tried to convince them of his born-again experience and Biblical insight—that salvation is through God's grace and faith, and not by works.

But the Church adamantly disagreed with Luther and his new doctrines, in which he insisted that salvation was by grace and faith *alone*, and people were not to do any works of righteousness for salvation. This was a stark contradiction to the salvation doctrines the Church and Christians had always believed. So, their controversy continued.

Then, in 1517 Luther wrote down his grievances regarding the abuses and false doctrines he saw in the Catholic Church, as his famous *Ninety-five Theses*—and nailed them to the door of the Wittenberg Church. Luther's theses were widely copied by others who had become disgruntled with the Catholic Church, and they spread quickly throughout Europe. Finally, in 1521 the Pope declared Luther a heretic, and he was excommunicated from the Catholic Church. So, Luther took his doctrines to the people, launching the Protestant Reformation!

What exactly were Luther's new doctrines that the Catholic Church was so adamantly against?

After reflecting on his born-again experience and subsequent study of scripture, Martin Luther decided that Christians are saved by grace *alone*, through faith *alone*, in Christ *alone*, under the authority of scripture *alone*. He wanted to believe that God, Himself, saves us unilaterally. In other words, God does *all* the work for us and we are to do nothing, except believe on Jesus. Luther's doctrines actually created a new paradigm for salvation that was opposite from the view of salvation that Christians had believed since the time of the apostles. Luther's unilateral model has been labeled *monergism*, which basically means *one energy or entity—unilateral work*. This is how Wikipedia describes it:

Monergism is the view in Christian theology that holds that the Holy Spirit is the only agent that effects the regeneration of Christians. It is contrasted with synergism; the view that there is a cooperation between the divine and the human in the regeneration process.

From the time of the apostles until Martin Luther (over 1,400 years), Christians had believed in more of a *synergism* paradigm for salvation which is cooperative, not unilateral. Christian salvation was viewed more like a marriage—where the bride (the Church) must make herself ready and worthy for the groom, Jesus. Whomever the Father regenerates and calls as a bridal candidate for His Son must love His Son and begin sanctifying herself to become like Him.

She must begin acquiring "fine linen" for her glorious wedding dress. How does she do so? By doing "righteous acts" and good works—the kind of things that the Son does. She must develop a character and heart like His, if she is to be a compatible, worthy spouse for Him. This takes devotion and concerted effort on her part. The Father and Son give her gracious gifts to help and encourage her, but they do not do everything for her. She must make herself ready. This picture is beautifully presented in the recent movie *Before the Wrath*, which may still be available on YouTube, Netflix, or other television platforms.

And I heard, as it were, the voice of a great multitude, as the sound of many waters and as the sound of mighty thunderings, saying, "Alleluia! For the Lord God Omnipotent reigns! Let us be glad and rejoice and give Him glory, for the marriage of the Lamb has come, and His wife has made herself ready." And to her it was granted to be arrayed in fine linen, clean and bright, for the fine linen is the righteous acts of the saints. (Revelation 19:6-8)

Luther actually created several problems with his new "sola" doctrines. He insisted that salvation is by God's grace *alone*—He either chooses you or He doesn't and there is nothing you can do to seek God yourself. If God does choose you, He gives you faith through which you are saved and you must not add your own good works to faith—you are saved by faith *alone*. And, the only righteousness you are to have is Jesus's righteousness—not your own. Luther believed that God imputes the righteousness of Jesus over those whom He chooses. He said that a person must not add their own efforts ("filthy rags") or good works to Jesus's righteousness. That would be practicing "works righteousness," which he labeled a heresy. Just believe on Jesus—He has already done everything necessary to make you righteous and justified before God. You should not do righteous acts proactively—out of a sense of duty, righteousness, or obedience to Jesus's commandments, according to Luther's theories. He said that would be practicing "the Law," as in the Old Testament Law of Moses.

Luther had obviously turned the salvation doctrines upside down, and created a very different model for salvation with his new *sola* doctrines. And, that was said to be the major issue the Catholic Church had with Luther. They believed and taught that salvation is through grace and faith but not "alone." The Church adamantly believed that it was a cooperative or *synergistic* interplay in which the believer had to participate with the Holy Spirit to become more like Jesus.

But the Church had fallen into transgression with the works side of that picture, creating unbiblical and self-serving doctrines that were abusive and heretical. Doctrines like *selling indulgences* and requiring other burdensome works from the people. These practices so angered Luther that I believe it pushed him toward the opposite extreme—*no works* were required in his paradigm for salvation—from beginning to end. Borrowing from the theories of St. Augustine of Hippo, no works of righteousness or obedience are to be done by the believer—only Jesus's righteousness is required for salvation, according to Luther. And, he was so convinced his theories were right that he decided to revamp the Bible!

Martin Luther had started out very well. The Lord had given him tremendous grace and power to do His will. And, Luther passionately followed the Holy Spirit's promptings to confront the Vatican with their sins and violations of God's word. He was a devoted warrior for the truth, and contributed many wonderful insights, wrote beautiful hymns, and was instrumental in bringing the Bible to the masses. But then he went too far, and assumed the right to do something that God adamantly forbids. As I shared earlier in "The Bride and the Kingdom," he began arbitrarily editing and reframing God's written word to create his own Bible, and a different foundation for salvation!

Luther decided that the Bible had been corrupted, and he was going to straighten it out by producing his own German-language Bible for the people. He began by editing the written word, adding the word "sola" into certain New Testament scriptures regarding salvation. His audacious behavior was not only shocking—it changed salvation doctrines! But he didn't stop there. Luther then took a hatchet to the Biblical canon that had been in place for over one thousand years, and removed seven books that he didn't like.

Those seven books became part of the apocrypha, and have been effectively removed from the purview of most Protestants ever since. He then tried to take out several more books from the New Testament—most of the books from Hebrews through Revelation. But other theologians stood up against him until he relented. So, he relegated them to the back of the Bible instead, and tried to marginalize and denigrate them. Why? Because they contained scriptures he didn't like or that contradicted his new doctrines. Did God tell him to do any of this? No! He arrogantly assumed he knew best and could do whatever he wanted!

What was so bad about Martin Luther's behavior?

Altering or mishandling God's written word is one of the most egregious sins a person can commit! As graphically illustrated throughout the Old Testament, God severely punished those who mishandled His written word or His sacred protocols. For example:

+ The Ten Commandments were handled in a very strict manner: the tablets were placed inside the Ark of the Covenant and carried about on long poles and/or carts by those who had been specifically called and anointed to do this task. If any unauthorized person even touched it, they could be instantly killed by the power of the Holy Spirit! And, throughout the Old Testament, God's written word encased in the Ark of the Covenant, brought terrible judgments and plagues upon those people or societies who misused it, or had illegitimately acquired it.

+ God also judged King Saul harshly for disobeying His words and violating His protocols. The Lord stripped the kingdom from Saul and gave it to David, because Saul's sins of disobedience, arrogance, and irreverence for God's protocols and commandments were so serious. Then, He cursed Saul by removing the Holy Spirit from him, and sending an evil spirit upon him instead! Saul continued in a downward spiral from there, ending in his ignominious defeat and death by suicide!

For rebellion is as the sin of witchcraft, and stubbornness is as iniquity and idolatry. Because you have rejected the word of the LORD, He also has rejected you from being king." (1 Samuel 15:23)

+ The Bible is God's inerrant word, which is living, active, and empowered by the Holy Spirit. Man is not to tamper with it or alter it in any way, as emphatically taught and meticulously adhered to during Old Testament times. When copying the sacred texts, Hebrew scribes were said to repeatedly count every letter, jot, tittle, and space on each line of text forward and backward again and again, to make sure they had not committed the egregious sin of adding to or taking away from God's written word. They were terrified of God's judgment if they did!

You may be thinking: "*Well, that all happened under the Old Covenant, when God's people were governed by the Law of Moses. But do those same precepts apply under God's New Covenant of grace?*"

Yes, they do! As if doubling down on this precept, the Lord reiterates these principles even more emphatically at the very end of the New Testament:

> *For I testify to everyone who hears the words of the prophecy of this book: If anyone adds to these things, God will add to him the plagues that are written in this book; and if anyone takes away from the words of the book of this prophecy, God shall take away his part from the Book of Life, from the holy city, and from the things which are written in this book.* (Revelation 22:18-19)

The Lord has established these foundational precepts like bookends on His written word, the Bible, encapsulating every word within. Here, in the last chapter of Revelation, God proclaims His strongest warning and curses upon anyone who dares to tamper with His written word! Whether it is doing violence to His established canon, laying another gospel foundation, adding to his written words, or taking away from His written words, such acts are vehemently forbidden. But some men have been so foolish and arrogant that they have done these things and more. It really goes without saying that such persons should have been immediately rejected—and their doctrines should never have been considered!

But unfortunately, that's not what happened in the Protestant Reformation. People were ignorant of these Biblical precepts because the Catholic Church had effectively prevented the masses from knowing God's word for themselves. And, these oppressed people loved Luther's new doctrines because they essentially told them exactly what they wanted to hear: "*You can live as you please, engage in the lusts of the world, and still get into Heaven. And, you don't have to do any good works—just believe on Jesus!*"

What is it about Martin Luther's and John Calvin's doctrines that cause believers to end up in Hell?

Here are a few things that come to my mind, but this is certainly not an exhaustive list:

+ First of all, both Luther's and Calvin's doctrines are based on the faulty foundation of *monergism* created by Martin Luther—a man who arrogantly did great violence to the Bible in an attempt to establish his own doctrines. He would then have incurred God's judgment and curses for his disrespect of God's written word. Therefore, *Luther's radical new doctrines are not from God—nor are Calvin's doctrines, which are also based on the erroneous monergism foundation.* Both men and their doctrines should be rejected, in my humble opinion.

+ But to prove if my assessment is correct: Jesus tells us to judge such persons by the fruits they produce. An evil tree will produce evil fruit. So, let's briefly look at some of the fruit produced by Luther's and Calvin's doctrines:

1. Martin Luther introduced another foundation and paradigm for salvation—monergism. A few years later Calvin based his doctrines on that foundation as well. Monergism is a reversal of the synergistic paradigm for salvation that Christians had believed since the time of the apostles. Luther's new doctrine has brought division and confusion into the body of Christ, causing it to splinter into many different factions.

2. If Luther had not introduced these doctrines into his treatises, the Catholic Church may have come to terms with Luther's legitimate grievances, and repented. There may have been

healing and blessing, instead of the disaster Christianity has been dealing with for the last five hundred years.

3. Luther's and Calvin's doctrines turn salvation upside down. They absolve believers of responsibility and accountability for their sins, and make their sins the responsibility of Jesus instead. "You don't have to repent or do any righteous works—just believe my new doctrine and you are saved," they tell their followers. But that isn't what the Bible teaches. Jesus preached repentance, faith in Him, righteous works, and obedience as requirements for salvation, and so did the apostles. And, only Biblical doctrine is to be followed—as modeled by Jesus and the apostles! (Matthew 4:17; Luke 13:3; Mark 6:12; Luke 24:46-47; John 14:21; John 15:10; Acts 2:38; 3:19; 8:32; 17:30; 26:20)

+ *You see that a person is justified by works and not by faith alone. (James 2:24 NAS)*

+ *As many as I love, I rebuke and chasten. Therefore be zealous and repent. (Revelation 3:19)*

+ *If we say that we have no sin, we deceive ourselves, and the truth is not in us. If we confess our sins, He is faithful and just to forgive us our sins and to cleanse us from all unrighteousness. (1 John 1:8-9)*

4. Their upside-down dogmas actually call good evil, and evil good, in my humble opinion. Luther's and Calvin's doctrines tacitly encourage sin. They promise Heaven regardless of how a believer lives, then tell their followers not to proactively do righteous works ("*works-righteousness*")—quashing obedience to Jesus's commandments to demonstrate their love for God. The Bible says that sin separates us from God—and that the way we prove our love for God is by obeying all that Jesus commands us.

So, those who follow Luther's and Calvin's "no works" dogma will likely be sin-laden, and have no deliberate acts of obedience proving that they loved God—when Jesus judges the Church!

5. Another evil fruit is that Luther's and Calvin's Cessationism sentiments and teachings have taught their believers to resist and deny the full ministry of the Holy Spirit—our supernatural Helper and power of God! Thus, robbing millions of believers of His gifts, miracles, and possibly their salvation. Calvin is credited with promoting this teaching, while Luther vacillated back and forth on it.

   However, most Calvinists and Lutherans today tend to believe in the false doctrine of Cessationism—and the lack of the Holy Spirit's power and presence is obvious in most of their congregations. The apostle Paul prophesied about such people in today's world, saying: *"But understand this: In the last days terrible times will come. For men will be lovers of themselves . . . having a form of godliness but denying its power. Turn away from such as these."* (2 Timothy 3:1-5 BSB)

6. Jesus taught that offending, denying, or speaking against the Holy Spirit and His power is one of the most dangerous things a person can do. Christians are commanded to resist the devil—not the Holy Spirit! Furthermore, the scriptures in 1 Corinthians 13:8-10, which Cessationists use in an attempt to justify that heretical doctrine, are a laughably erroneous interpretation of those scriptures and their subject matter. It is obvious to anyone with spiritual discernment that they are "grasping at straws" in an effort to justify that ungodly teaching—and resist the power of the Holy Spirit! *Who would do that?*

7. People who believe and practice these men's doctrines are not usually concerned about sin. They believe their salvation is assured because they believe the *truth* (their leader's doctrines).

Whether it is Luther's "alone" doctrines, Calvin's "once-saved-always-saved" doctrines, Joseph Smith's "restored" doctrines, or Peter Drucker's "seeker-sensitive" model—all of these men assure their followers salvation and/or success, if they follow their unique paradigm. So, their believers tend to live according to the doctrines of the man they are following, thinking they are guaranteed salvation. But their doctrines are all different from each other and the Bible. So, who is lying? *Indeed, let God be true but every man a liar. (Romans 3:4)*

8. Practicing sin and hypocrisy are two major reasons these believers end up in Hell, but there is an even bigger reason that is more insidious—deception. The final words and warning Jesus gave to His people at the end of the book of Revelation is this:

Blessed are those who do His commandments, that they may have the right to the tree of life, and may enter through the gates into the city. But outside are dogs and sorcerers and sexually immoral and murderers and idolaters, and whoever loves and practices a lie. (Revelation 22:14-15)

The angel of God makes it crystal clear that we *must* "do His commandments" and those who commit various sins, or *whoever loves and practices a lie* (false doctrines), will not enter Heaven. Jesus's final warning to the Church is also the final nail in the coffin for the doctrines of Martin Luther and John Calvin, in my opinion. Jesus expects His people to obey Him, live a righteous life, and not love a lie—such as false doctrines of men, built on a different salvation platform.

For no other foundation can anyone lay than that which is laid, which is Jesus Christ. (1 Corinthians 3:11)

For the leaders of this people cause them to err, And those who are led by them are destroyed. (Isaiah 9:16)

Take Back Your Power

As a born-again Christian, you live under the New Covenant of grace. Throughout the Old Testament God promised again and again that He was going to replace the Old Mosaic Covenant with something much better—the New Covenant—which is described in the book of Hebrews:

> *"For this is the covenant that I will make with the house of Israel after those days, says the LORD; I will put My laws in their mind and write them on their hearts; and I will be their God, and they shall be My people. None of them shall teach his neighbor, and none his brother, saying, 'Know the LORD,' for all shall know Me, from the least of them to the greatest of them. For I will be merciful to their unrighteousness, and their sins and their lawless deeds I will remember no more." (Hebrews 8:10-12)*

This promise is fulfilled when you hear the gospel, believe, and are born-again. The Holy Spirit enters you and begins cleansing your heart and renewing your mind. He starts putting God's righteous laws into your mind and writes them on your heart. His presence within makes you love the Lord and want to obey His teachings and do His will. The Holy Spirit is your teacher, counselor, and the One who connects you with Jesus and gives you understanding—*so you won't need men to tell you how to "know the LORD."* He also keeps you in God's grace, forgiving and cleansing your sins, as you confess them and repent. He enables you to believe and obey the Biblical Jesus—so you don't believe "another gospel" or follow a false Christ!

But you, do not be called 'Rabbi'; for One is your Teacher, the Christ, and you are all brethren. Do not call anyone on earth your father; for One is your Father, He who is in heaven. And do not be called teachers; for One is your Teacher, the Christ. (Matthew 23:8-10)

We all need to take back our power—the power of the Holy Spirit! Stop letting the doctrines of men rob you of your God-given gifts, power, and possibly your salvation! Read and study God's word for yourself, and ask the Holy Spirit to give you understanding. It's time to stop allowing ourselves to be deceived and misled by the twisted doctrines of arrogant men. We don't need them—we have the all-powerful Holy Spirit!!

+ *My people are destroyed for lack of knowledge. Because you have rejected knowledge, I also will reject you from being priest for Me . . . (Hosea 4:6)*

+ *For the time will come when people will not put up with sound doctrine. Instead, to suit their own desires, they will gather around them a great number of teachers to say what their itching ears want to hear. They will turn their ears away from the truth and turn aside to myths. (2 Timothy 4:3-4 NIV)*

My Conclusion:

I believe that Jesus Christ's Church has been massively deceived—both Catholics and Protestants. The Catholics have been misled by all of the false doctrines and practices that Martin Luther railed against: idol worship; polytheism (praying to "saints" as demigods); over-emphasizing works rather than grace and faith as the key to salvation; and teaching many false doctrines. Protestants have also been massively misled by Luther, Calvin, Smith, Drucker, and many other deceivers teaching dangerous upside-down doctrines. Their believers read the Bible with a filter over God's words—straining it through the doctrines of the man they are following. As a result, they don't understand, believe, or obey God's precepts and doctrines—and they may even reject Jesus and His words. This is especially dangerous because He tells us:

> He who rejects Me, and does not receive My words, has that which judges him—the word that I have spoken will judge him in the last day. (John 12:48)

So, if their leader teaches them to ignore or wrongly interpret different words or Biblical doctrines, the people will suffer judgment for unbelief and practicing a lie. They didn't take heed—and were deceived! Both Catholics and Protestants have been corrupted by the doctrines of men, and as a result many believers are ending up in Hell! Christians need to remove these filters from their Bibles and ask the Holy Spirit to give them understanding, in my opinion.

Jesus is about to shake the world—we must wake up now! We can still repent and take back our spiritual power, the Holy Spirit. But our time is running out fast! Read and study God's word for yourself—and don't fall for the doctrines of these men. Remember *the simplicity of Christ,* as the apostle Paul tells us:

> But I fear, lest somehow, as the serpent deceived Eve by his craftiness, so your minds may be corrupted from the simplicity that is in Christ. (2 Corinthians 11:3)

> Thus also faith by itself, if it does not have works, is dead. (James 2:17)

> You see that a person is considered righteous by what they do and not by faith alone. (James 2:24 NIV)

... *'This people honors Me with their lips,*
But their heart is far from Me.
And in vain they worship Me,
Teaching as doctrines the commandments of men.'
(*Mark 7:6-7*)

Conclusion

In conclusion, *God is for real* and so are Heaven and Hell! I believe that the abundance of evidence presented in this book effectively proves this statement to be true. The numerous prophetic visions, dreams, revelations, fulfilled prophecies, miracles, wonders, and witness testimonies are more than enough evidence to convince any honest jury in the world. And most scientists would likely agree, especially when the mathematical laws of probability are applied to all of these supernatural events and evidence. Then, when we add the multitude of Biblical, historical, and witness testimonies over the last two thousand years to all of this, there is only one intelligent conclusion: God, Heaven, and Hell are absolutely for real—the proof is overwhelming. And, the common thread that runs through all of these events and testimonies is shown to be Jesus Christ.

If you believe these statements are true, the next logical question becomes: "So, what should I do?" You need to hear (or read) the gospel of Jesus Christ, presented in the Bible. I especially recommend the Gospel of John, chapters 1-3. You will realize that Jesus Christ is God the Word, the Son sent by God the Father to redeem His people from the claim of Satan and Hell. Jesus is the Lover of your soul, who became a human being in order to pay for the sins of His people. He lived the perfect life required, then He laid down His life for yours—and took your punishment, so you don't have to suffer at the hands of demons for every sin you committed. Once you hear the gospel and believe in Jesus, ask Him to forgive your sins and save you—then follow and obey Him the rest of your life. And you will spend eternity in the marvelous reality called Heaven!

You are saved through faith in the Lord Jesus Christ when you are born-again and the Holy Spirit enters your heart. But saving faith is not just believing that something is true. And it is certainly not belief in the doctrines of men. It is a gift of God's grace received when you hear and believe the Biblical gospel. The Greek word *pisteuo* is used to describe this kind of faith, which implies a holistic type of belief and trust that comes from your heart and governs your entire life—your values, standards, interests, thoughts, and behavior. It is the kind of faith that makes you a disciple of Jesus Christ, not just a "believer."

Pisteuo is the type of faith that will withstand many tests and trials in life, and develop your character through perseverance. No matter what happens, hold onto your faith! It is impossible to please God or be saved without it. But you are not saved by faith alone—it must be accompanied by repentance, righteous acts, and a new nature, which are the evidence of saving faith, as described in James 2:17-24. This kind of faith is greatly rewarded in Heaven!

As a result of our salvation, Jesus expects certain things from His people. Here are a few of them:

+ **Live a righteous lifestyle:** *Or do you not know that your body is the temple of the Holy Spirit who is in you, whom you have from God, and you are not your own? For you were bought at a price; therefore, glorify God in your body and in your spirit, which are God's. (1 Corinthians 6:19-20)*

+ **Walk in the Spirit:** *So I say, walk by the Spirit, and you will not gratify the desires of the flesh. For the flesh desires what is contrary to the Spirit, and the Spirit what is contrary to the flesh. They are in*

conflict with each other, so that you are not to do whatever you want.
(Galatians 5:16-17 NIV)

✦ **Make disciples and teach them to obey:** *"Therefore, go and make disciples of all nations, baptizing them in the name of the Father and of the Son and of the Holy Spirit, and teaching them to obey everything I have commanded you. And surely I am with you always, to the very end of the age." (Matthew 28:19-20 NIV)*

Contrary to the doctrines of Luther and Calvin, the Lord expects us to discipline ourselves to live a righteous life and walk in the Spirit. Obedience is how we prove we love God, as Jesus taught: "Whoever has my commands and keeps them is the one who loves me . . ." (John 14:21 NIV) *We cannot do whatever we want.* We have been bought with a very high price, and He expects us to obey Him and show our love and gratitude by leading others to Him. We are to make them disciples as well and teach them to obey everything He has commanded.

I am guessing that most of us fall short of doing these things because we thought we didn't have to. That's what many of us were told. We have been deceived, but it's not too late! We can confess our sins, repent, *and start doing what Jesus has commanded us now!*

The Eagle has Officially Imploded

As I am finishing this book in late September 2024, the Lord has just made me aware that the eagle representing the United States in my testimony "The Eagle in the Cloud" has now officially imploded. This occurred on September 22, 2024, at the United Nations in New York City.

The United States of America is no longer a sovereign country; it is now a vassal of the United Nations, along with approximately 195 other nations of the world. This official event called "The Summit of the Future" did not receive the attention it warranted from the media or our congressional representatives, given the monumental impact it will have on every citizen of the United States.

It seemed to be handled in a stealth manner, just below public radar. But you can find stories and videos talking about this meeting on the Internet, so please do your own research to learn about what has happened. You will be stunned to see our government's profound betrayal of the American people while keeping us distracted with political theater and frivolous banter!

Of course, they are presenting this "Pact for the Future" as a good thing—like a global "kumbaya" that will result in equality, peace, and prosperity for all. But the American people are not that stupid, we can read between the lines. They want to take from us to give to the poorer countries, leveling the playing field—until everyone is equal. And that's just the beginning of the global reset they have planned for us.

We will likely see the two swirling black circles that I saw in my 2011 vision emerge soon, as America descends into civil unrest.

When the Lord brought this information to my awareness, the events described in Revelation 17:12-13 began flooding my mind:

> "The ten horns which you saw are ten kings who have received no kingdom as yet, but they receive authority for one hour as kings with the beast. These are of one mind, and they will give their power and authority to the beast."

This is exactly what has happened at the UN—the leaders of the world are of one mind and have given their nation's power and authority (sovereignty) over to the beast, the United Nations. Will we also see a woman riding the beast and the events that follow (Revelation 17:1-7)?

Get Ready to Meet the Lord!

Our world is rapidly changing in every way: geopolitically, physically, socially, and spiritually, as most people can see. We are moving into the most challenging time in Earth's history—the end-days. I believe we will soon know who the Antichrist is. He will be in power before Jesus returns for His people, and Christians must prepare to not take the "mark of the beast." As we are told in the book of Revelation, the Antichrist will prevent people from being able to buy or sell unless they have the "mark," making life very difficult for those who refuse it. But the Bible says that those who do take it will be damned. *Those who take the mark have chosen to believe and obey Satan, rather than Jesus.* Please do what you can to prepare now, so you can resist the mark! (Revelation 13:15-18; 14:9-12)

Hopefully, the testimonies and information shared in this book together with God's word, the Bible, will help you understand what is happening. Then, when certain events begin to occur, your faith will be strengthened, as you remember God's prophetic forewarnings. Many Christians will also experience the supernatural promises of Psalm 91, as the world becomes increasingly chaotic. Try to be like the person described in that Psalm; take time to dwell in your secret place with the Lord, and you will receive those promises! And, get ready for the Wedding—make sure you are one of the five *wise* virgins who prepared, and not a presumptuous foolish virgin who thought she didn't have to! (Matthew 25:1-13)

A spiritual battle between the forces of good and evil is converging upon our world, and Christians need to learn how to *"put on the whole armor of God, that you may be able to stand against the wiles of the devil"* (*Ephesians 6:11*). Determine in your mind and heart now that you will be a victor and not a victim! Build up your faith and learn how to engage in spiritual warfare, which is very different from physical warfare.

Find a good church who is hearing and following the Holy Spirit, and will teach you what you need to learn and do. If you can't find such a congregation, then read the book of Ephesians, especially chapter 6. Also study the book of Acts and the gospels to learn how Jesus and the apostles walked in the supernatural power of the Holy Spirit.

Prepare yourself to stand in faith, and not cower in fear. Faith is the power of the Holy Spirit—fear is the power of Satan. Who do you want empowering your life? Take a few minutes and memorize these important scriptures. They will help you stay in faith as you apply them in your life:

+ *Trust in the LORD with all your heart, and lean not on your own understanding; in all your ways acknowledge Him, and He shall direct your paths. (Proverbs 3:5-6)*

+ *Be anxious for nothing, but in everything by prayer and supplication, with thanksgiving, let your requests be made known to God; and the peace of God, which surpasses all understanding, will guard your hearts and minds through Christ Jesus. (Philippians 4:6-7)*

+ *Behold, I give you the authority to trample on serpents and scorpions, and over all the power of the enemy, and nothing shall by any means hurt you. (Luke 10:19)*

It is essential that you keep your eyes on Heaven and the glorious, thrilling life that awaits you for eternity. Hope of Heaven, together with your faith and trust in the Lord Jesus, will pull you through the difficult times ahead. Set your mind on the things of Heaven—its beauty, love, ecstasy beyond your wildest imagination—and the euphoria of being in the presence of God! Read the witness testimonies of Heaven shared in Part III again and again, as well as the descriptions found in the New Testament, until those visions are firmly implanted in your mind. But if you are one of those people who need a little more motivation, then read the witness testimonies about Hell again and again. That should give you all the motivation you need to make sure you go to Heaven and bring others with you! Then, be like the apostle Paul:

I have fought the good fight, I have finished the race, I have kept the faith. Finally, there is laid up for me the crown of righteousness, which the Lord, the righteous Judge, will give to me on that Day, and not to me only but also to all who have loved His appearing. (2 Timothy 4:7-8)

Finally, be sure to share your testimony of Jesus Christ with others. Tell them how you became a believer and the wonderful things the Lord has done for you! Doing so will strengthen your faith and the faith of those who hear your testimony. It is also one of the most powerful ways to lead others to Christ, and to ensure that you will be an overcomer!

And they overcame him [Satan] by the blood of the Lamb
and by the word of their testimony,
and they did not love their lives to the death.
(Revelation 12:11)

And He told me, "It is done! I am the Alpha and the Omega,
the Beginning and the End.
To the thirsty I will give freely from the spring of the water of life.
The one who overcomes will inherit all things, and I will be his God,
and he will be My son.

"But to the cowardly and unbelieving and abominable and murderers
and sexually immoral and sorcerers and idolaters and all liars,
their place will be in the lake that burns with fire and sulfur.
This is the second death."
(Revelation 21:6-8 BSB)

"The one you obey is the one you love
and will be with for eternity!"
~Rhett Miller

Do You Want to Be Saved?

F*ollowing are some essential truths* from the Gospel of John and the book of Ephesians that you need to hear and believe:

+ *In the beginning was the Word, and the Word was with God, and the Word was God. He was in the beginning with God. All things were made through Him, and without Him nothing was made that was made. In Him was life, and the life was the light of men.* (John 1: 1-4)

+ *He was in the world, and the world was made through Him, and the world did not know Him. He came to His own, and His own did not receive Him. But as many as received Him, to them He gave the right to become children of God, to those who believe in His name: who were born, not of blood, nor of the will of the flesh, nor of the will of man, but of God.* (John 1:10-13)

+ *Jesus answered and said to him, "Most assuredly, I say to you, unless one is born again, he cannot see the kingdom of God."* (John 3:3)

+ *"For God so loved the world that He gave His only begotten Son, that whoever believes in Him should not perish but have everlasting life."* (John 3:16)

+ *For by grace you have been saved through faith, and that not of yourselves; it is the gift of God, not of works, lest anyone should boast. For we are His workmanship, created in Christ Jesus for good works, which God prepared beforehand that we should walk in them.* (Ephesians 2:8-10)

Do you believe that Jesus is God the Word, the only begotten of God the Father, who came into this world to pay for the sins of His people and redeem them from Satan's claim?

Do you want to be forgiven and cleansed of your sins?

Do you want to receive Jesus and be born-again, so you can know God and enter into Heaven when you leave this world?

If you answered "yes" to these questions, confess your beliefs by humbly praying to God, as suggested in the following prayer:

The Sinner's Prayer

"Father in Heaven,

I believe You are Almighty God and I believe You sent Your Son, Jesus Christ—God the Word, to save Your people. I confess that I am a sinner and cannot save myself.

Lord Jesus, I ask You to forgive my sins, come into my heart and be the Lord of my life. Please help me to become the person You created me to be.

Father, I ask you to hear my prayer in Jesus's name. Amen."

For with the heart one believes unto righteousness, and with the mouth confession is made unto salvation . . . For "whoever calls on the name of the LORD shall be saved." (Romans 10:10; 13)

Congratulations!

If you sincerely meant the words you prayed, the Holy Spirit has entered you and you are born-again! Get yourself a good Bible and begin reading it and praying. The Holy Spirit will give you understanding and you will begin to love God and be drawn deeper and deeper into His word, the Bible. As you seek to know Jesus, be sure to do as He teaches. Obedience is how you prove your love for God! (John 14:21)

Ask the Lord to lead you to a good Bible-believing church, and become an active part of God's family on Earth.

He who overcomes shall be clothed in white garments, and I will not blot out his name from the Book of Life; but I will confess his name before My Father and before His angels. (Revelation 3:5)

"There are only two things [authorities]
in this world—Jesus and Satan.
The one you obey is the one you love
and will be with for eternity!"

"Be sure to forgive others—
do not hold any unforgiveness or hatred in your heart!"

~ Rhett Miller

I hope you enjoyed this book. Would you do me a favor?

Like all authors, I rely on online reviews to promote my book and get it out to as many people as possible. If you feel that the material I have shared would be beneficial for others to read, I would greatly appreciate your help. Would you kindly take a few moments now, to share your honest opinion and assessment of my book at the book review site of your choice?

I also invite you to follow my blog posts and continuing information on my website:

Annmillerbooks.com

Thank you very much, and may God bless you!
Ann Miller

About the Author

Ann Miller has been a devoted disciple of Jesus Christ since 1983, when the Lord began revealing Himself to her through a series of prophetic visions, dreams, and miracles that continued over the next forty years. In 2013, God revealed that He had made her a watchman, and had given her these experiences as a testimony to be shared with others in these end-days.

Ann holds a business management degree and worked many years in the corporate and financial arena, from which she has retired. She now enjoys spending time with her four children and nine grandchildren and writing about God, as the Holy Spirit leads. Her husband, Rhett, passed away in 2016, after the Lord gave him some astounding spiritual experiences, which she also shares in her book *God Is for Real . . . And So Are Heaven and Hell.*

About Rhett Miller

The *attached photo was taken* in 2015, one year before Rhett Miller went to be with the Lord. Although his health was deteriorating and he was on oxygen 24/7, the joy of the Lord radiates through his face.

As shared in his in-depth testimonies, Rhett was given some extraordinary spiritual experiences with Jesus, Heaven, and Hell, as detailed in this book. The information he shared about the things he experienced and learned are astounding and essential information for everyone to read!